PERSPECTIVES IN CONTROVERSY:

Selected Essays from
Contemporary Argumentation and Debate

PERSPECTIVES IN CONTROVERSY:
Selected Essays from
Contemporary Argumentation and Debate

KENNETH BRODA-BAHM, EDITOR

International Debate Education Association
New York • Amsterdam • Brussels

Published in 2002 by
The International Debate Education Association
400 West 59th Street
New York, NY 10019

ISBN 0-9702130-5-0

Library of Congress Cataloging-in-Publication Data

    Perspectives in Controversy: Selected Essays from
        Contemporary Argumentation and Debate/ editor, Kenneth
        Broda-Bahm,
                P.cm.
        Includes bibliographical references.
        ISBN 0-9702130-5-0
            1. Debates and debating. I. Broda-Bahm, Kenneth, 1963-
        II. Contemporary Argumentation and Debate
    PN4181 .P433 2002
    808.53–dc21

        2002023339

Printed in the United States of America

TABLE OF CONTENTS

INTRODUCTION

One aspect of any community is that it develops and communicates knowledge. For a community of debaters, teachers, coaches, and scholars, one way that knowledge is developed and communicated is through a body of literature: published essays about the theory and practice of academic debate. In an academic debate community, focusing as it does on direct instruction, preparation, and practice, the role of scholarship is not always clear. There are several reasons, however, for developing a published body of opinion, a dialogue on important questions relating to the philosophy and pragmatics of educational debating.

First, published scholarship plays a role in developing instructional pedagogy. In order to address questions of policy, for example, students need to address the concept of fiat, or the ability to assume that a given action has taken place. As several of the authors in the fourth section in this text note, practical ways of giving life to this assumption in the context of academic debate have not always been simple or clear. By developing and offering several models for conceiving and applying fiat, these essays seek to provide practical tools for teachers and arguers.

Second, published scholarship serves as a vehicle for addressing community-wide concerns. As educational accountability has increased in salience, debate educators have felt the need to investigate and communicate a more thoroughly grounded defense of the educational value of competitive debate. The second section of this text includes two important essays which explore the question of whether academic debate educators can claim that their activity increases students' critical thinking.

Third, published scholarship offers a means to comment upon the development of theory by debaters. Since debate provides an open framework for argument, students frequently create and test novel arguments "in round," that is during the debate itself. One such emergent argument is the "Critique" (also known as the "Kritik" to reflect its underpinnings in Continental philosophy). The essays in the fifth section of this text reflect varying perspectives on this argument strategy while providing an example of scholars' efforts to offer critical advise to debaters who are developing "in round" theory.

Finally, published scholarship can serve as a vehicle for bringing the knowledge of other fields to bear on the practice of academic debate. While all of the essays to a greater or lesser extent serve to frame and apply concepts generated in other academic fields, the sections on argumentative support and causality are particularly illustrative of some of the opportunities, as well as challenges, of expanding debate theory through the exploration of other fields of inquiry.

The essays included in this text have all appeared in *Contemporary Argumentation and Debate: The Journal of the Cross Examination Debate Association*. The precursor to this journal was first published in 1980 as a collection of essays by instructors involved in teaching and coaching within what was then a new debate organization: the Cross Examination Debate Association, or CEDA. Initial collections of essays appeared under the title Perspectives on Non-Policy Argument in 1980 and as *Contributions on the Philosophy and Practice of CEDA* in 1981. In 1982, the journal became an annual publication, and its title was changed to *CEDA Yearbook*. In 1994 the journal began appearing under its current title. The essays included in this text were selected in order to reflect the breadth of perspectives offered in the most recent decade of the journal's existence, a decade that has witnessed substantial change within the CEDA debate community. Some of the essays assume a CEDA that distinguished itself through the use of non-policy or value topics, while others assume the more current practice of adopting policy topics. Some of the essays are broad in their perspective and generalizable to contexts outside of educational debate while others are quite unique to America's two-person, research oriented debate format. Some of the essays are very practical in identifying current difficulties and proposing solutions while others are more oriented toward defining and refining concepts. All of the essays, however, continue to carry relevance for debate educators, practitioners and others, and all provide a glimpse into the principle questions which continue to drive the journal's development and fuel the conversations of an academic community.

A great deal of thanks is due to all of the authors of the included essays and for the CEDA debate community itself which has provided these authors with an inspiration, a testing ground, and an audience. In addition, thanks is due to the Open Society Institute not only for supporting this publishing project but also for its many programs to reinvigorate debate in the United States and throughout the world.

PART ONE:
METHODS OF ARGUMENTATIVE SUPPORT

Academic debate is an educational activity which rests ultimately on an advocate's ability to prove or disprove a claim. Hence it rests centrally upon the idea of argumentative support. Debate has also been referred to as a "frame game" in the sense that virtually all arguments involve the importation of the ideas, standards and questions from other fields such as law, politics, or critical theory. The two essays in this section address this aspect of academic debate. Noting the debate community's heavy reliance on quoted testimony as evidence, **T.C. Winebrenner** in *Authority as Argument in Academic Debate* argues for a closer link between testimony and proof in the practice of debate. Because the debate community has embraced testimonial evidence but not applied the principles which support its use, Winebrenner claims that "the result has been testimony without proper foundation, appeals without argument, and evidence without comparison." Noting that the use of testimony as evidence requires that a foundation be laid, Winebrenner advances a number of specific standards for assessing the worth and validity of argument by authority in the academic debate context. In *Argument Borrowing and its Obligations*, **Carrie Crenshaw** observes that support in a debate context, both at the level of argument content and argument theory, is accomplished through the utilization of concepts from other literatures – a practice referred to as "argument borrowing." Noting the advantages and disadvantages of this practice, Crenshaw uses examples drawn from feminist literatures to show the tensions and inconsistencies that can result. She concludes by arguing for an expanded role for argumentative invention, the creative conceptual generation of ideas distinct from simple discovery through research.

AUTHORITY AS ARGUMENT IN
ACADEMIC DEBATE

T. C. Winebrenner

Once considered an unassailable postulate, the supposition that academic debate provides an environment in which students learn "to understand and communicate various forms of argument more effectively" (McBath, 11) has come under recent attack. For the most part, the charges grow out of a perceived rift between participant behavior and the argumentation theories academic debate supposedly embodies. While some scholars have stepped forward to defend the theoretical soundness of particular practices (Bahm & McGee; McGee & Simerly), as a general claim, Trapp's conclusion that "Debate is in trouble because its practitioners have lost their focus on argumentation" seems well founded (23).

One of the more obvious manifestations of academic debate having lost sight of its traditional grounding is found in the way participants use testimonial evidence in support of their asserted claims. Certainly, norms regarding the use of evidence cut to the very heart of the connection between academic debate and argumentation. The essential role of evidence in argument is attested to by Toulmin:

Let it be supposed that we make an assertion, and commit ourselves thereby to the claim which any assertion necessarily

PERSPECTIVES IN CONTROVERSY

involves. If this claim is challenged, we must be able to establish it — that is, make it good, and show that it was justifiable. How is this to be done? Unless the assertion was made quite wildly and irresponsibly, we shall normally have some facts to which we can point in its support: if the claim is challenged, it is up to us to appeal to these facts, and present them as the foundation upon which our claim is based. (1965, 97)

Testimony, or attributed facts and opinions, constitutes only one manner by which evidence may establish the foundation for a claim. Nonetheless, it seems to be the manner of evidence which academic debate embraces most enthusiastically. In fact, many contemporary debate texts use the terms "evidence" and "quotation" interchangeably, presuming that debate evidence will take the form of quoted facts and opinions (Bartanen & Frank; Branham, Church & Wilbanks; Freeley; Pfau, Thomas & Ulrich).

Trapp argues that the predominance of testimonial evidence has been detrimental to academic debate, pointing to an equivocation which he ascribes to a pedagogy more concerned with the *persuasiveness* of arguments than with their *soundness*. Expert opinion, Trapp argues, can be very persuasive. Public audiences are not well versed on all issues, and thus respond favorably to facts, opinions, and visions attributed to perceived experts. Unfortunately, once testimony is accepted as effective evidence it is not a long slide to equivocating compelling arguments with sound arguments. Trapp concludes that the practice of relying heavily on testimonial evidence is antithetical to the logical and dialectical argumentation constructs to which he would connect academic debate. It is my contention, however, that this antithesis is grounded in the ways debaters use testimony rather than the intrinsic nature of such evidence. I will argue that testimonial evidence has a logical-dialectical as well as a psychological dimension, and that when *properly employed,* testimony produces arguments which are both persuasive and sound. To that end, I will propose standards for using witness testimony which seek rapprochement between the epistemic substance of proof by authority and the practice of academic debate.

THE DEVALUATION OF WITNESS CREDIBILITY

At the center of this issue is a controversy relating to whether or not debaters are obliged to lay a foundation for testimonial evidence by addressing the qualifications of "expert witnesses." While it once might have been true that debaters were expected to qualify sources before presenting evidence (Sanders), that practice is no longer in vogue.

Among debate judges, there appears to be little consensus regarding if, when, or how witnesses should be qualified. The content of judge philosophy statements illustrates the range of expectations regarding the practice. At the 1994 CEDA National Tournament, fewer than 60% of the judges who made substantive comments about evidence even addressed the question of witness qualifications (Cross Examination Debate Association). For those who did, preferences ranged between instructing debaters to present source qualifications, affirming the importance of qualifications but failing to mention when or how they should be worked into the debate, allowing that qualifications need not be presented but should be available upon request, and instructing debaters not to present source qualifications.

Debaters seem more of a single mind. The norm for using testimonial evidence seems to be a convention in which testimony is introduced without reference to witness credibility. The 1990 CEDA championship debate illustrates. Of the 100 examples of testimony introduced into the debate, in only four instances did the debaters directly address witness qualifications, although there were seven subsequent references to those sources. In an additional six instances the evidence took the form of a report which contained internal qualifications, and in nine instances evidence was drawn from a nationally known publication which might lend some authority to the testimony. This majority of the testimony (74 instances) was introduced by citing a name and date, absent any reference to expert qualifications. This behavior is so prevalent in contemporary academic debate as to constitute a community norm (Trapp).

Support for the name-date convention normally is grounded in two metaphors. The more familiar metaphor compares academic debate to a judicial setting, and draws upon a practice Freeley calls *judicial notice* (103). In the court room, it is common practice for attorneys to stipulate certain facts, that is, to agree to accept a fact without a foundation having been laid. In circumstances in which expert witnesses are well known to the court, the qualifications of those witnesses often are stipulated so that counsel may forego the time and trouble of laying a foundation which opposing counsel has no intention of challenging. Freeley extends this to the practice of qualifying witnesses in academic debate, arguing that debaters, judges and audience members diligently research relevant issues, producing an extensive body of common knowledge. Thus, participants are likely to be conversant with the available authorities and evidence, allowing sources to be introduced with references "below the acceptable level for general argumentation" (390). Freeley concludes that "Time is precious in a debate and, given the choice between citing four pieces of evidence incompletely or two pieces of evidence completely, the experienced debater in this situation would take the risk of incomplete citation. The 'in-group,' the experienced judges and debaters, would understand why the choice was made and, for better or worse, accept it in this situation" (390). Setting aside the appeal to circumstances, the brunt of this argument seems to be that participants and judges can be expected to be familiar with available witnesses, making it unnecessary to lay a foundation for expert testimony.

The weakness of this comparison should be obvious. In the court room, the qualifications of witnesses are stipulated only when they are known to the court and when opposing counsel has no intention of impeaching the witness. Whether or not facts are stipulated remains the decision of opposing counsel, and the structure of the proceeding provides an opportunity for counsel to expedite examination of an expert witness by stipulating expertise. Furthermore, the court is likely to draw upon a small body of experts, increasing the likelihood opposing counsel will acknowledge the expertise of a particular witness. Academic debate is substantially different. It is the advocate, not the opponent, who decides whether to qualify a source, and should the opponent be willing to stipulate expertise there is no provision by which such stipulation might be recognized prior to laying the foundation. Even were such not the case, the virtually infinite profusion of potential sources from which debate testimony could be drawn mitigates the possibility that the "court" would be familiar with the witness. In addition, opponents are likely to have expert witnesses of their own, and must lay the groundwork for comparing witness testimony. In such a situation, stipulating witness qualifications would be foolish. Unlike academic debate, the judicial setting recognizes the fundamental importance of laying a foundation for deference, and forgoes that step only when no exception is to be taken.

The second metaphor compares academic debate to academic writing. It is the norm for scholarly publications to cite references by last name and date of publication. Academic debate is a scholarly activity, or so the argument goes, and should be subject to the same norms. The description of academic writing upon which the metaphor is based is accurate. Both the American Psychological Association and the Modern Language Association, whose manuscript conventions are considered standard for writing in the social sciences and humanities, subscribe to some form of name-date reference citations (American Psychological Association; Gibaldi & Achtert). While there are minor differences in the way the two stylebooks employ the convention, they both prescribe that attributed, paraphrased and quoted sources should be cited by author and date of publication. The assumption of the metaphor is that academic debate involves a kind of oral scholarship in which source references should be subject to the same conventions as would apply were the arguments presented in written form.

What this comparison forgets is that the purpose of source references in academic writing is different than the role of references in academic debate. Scholars engage in acts of attribution. That is, sources are cited to distinguish between original thought and ideas borrowed from other scholars. Reference citations are just that, references; they protect writers from claims of plagiarism and point readers to additional works by connecting ideas with particular sources. Academic arguments are grounded in the substance of scholarly ideas rather than attribution to previous publications. In academic debate, references often *are* the substance of arguments, and there is little proof beyond that revealed through testimony. Furthermore, when scholars propose to derive some advantage from presumed deference, their references to authoritative works commonly extend into textual commentary. Oddly enough, when debaters introduce evidence which depends upon presumed deference, they point to scholarly behavior as their license to avoid commentary.

All that remains is Freeley's circumstantial argument: Time is at a premium in academic debate, and qualifying witnesses is time consuming. His premises are true, but Freeley's conclusion begs the question of whether academic debate should inexorably yield pedagogy to convenience. The urge to reject outright an appeal to circumstance, which Richard Weaver described as "a surrender of reason," (qtd. in Johannesen, 130) is tremendous. While accepting the transcendence of convenience might put a quick end to any number of disputes about academic debate practices, it also would call to question the activity's right to the moniker "academic." Nonetheless, time is a constraint, and any reasonable standard for qualifying witnesses must be fully cognizant of that fact.

The problem with both metaphors used to justify name-date references is that the situations which dictate legal and academic citation conventions are unlike that which ought to dictate conventions in academic debate. Furthermore, when placed in a context similar to academic debate, both court room and academic writing behaviors conform to a higher standard of source qualification than otherwise would be the case. In essence, the metaphors fail because they are not attuned to the logical-dialectical dimension of proof by authority, which ought to be the basis upon which testimonial evidence is offered in an argumentation setting.

PROOF BY AUTHORITY

Testimony generally is thought to have its grounding in the Aristotelian doctrine of *ethos,* the classical counterpart of *source credibility.* Basically, this doctrine holds that the credibility of a message can be influenced by an audience's assessment of the intelligence, character, and good will of the messenger. Trapp implies that grounding judgments of testimony in *ethos* reflects the persuasive orientation of contemporary academic debate — public audiences are more likely to be *persuaded* by testimony from sources thought to be "competent, trustworthy, and dynamic" (29). It is from this point, claims Trapp, that the slide begins: Testimony from a more credible source is better than testimony from a less credible source; testimony from a less credible source is better than testimony from an unknown source; testimony from any source is better than no testimony at all. From there it is a fairly minor leap to the assumption that it is the *fact* of testimony rather that its *substance* and the *credibility* of the witness which constitutes logical proof. Although debaters may be cautioned that "The mere fact that a statement appears in print lends not one atom to its value," (Foster, qtd. in Branham, 77), reliance on conclusionary testimony and name-date references leaves little else upon which to base an appeal. These practices are reinforced by textbooks that refer to witness qualifications as a *comparative dimension* of evidence rather than a *necessary foundation* for witness testimony.

A somewhat different bent on testimony can be drawn from Whately's theory of presumption. That something is presumed, Whately reminds, does not mean a "preponderance of probability in its favour [sic]," but rather that it must "stand good till some sufficient reason is adduced against it" (qtd. in Golden & Corbett, 342). Presumptions preoccupy argumentative ground and are not to be disturbed until a good and sufficient claim to the contrary can be constructed. Whately refers to one such presumption as "deference" (Golden & Corbett, 346-7). That is, some persons, bodies or works are accorded a mantle of Authority. As learned persons or institutions, Authorities occupy a ground that favors their decisions or opinions. As such, to the extent to which learned persons are regarded as Authorities, they are accorded a degree of deference manifested in a presumption favoring their ideas.

While presumptions exist independent of arguers, it remains for arguers to find those presumptions that can be used to defend argumentative ground. Presumptions are derived from associations, but given the many associations that may exist in respect to any topic, arguers are confronted by presumptions that defend and presumptions which counter occupation. Arguers construct presumptions in the same sense that substantive arguments are constructed — topics are connected to relevant presumptions in an attempt to overthrow other presumptions and transfer burdens of proof. For instance, academic debate accepts the ubiquitous presumption against assertions, literally requiring that whoever asserts must prove. Authoritative proof can be generated by associating an assertion with a learned person to whom one might reasonably defer. In this sense, arguers *construct* a presumption of deference.

Ehninger and Brockriede describe the inferencing involved in associating ideas with learned Authorities as generating proof in the same manner as substantive logics generate proof — a claim (belief) is reasoned from specific evidence (expert opinion) by virtue of logical license (deference). The exigence for such proof is explained by Toulmin, Rieke and Janik:

> In a world of such complexity as ours, it would make no sense not to recognize the need to call upon expert judgment from time to time. If causes of death were judged only by lawyers and jurors, much would be lost from our system of justice. If only politicians judged the qualities of space vehicles or economic analyses, our government would have even more trouble than it has. Accordingly, we do rest claims upon the judgment of authorities. . . . (230)

The fact that an opinion is grounded in the judgment of an authority does not establish a probability that it is true, merely the *presumption* that it is so. Thus, the judgment of an authority preoccupies argumentative ground, and remains upon that ground until good and sufficient reason is advanced to challenge the occupation. The problem, as Toulmin (1972) explains, is determining to whom audiences should defer:

> All accredited members of a scientific profession may, in theory, be equal; but some turn out to be 'more equal' than others. On the one hand, there are the men [sic] whose word carries weight in the profession — the men whose judgements [sic] are accepted as authoritative by other workers in the field, and who come to speak 'for and in the name of' the science concerned. On the other hand, there are the men who have no such influence . . . [and] are in no position to act as spokesmen for the science they all serve. (264)

It follows that a claim to Authority must be established in order to construct a proof out of deference. As Toulmin, Rieke and Janik put it:

> The problem with such arguments is not the use of authority *per se;* it is the failure to establish an adequate *foundation* for the authority. To justify a claim with any cogency, the authority cited must be qualified as capable of providing expert judgment on the subject of the claim. If the claim is used in the court to express the cause of death in a murder case, the authority must be qualified as a physician, specializing in forensic medicine, with experience in determining death caused under questionable circumstances, with extensive experience in recent times, and with a reputation among those qualified to judge as an expert in this area. (230)

Thus, arguers who attempt to prove by testimony must lay a foundation for the inference by establishing that a witness should be accorded the presumption of deference. In effect, it is the qualifications of the witness which warrants an inference. Ehninger and Brockriede explain how this idea transfers to academic debate:

> In college debating and elsewhere the support for the warrant of an authoritative proof is quite important. All too often a college debater will support a contention with a few 'quotes' from 'noted authorities,' without taking the trouble to inform his [sic] listeners of the qualifications that make the opinions and information of his experts worth believing. Such a debater might as well attribute the statements to himself. Unless an authoritative warrant is supported adequately, no proof exists at all. For it is the warrant certifying the credibility of the source that carries testimonial evidence to the status of a claim. (160)

In an early treatment of Toulmin's model of argument, Trent discusses several extended variations of the DATA-WARRANT-

CLAIM relationship. In each, he adds to the basic structure an element he terms "backing for the data" (256). Toulmin's model, Trent claims, is not satisfactory for examining the material validity of the evidence upon which inferences are grounded. Rather than treating indicators of material validity as separate arguments, Trent opts for a holistic model in which such indicators are viewed as statements supporting the evidence. In the case of academic debate, this extension of the Toulmin model paves the way for understanding the symbiosis of presumption and substance in testimonial evidence.

When debaters establish constructive premises (data from which they will draw an inference), the material validity of those premises is always at question. As such, they ordinarily are drawn from testimonial evidence. To wit, when a debater reasons that AIDS has reached epidemic proportions, that claim might be constructed from the premise that a significant number of individuals have been infected with the virus. Barring the unlikely circumstance that the infection rate is common knowledge or that an opponent is willing to stipulate the premise, the material validity of the premise will rest on the ability of the debater to document the incidence of the disease. Since the warrant for this argument is substantive rather than authoritative, it would appear that the documentation does not constitute testimony in the traditional sense, and that no presumption of deference need be established. However, the acceptability of the *premise* is at question, and is supported only by the testimony of an individual or institutional authority. Thus, witness qualifications remain at issue even when evidence takes the form of a constructive premise.

In a similar fashion, when debaters rely on expert opinion, substantive reasoning ought to be involved. While it may be popular to rely on conclusionary evidence, such arguments are grounded solely in presumed deference. What is the epistemic weight assigned to that presumption? Deference should be viewed as one strand in a web of proofs that give force to an idea. Conclusionary evidence establishes only the *fact* of expert opinion, it does not consider the *substance* of the opinion. Upon what did the witness base this judgment? How soundly did the witness reason? Authoritative inferences (testimony revealing the reasoning by which a witness arrived at a conclusion) provide a basis for answering such questions by requiring a witness to explain a judgment. Such an explanation serves as substantive backing for the data, constructing a stronger web of proof for an arguer's claim.

It is only in the case of conclusionary evidence (assertions by authorities) that deference is isolated from substance. When such testimony is introduced into a debate, it has no force other than that given to it by the authority of the witness. Any backing for such evidence would have to come from the corroborative effect of similar conclusions reached by other witnesses.

Viewed from this perspective, proof by authority is consistent with both logical and dialectical notions of argumentation. Authority provides a basis for generating reasoned discourse. To prove by authority, an arguer must construct an inference in which testimony is connected to a claim by virtue of presumed deference, a warrant that exists only once a proper foundation has been laid by explicit reference to the expertise of the witness. By so doing, the arguer has facilitated inspection, evaluation and discussion of both the claim and the inferential process from which it was derived. Whether or not the argument is psychologically compelling, it is laid open in such a fashion that its intuitive soundness can be addressed by both parties to the dispute. Proofs by authority not only can be argued, they can be argued about.

STANDARDS FOR TESTIMONIAL EVIDENCE

How then, ought witness testimony be employed in academic debate? Any answer ought to reflect four basic assumptions evolving from the preceding discussion: First, a foundation must be laid which gives some basis for assuming expertise. Proof by authority is grounded in deference, but there is no presumption to defer absent some sign that testimony is taken from a learned person, institution or work. Second, witnesses must be introduced in such a way as to make a challenge to Authority feasible. Presumptions are open to challenge, and witnesses ought to be introduced in such a way that opponents know who is being questioned and what Authority they represent. Ambiguous references fail to identify the person, institution or work from which testimony has been drawn, thus insulating the witness from impeachment. By its very nature, ambiguous reference encourages *argumentum ad ignoratum* (the witness is assumed qualified until demonstrated otherwise). Third, preference should be given to strong testimony. Strong testimony is a symbiotic product of deference and substance in which both the expertise and reasoning of a witness stand up to critical scrutiny. While deference can be constructed without addressing the internal validity of an expert opinion, such arguments are supported by a weaker form of proof. Fourth, the implementation must be feasible within the practical constraints of competition. While preferences ought not be abandoned in the name of circumstance, they must be tempered by concerns with the real. Standards for introducing evidence that place unreasonable demands on competitors will be summarily ignored.

From these assumptions are derived five standards for using testimonial evidence in academic debate.

1. All sources must be clearly identified. Opponents have the right to know who has been called to testify, from which work that testimony was drawn, and when that work was published. Witnesses can be impeached on personal, temporal and substantive grounds. Evidence drawn from sources ambiguously identified hides the person and obscures the context of the testimony. While name and date may suffice to identify evidence drawn from commonly quoted works, a more complete citation should be readily available should the work prove to be unfamiliar. The ability to provide a suitable reference citation upon demand should be considered a minimum condition for introducing testimony
.

2. The initial testimony from any witness must include some sign that the witness is qualified to testify. The deferential grounding for testimonial evidence is not altered by the way that testimony is used. The force of authoritative inferences is derived both from the authority of the witness and the intuitiveness of the inference. When testimony is being used to establish a constructive premise, the material validity of the premise rests on the authority of the witness. Conclusionary testimony has no force other that taken from the authority of the witness. In each instance, the epistemic value of the testimony is connected in some significant way to the authority of the witness. No such authority exists absent a proper foundation. Source qualifications provide that foundation.

3. Direct signs of expertise are to be preferred over indirect signs. Without reference to signs of expertise, testimonial evidence produces unwarranted claims. The crucial question becomes, what constitutes a sign of expertise? Showing due concern for time constraints, I propose the following hierarchy of signs:

Direct evidence of expertise
Associative evidence of expertise
Evidence of accepted expertise

Direct evidence of expertise includes signs that the substance of the testimony is within a source's field of competence. Professional or professorial status in a relevant field constitutes one such sign. For instance, drawing testimony concerning economic theories from a professor of economics, testimony concerning legal principles from a court majority opinion, and testimony regarding carcinogens in a food substance from the Food and Drug Administration, would be examples of direct signs. Direct signs are more or less fallible, i.e., professor of urban studies would be a less fallible sign than would professor of sociology when considering urban culture, and the text of a majority opinion would be less fallible than the opinion of a legal expert when considering a particular Supreme Court decision. The more specifically a sign connects established expertise to the fact or opinion at question, the greater the presumption which that sign constructs.

Associative evidence of expertise includes indications that a witness is, represents, or is associated with an institution with general connections to the substance of the testimony. In this case, the sign of expertise is indirect. Congressmen, for instance, are assumed to have some knowledge about matters that fall within the purview of their committees, and research fellows from policy research centers are assumed to have some knowledge about policies they have investigated. However, such qualifications do not constitute signs of direct expertise. Associative signs also are more or less fallible; the long-time chair of the Senate Foreign Relations Committee might be presumed to speak with greater Authority than would a member of the Senate at large when addressing foreign policy issues. With an associative sign, the more closely the institution is connected to the issue at hand, the greater the presumption which an association with that institution would construct.

Evidence of accepted expertise covers a far broader range of signs. Into this category would fall witnesses who testify before investigatory committees, staff writers for recognized publications, news reports from recognized agencies, etc. In this case, arguers do not establish expertise directly or by association. Instead, they establish that reliable proxies have accepted the expertise of the witness, and interpret this prior acceptance as a sign that extends credibility to the case at hand. Once again, the signs are more or less fallible. Testimony drawn from a news report printed in the *New York Times* might be more authoritative than had it been drawn from a local newspaper, evidence drawn from a witness testifying before a Senate committee would be more authoritative than evidence drawn from a staff writer, and evidence drawn from a known publication would be more authoritative than evidence drawn from an unknown publication. The fallibility of accepted expertise is related to the credibility of the institution that made the prior determination.

Two additional points need to be made about the hierarchy. First, the weight of presumption attached to any witness is a function of the directness as well as the fallibility of the sign used to lay a foundation for the testimony. Stronger presumptions are harder to challenge than are weaker presumptions, and thus are to be preferred. Since less fallible signs create greater presumptions than do more fallible signs, a strong associative sign might create a greater presumption than would a weak direct sign. Second, witnesses may have connections to any number of signs. An expert testifying before a congressional committee, for instance, would have been accepted as a credible witness for some reason. Whatever that reason, it is likely to be more direct than the sign derived from having been called to testify, and should create a stronger presumption. The congressional testimony merely enhances that effect. It should be the responsibility of debaters to seek out the strongest signs so as to create the greatest presumption. Debate ought to involve a search for strong arguments, and making debaters responsible for the strength of the foundation they can lay for their testimonial evidence reinforces the epistemic dimension of the activity.

Requiring that some sign be used to lay a foundation for testimony does not place an undue burden on debaters. A phrase the equivalent of "Professor of Government at Harvard," or "testifying before the Joint Committee on Intelligence," falls easily within the bounds of reasonable expectations. Subsequent references to a witness, of course, require only some indication that the evidence is drawn from a source for whom a foundation already has been laid.

4. The substance of testimony is as important as the expertise of the witness. In academic debate, the symbiosis of substance and deference produces three distinct types of testimonial evidence. As a logical-dialectical experience, the relationship between substance and deference should create a clear hierarchy of preference.

Constructive Premises
Authoritative Inferences
Conclusionary Evidence

In academic debate, constructive premises ought to be preferred over all other uses of testimonial evidence because such usage places the greatest epistemic burden on the arguer. Rather than delegating the burden of argument to witnesses and depending upon expert opinion to confirm an asserted claim, constructive premises rely on witnesses only as sources of information from which claims might be inferred. Thus, a debater who asserts that underdeveloped nations should establish population control measures would be responsible for determining the premises upon which such a claim might reasonably be based, providing support for those premises, and defending the intuitive soundness of the argument. Testimony enters the debate only as a way of validating the premises.

An authoritative inference involves expert opinion, but presents that opinion in a manner that reveals the thinking of the authority. Upon what evidence is the opinion based? Is the opinion intuitively sound? Such testimony not only identifies the opinion a witness holds, it identifies the inference upon which that opinion has been based. Opinions that combine substance with deference create a stronger web of proof than do opinions which rely upon deference alone. Such opinions are harder to overturn, and thus are to be preferred over opinions which construct no argument. On the other hand, with an authoritative inference the burden to construct the argument has been delegated to an expert witness, and should be considered inferior to discourse in which that responsibility is assumed by an advocate.

Conclusionary evidence is the weakest form of testimony. Since neither the debater nor the witness makes a substantive argument, such evidence constitutes proof solely by presumption. As expert opinion, conclusionary evidence merely confirms that an expert has reached a conclusion convenient for the debater who introduces the testimony. The strength of the opinion rests entirely upon the credibility of the witness, and can be validated only by introducing confirming opinions, which themselves might rest solely upon the credibility of the witnesses. For conclusionary evidence to play an epistemic role in academic debate, it should be limited to testimony that addresses questions of what (fact) rather than questions of why or whether (opinion). It is what the witness has observed rather than what the witness has inferred which is entered into evidence, so the probative weight of the testimony is more likely to be determined by position than by preference. In this case, expertise alone may be sufficient to validate the observation.

5. Advocates must be prepared to compare evidence. Matters of expertise and substance are arguable. Who is a more reliable witness in a given situation? Which source presents the more sound argument? Where does the predominant opinion lie? When evidence is treated as absolute proof, evidence comparisons are unlikely. The fact that expert testimony confirms an assertion gives it some force, but that force is variable. Contemporary debate practice, with few exceptions, treats all testimony as equal. An evidence claim, no matter how poorly reasoned, is assumed superior to an unevidenced claim, no matter how well intuitively sound that claim might be. More recent testimony, no matter its force, is assumed superior to less recent testimony. These unwritten assumptions of contemporary debate do not lend themselves well to meaningful comparisons of evidence. Accepting the principles that experts are more or less credible, and that their opinions are more or less reasonable, paves the way for challenging testimonial evidence. The strength of evidence ought to be as much a matter of argument as are the issues of a resolution. Contemporary practice, however, does not give debaters the tools with which to challenge and compare testimony.

Adhered to on a community wide basis, these five standards would create a new environment for employing testimonial evidence in academic debate. Standards one and two are prescriptive norms, intended to establish minimum conditions for introducing testimony in academic debate. Standards three and four are comparative norms, intended to establish hierarchies of preference for making logical-dialectical choices between alternative witnesses and testimony. Standard five is a descriptive norm, intended to reflect he way testimony ought to be processed in the interaction between opposing advocates. Taken together, these new norms reconceptualize the relationship between evidence and claim, and should force debaters to rethink the ways they select, use and argue about evidence.

SUMMARY

Trapp argues that academic debate should subscribe to argumentation as a "master perspective" (26). His contention that notions of argumentation are central to the act of debating, and thus constitute the most appropriate perspective from which to critique academic debate, is well taken. Such a presumption pervades this essay. However, Trapp views the use of testimonial evidence, the predominate form of evidence in academic debate, as a manifestation of a debate pedagogy which overemphasizes rhetorical argument at the expense of logical-dialectical argument. While the connections between testimonial evidence and persuasive discourse are obvious, I have attempted to demonstrate that testimony has an epistemic dimension as well. The logic of testimony, derived from Whately's discussion of deference to learned persons, requires arguers to construct authoritative proofs in much the same way that they construct substantive proofs. Properly conceived, testimonial evidence involves *argument* from authority more than *appeal* to authority.

The problems that arise from testimonial evidence relate not to questions about its legitimate place in argumentation, but to the way it is employed in academic debate. Questions about witness credibility, the essential ingredient in epistemic testimony, have been sidetracked by inappropriate metaphors and arguments of convenience. The result has been testimony without proper foundation, appeals without argument, and evidence without comparison. If testimonial evidence is to play a role in academic debate, credibility must be revived as an issue so to reconnect testimony with presumption and substance. Community norms should encourage debaters to examine, evaluate and argue about evidence. The current practice of ignoring credibility issues while assuming that all testimony has the same probative value discourages arguments about evidence. To that end, I have proposed five standards for using testimonial evidence that recognize the logical-dialectical dimension of testimony, and create an environment where debaters may argue about evidence as well as argue with evidence.

WORKS CITED

American Psychological Association. *Publication Manual of the American Psychological Association* 3rd ed. Washington, DC: American Psychological Association, 1983.

Bahm (Broda-Bahm), Ken and Brian McGee. "CEDA Assessment Conference: The Brat-Pack and the Buffalos." *CEDA Report* (October 1, 1991): N. pag. (Mimeographed).

Bartanen, Michael D. and David A. Frank. *Nonpolicy Debate* 2nd ed.

Scottsdale, AZ: Gorsuch Scarisbrick, 1994.

Branham, Robert James. *Debate and Critical Analysis.* Hillsdale, NJ: Lawrence Erlbaum, 1991.

Church, Russell T. and Charles Wilbanks. *Values and Policies in Controversy.* Scottsdale, AZ: Gorsuch Scarisbrick, 1986.

Cross Examination Debate Association. *CEDA Nationals Judging Philosophies Booklet.* N.p.: Cross Examination Debate Association, 1994.

Ehninger, Douglas. *Influence, Belief, and Argument.* Glenview, IL: Scott, Foresman, 1974.

Ehninger, Douglas and Wayne Brockriede. *Decision by Debate.* New York: Dodd, Mead, 1963.

Freeley, Austin J. *Argumentation and Debate* 8th ed. Belmont, CA: Wadsworth, 1993.

Gibaldi, Joseph and Walter S. Achtert. *MLA Handbook for Writers of Research Papers,* 2nd edition. New York: Modern Language Association, 1984.

Golden, James L., Goodwin F. Berquist and William E. Coleman. *The Rhetoric of Western Thought* 4th ed. Dubuque, IA: Kendall/Hunt, 1989.

Golden, James L. and Edward P. J. Corbett. *The Rhetoric of Blair, Campbell and Whately.* New York: Holt, Rinehart and Winston, 1968.

McBath, James H., ed. *Forensics as Communication: The Argumentation Perspective.* Skokie, IL: National Textbook Company, 1975.

McGee, Brian R. and Greggory Simerly. "Intuition, Common Sense, and Judgment." *CEDA Yearbook* 15 (1994): 86-97.

Pfau, Michael, David A. Thomas and Walter Ulrich. *Debate and Argument.* Glenview, IL: Scott, Foresman, 1987.

Sanders, Gerald H. "Misuse of Evidence in Academic Debate." *Advanced Debate.* David A. Thomas, ed. Skokie, IL: National Textbook Company, 1975: 220-227.

Toulmin, Stephen. *Human Understanding* Volume I. Princeton: Princeton University Press, 1972.

_____. *The Uses of Argument.* Cambridge: Cambridge University Press, 1964.

Toulmin, Stephen, Richard Rieke and Allan Janik. *An Introduction to Reasoning* 2nd ed. New York: Macmillan, 1984.

Trapp, Robert. "The Need for an Argumentative Perspective for Academic Debate." *CEDA Yearbook* 14 (1993): 23-33.

Trent, Jimmie D. "Toulmin's Model of an Argument: An Examination and Extension." *Quarterly Journal of Speech* 54 (October 1968): 252-259.

Wenzel, Joseph W. "Three Perspectives on Argument." *Perspectives on Argument: Essays in Honor of Wayne Brockriede.*

T.C Winebrenner (Ph.D., Ohio State University) is Professor of Speech Communications and Director of Debate at California Polytechnic State University, San Luis Obispo. This essay was originally published in volume 16 (1995) of *Contemporary Arguementation and Debate*, pp. 14-29

ARGUMENT BORROWING
AND ITS OBLIGATIONS
Carrie Crenshaw

W hile many authors have elaborated on the relationship between argumentation theory and debate, Robert Trapp issued one of the most recent calls for a reevaluation of the alliance. He argues that we must recover a consensual argumentative perspective for academic debate to cure our "diseases" rather than merely suppress the symptoms of what ails the CEDA community. I would like to contribute to the discussion by suggesting the usefulness of the concept "argument borrowing" for conceptualizing the relationship between argumentation and debate. Such a conceptualization will assist both our theoretical and pedagogical efforts to flesh out the meanings of the argumentation metaphor for our activity.

Willard initially emphasized the significance of borrowing arguments in his elaboration on argument fields (71). While there is some dispute about the exact meaning of argument fields (McKerrow; Rowland; Toulmin; Willard; Zarefsky), continued attempts to conceptualize them recommend their utility for argument theory. Setting aside for the moment the issue of the exact definition of argument fields, I suggest that the concept of argument borrowing generated from fields research has much to offer our discussion of the argumentation metaphor for debate.

Accordingly, this essay explores the meaning of the term "argument borrowing" by describing the various instances of the practice and investigates its implications. Because the process of argument borrowing is so prevalent and arguably inherent in intercollegiate debate, I argue for the necessity of exploring its possibilities for better debate pedagogy.

ARGUMENT BORROWING IN DEBATE

Argument borrowing occurs on both theoretical and substantive levels. Scholars often utilize concepts from other literatures to advance the progress of debate theory. Hollihan and Riley describe this borrowing process as grafting the principles of related disciplines onto debate theory. They argue that the intent is to develop analogies "that mimic decision making in other arenas" (399). For example, the introduction of systems analysis as a way of theorizing debate about public policy making was very influential in the development of NDT debate (Brock, Chesebro, Cragan and Klumpp). A more recent example of this phenomenon is found in the work of Bile and Bahm. Bile's conception of the "whole resolution" borrowed from educational literature and general semantics, and Bahm's intrinsicness arguments initially borrowed from literature devoted to phenomenology. Each of these theoretical proposals have spawned challenges to the appropriateness and success of the borrowing process and have resulted in a productive theoretical discussion (see for example Klumpp; Hollihan and Riley; Madsen and Chandler; Bahm 1991 and 1993; Hill and Leeman 1990 and 1993).

Debate students as well as established scholars have engaged in the process of argument borrowing to improve the practice of debate theory. For example, debaters have imported "critique theory." Debaters justify their critical stance by borrowing from some of the literature in the field of critical theory. Some argue that there should be no burden to advocate a totalizing universal solution and that such universalized solutions have only contributed to the reification of current oppressive hierarchies. Others take the argument a step further by advocating the position that only a critical stance can open a discursive space for appropriate solutions to arise. The strategic lure of the importation seems to be its ability to transcend the limitations of policy burdens. Questions about the appropriateness of this practice have also resulted in a lively on-going dispute (see for example Lake and Haynie; Harris and Rowland; Panetta and Herbeck; Tucker).

Argument borrowing also occurs on the substantive level. When researching specific resolutions, debaters typically immerse them in relevant literatures and engage in a process of argument discovery. For example, research of the Spring 1994 resolution ("Resolved: that U.S. military intervention to foster democratic government is appropriate in a post cold war world") revealed that commentators most often talked about the cases of Bosnia, Haiti, and North Korea. As a result, these were very popular cases—easily researched and defended with evidence. Disadvantages frequently reflected current disputes in the literature over military strategy. Debates over commonly recurring arguments also indicate the presence of argument borrowing. For example, the debates over nuclear proliferation commonly mirror disputes in the nuclear-proliferation literature. The rate or inevitability of proliferation, the United States' role in anti-proliferation, the likelihood of specific scenarios of nuclear use—issues that recur in the proliferation literature also recur in debate rounds. The research process as it is practiced is often the heart of argument construction.

THE BENEFITS AND DRAWBACKS OF ARGUMENT BORROWING: SOME PEDAGOGICAL CONCERNS

Willard described the advantages of such argument borrowing, noting that importation of concepts from other fields performs a check of our thinking against new standards. "The motive is 'getting epistemically better'" (Willard 71). Argument borrowing can point to "new lines of argument, implications, and truths that were obscured by the logic being used" (Willard 71). Argument borrowing enables the transcendence of local argument obstacles. Yet, such borrowing has its limitations.

> Imported concepts have no value unless they have to some extent their own meanings. Fields borrow concepts to transcend local obstacles; this would not succeed unless the whole

apparatus of the borrowed concept were imported. This permits the inference that a field that wants the advantages of importation assumes the logical burdens of the imported concept (Willard 71).

Successful argument "borrowing incurs obligations" (Willard 71).

As it is practiced in intercollegiate debate, argument borrowing has its benefits and drawbacks. Argument borrowing offers the unique pedagogical benefit of direct student participation in the development of theory. Students participate in and contribute to the development of debate/argument theory through their efforts to overcome local argument obstacles. They do so both by "testing" the theoretical concepts of scholars in actual debate practice and by developing theoretical arguments of their own or in concert with their coaches. Often the result is advances in debate theory.

The importance of articulating the pedagogical advantages of intercollegiate debate cannot be understated. In a recent call for accountability, Hill persuasively argues that justification for intercollegiate debate in higher education must be grounded in a commitment to a pedagogical mission. Citing several authors (Herbeck; Kay; Sillars and Zarefsky; Sproule), Hill argues that the very existence of intercollegiate debate in higher education is dependent upon our ability to effectively articulate a pedagogical justification for the activity. This is increasingly the case because of the decreasing availability of resources in the academy. Questions about the educational value of debate require competent, well-supported answers. Hill notes "not only is it reasonable that, as educators, we be expected to address those questions seriously, it may well be imperative to the existence of our programs" (1-2).

Most pedagogical justifications of debate are based on the idea that debate should teach students argument skills to prepare them for future life. Colbert and Biggers illustrate this contention by drawing upon various sources to construct a coherent rationale for the activity. They offer three justifications for the continuation of intercollegiate debate in the face of institutional financial pressures. Each justification assumes that debaters are better prepared than their collegiate counterparts to engage in argument.

The first justification is that debate "improves the students' communication skills" (235). The second justification, debate promotes "depth of educational experience," relies heavily upon the importance of critical-thinking skills in order to make collective decisions (235). The third justification argues that debate is excellent "pre-professional preparation." These justifications appear to be a relatively straightforward list of the distinct merits of intercollegiate debate. Yet the authors primarily emphasize the importance of promoting critical thinking about argument. Colbert and Biggers quote Ehninger and Brockriede at length.

> The function of debate is to enable [humans] to make collective choices and decisions critically when inferential questions become subjects for dispute... When collective choices and decisions will be made critically . . . a critical decision is more "human" i.e., rational, than an uncritical one. The ability to arrive at decisions critically is that trait that chiefly distinguishes [human] from animal (15).

Critical decision making or argumentation is most significant when tied to collective choices. Debate prepares our students for making such choices.

Complaints about debate moving away from a public-speaking orientation might seem to contradict the claim that debate is justified by a conception of collective argument. However, as Rowland and Deatherage point out, "debate is now aimed at sharpening the research, critical thinking and organizational skills of students so that they can become effective advocates before government commissions, courts, and other decision-making bodies" (247). Despite disagreement over debate's public-speaking orientation, there still seems to be agreement on debate's promotion of critical-thinking in preparation for group critical decision making. Thus, the raison d'être of intercollegiate debate still resides in the value of attaining argument skills.

Student participation in the development of debate/argument theory through argument borrowing enhances the attainment of this goal. By participating in the development of this theory, students not only can learn argument "skills" per se but also can master the intricacies of argumentation theory. The debate "laboratory" provides the opportunity for students to see as well as participate in the construction of the direct relationship between argumentation theory and argument practice.

Yet the process of argument borrowing, if done poorly, also has its drawbacks. There can be no doubt that a major educational advantage of intercollegiate debate is the knowledge gained about different subjects. However, if the practice of argument borrowing privileges the discovery of arguments already existing in various literatures to the exclusion of the invention of arguments, then we have sacrificed a unique educational benefit of debate. Borrowing as a substitute for invention is seen most clearly in research practice and the use of evidence.

Tuman provides an in-depth analysis of some of the problems associated with reductionism in the research phase of debate. He argues that our lack of scrutiny of the claims, methodological choices, and reasoning of the authors cited in debate rounds predictably results in poor argument practice. Conducting the research phase of debate solely as a process of discovering what arguments already exist in the literature in order to mimic those arguments in rounds is a substantially impoverished approach. It is argument borrowing *reductio ad absurdum* and often results in fallacious appeal to authority. Instead, we should privilege the invention of argument informed by argument borrowing. Research should serve not as a replacement for the invention of arguments but rather as a process of finding support for building the invented argument.[1] Argument borrowing then would perform its appropriate role by enabling the transcendence of local argument obstacles.

Another difficulty associated with the practice of argument borrowing concerns the obligations of the importations. Inconsistency sometimes results from a poorly executed practice of argument borrowing. These inconsistencies can occur on both the substantive and procedural levels. Additional inconsistencies may occur between the assumptions of certain substantive and theoretical arguments. To illustrate the inherent risk of inconsistency associated with the practice of argument borrowing, I suggest that we consider the borrowing of arguments from feminist literatures for two reasons.

First, feminist theory and criticism is one field of inquiry from which debaters frequently borrow for both substantive and procedural arguments. Second, most feminist theories are uniquely reflective about the relationship between theory and practice. A consistent theme of many feminists is

> The interplay between theory and practice, a problematic that Showalter nominates as the central concern of feminist criticism (4) and Jane Marcus identifies as the "most serious issue facing feminist critics today" (218). Indeed, within an increasingly unstable and fractious movement, the discovery of "intersections" and "synthesis" between theory and practice seems to be one of the very few surviving consensual imperatives (103).

Warren argues that feminist emphasis on the relationship between theory and practice is both valuable and unique. The conventions of many feminists "place a high premium on 'practical theory,' and direct attention to the 'practice of theory,' two constructions rarely encountered in discussions of theory and theorizing" (103).

The initial importation of arguments from feminist literatures began on the substantive level. Debaters made and continue to make arguments about feminists. Such arguments often refer to literature regarding women's movement in the United States and abroad. At the link level, debaters identify causal agents that encourage or discourage feminist movement. At the impact level, debaters defend arguments about the implications of feminist movement. For example, a typical disadvantage of this sort argues that the affirmative causes a decline in feminist movement, which has serious enough results to weigh against the affirmative case scenarios. Other examples include but are not limited to discussions about eco-feminist movement, feminist human rights movement, and the absence of women in various institutions relevant to the topics debated.

A second and distinct round of importation began when debaters initiated procedural arguments based on feminist claims. These feminist arguments are somewhat different from (though related to) what I have described as arguments about feminists. Feminist arguments embrace various tenets of feminist theories to generate normative reasons for or against various debate practices. While a comprehensive theory of feminist argument has yet to be produced, several developments in feminist communication and rhetorical theory point to the usefulness of exploring the relationship between research about women and feminist research.

Communication theorists have described feminist communication research as characterized by 1) the interrogation of existing research practice by comparing it to actual women's experiences; 2) developing research procedures within traditional boundaries that correspond to women's communication behaviors; and 3) development of explicitly feminist methodologies which include critiques of the politics of androcentrism (Carter and Spitzack). Similarly, feminist rhetorical scholars have described feminist rhetorical theory as designed to analyze and evaluate the use of rhetoric to construct and maintain particular gender definitions for women and men. Feminist rhetorical theory attempts to re-vision traditional rhetorical theory with a new feminist consciousness of its drawbacks in order to create and sustain a new rhetorical theory and practice that includes the interests and perspectives of all people (Foss).

These authors make clear that feminist communication and rhetorical theories are not merely a discussion of women's communication practices (Spitzack and Carter). Instead, feminist communication and rhetorical theories address how communication research is practiced and how rhetorical theory functions to include or exclude persons on the basis of gender difference. Feminist argument is not just a set of claims "about women." It is a set of normative assumption about our societal constructions of gender.

In intercollegiate debate, discussions concerning feminist movement on the substantive level, as they are currently practiced, are not necessarily perceived as feminist argument. (I will return to the consistency of this issue a bit later.) Rather, feminist arguments explicitly question the basis of debate practice, referencing normative reasons for or against certain procedural practices in the debate round itself. Initially, these arguments appeared in the form of language-linked value objections or reasons to reject grammar standards for topicality.

For example, a debater might have argued that the Fall 1993 resolution "Resolved: that the national news media in the United States impair the public's understanding of political issues" is flawed in some sense because it contains a conceptualization of "public" that is centered in a sexist public/private dichotomy. The debater might have argued that the rhetorical practice of maintaining the gendered dichotomy perpetuates, reflects and/or buttresses the oppression of women. One past resolution contained the phrase "race or gender." Some negatives argued that the dichotomous construction of this topic excluded women of color. The identity of women of color is erased in a phrase that forces a choice between ethnicity and gender. In addition, some discussions of topicality have included normative reasons to reject a grammar standard for the interpretation of the resolution. Some affirmatives have argued that traditional rules of grammar have functioned hegemonically to undergird a sexist language structure that results in the exclusion of women. One final example: some debaters argue decision rules that ask the judge to reject any instantiation of patriarchy. Each individual must, so the argument goes, reject manifestations of patriarchy whenever the opportunity arises and especially in the case of that particular debate round.

In each of these instances, debaters have borrowed from feminist literature to make normative arguments about the worth of certain debate practices. While I am encouraged that our students are exposed to emancipatory feminist literatures, I also am concerned about the loose way in which these (and other) literatures are borrowed and applied in debate practice. Inconsistencies resulting from these importations have three dimensions. The first two, though rather obvious, are nonetheless important. The third necessitates a more sophisticated consideration of what it means to be a consistent advocate.

First, argument borrowing from feminist literatures for the development of substantive arguments often results in inconsistencies. Various feminists disagree about the meaning and impact of feminist movement, and as a result, their assumptions are often contradictory. For example, some feminists believe that feminist movement should be designed to include women in liberal political tradition. Jaggar calls these authors "liberal feminists." Liberal feminist movement is based on the assumption that women too can be rational decision makers in a liberal citizenship-based polity. The goal of the feminist movement is to treat women equally to men. Consequently, it involves a rights-based understanding of the success of each movement. Victories are achieved when women are accorded the same rights as men. Jaggar calls another segment of the feminist community "radical." Radical feminists base their theories of feminist movement in essentialist assumptions. Women are tied to nature in a way that men are not because of their reproductive capacity. As a result, feminist movement can provide solutions to environmental devastation and the pervasive militarism inherent in male hierarchies.

When debaters borrow from each of these literatures with the intent of developing coherent positions, inconsistencies often result. For example, the combination of an argument that the causal agent in the resolution spurs liberal feminist movement with an impact consisting of a defense of radical feminism as the solution to all of our environmental troubles lacks internally consistent links. Borrowing from inconsistent literatures in this instance results in the absence of internal links needed to establish a coherent position.

Second, such inconsistencies exist also on the procedural level. In the previous case of language-linked value objections or grammar standards, I have witnessed more than one debate round in which the standard was inconsistently applied. Debaters defending non-sexist linguistic standards as a reason to vote against their opponents would often engage in gender-specific language themselves or read evidence from the authors with the generic *he*. In addition, the assumptions of some of the feminist authors who object to the use of sexist language might be inconsistent with the assumptions of the impact to this procedural argument. The team defending this position often asks the judge to "punish" the opposing team for the use of exclusive language with a loss. Indeed, the assumptions of some feminist authors might be inconsistent with the assumptions of the debate format itself—the arguably dichotomous and even hierarchical construction of the inevitable win/loss.

Finally, poor borrowing practices can result in inconsistencies between the assumptions of substantive and theoretical positions. Let me return to the perceived but facile distinction I pointed out earlier between arguments about feminists and feminist argument. The current practice of borrowing from feminist literatures to construct arguments about feminist movement is often seen as a substantive argument absent of procedural implications. Yet most often the observations about patriarchy borrowed to impact the argument contain many assumptions that have implications for how every issue should be considered. For example, many "fem disads" are offered in the context of a simplistic cost/benefit analysis framework. But what if the feminist author who objects to the horror of patriarchal militarism also advocates as an inherent part of her or his claim that mindless cost/benefit analysis leads to such patriarchal military nightmares?

These sorts of inconsistencies certainly are not limited to arguments concerning feminists. My point is that it is a rare (perhaps nonexistent) instance in which factual claims are not tied to normative assessments. "Borrowing makes arguers accountable to the field from which the arguments were lifted" (Willard 71)—accountable for the normative assumptions underlying the claims that one borrows. This is particularly relevant to the way in which debaters argue for a particular decision calculus. Borrowing substantive impact evidence might oblige an advocate to adhere to the assumptive procedural decision calculus contained in the author's evaluation of that impact.

A return to an emphasis on argument invention instead of mere discovery would enable the avoidance of such inconsistencies and promote the development of coherent, and thus more strategically sound, argumentative approaches. We should teach our debaters advocacy through invention of arguments and (then) research skills that will provide supporting material. My point is not that debaters should be held responsible for every single belief ever held by an author. Instead, I stress the importance of the ability to discern which assumptions are relevant to the arguments made and the ability to invent and argue consistent claims.

CONCLUSION

In the end, I suppose I have engaged in a bit of argument borrowing myself in my pursuit of "getting epistemically better," for Willard initially observed that borrowing incurs obligations. Primarily, I have argued that exploring the process of argument borrowing in intercollegiate debate reveals some of the benefits and drawbacks to our current debate practices. It also provides a useful pedagogical construct for helping coaches and students alike to conceptualize the development of debate theory and the research process as well as the issue of argument consistency. It draws attention to the relative importance of argument invention over discovery.

It is my hope that understanding many of our current practices—good or bad—as argument borrowing will assist our self-reflexive attempts to recover an argumentative perspective for academic debate. Fundamentally, debate is process of reason giving. We can borrow all of our reasons, or we can do our best to invent good reasons and use argument borrowing to "check our thinking" in our pursuit of "getting epistemically better."

NOTES

1. Trapp provides a good conceptualization of the relationship between evidence and reasoning (31).

WORKS CITED

Bahm, Kenneth. "The Impractical Characterization of Intrinsic Justification: A Rebuttal." *Argumentation and Advocacy* 30 (Summer 1993): 43-49.

—. "Intrinsic Justification: Meaning and Method." *CEDA Yearbook* 9 (1988): 23-29.

—. "The Pragmatics of Intrinsic Justification: A Response to Hill and Leeman." *Argumentation and Advocacy* 27 (1991): 171-78.

Bile, Jeffery T. "When the Whole is Greater than the Sum of the Parts: The Implications of Wholistic Resolutional Focus." *CEDA Yearbook* 8 (1987): 8-15.

Brock, Bernard L., James W. Chesebro, John F. Cragan, and James F. Klumpp. *Public Policy Decision-Making:System Analysis and Comparative Advantages Debate*. New York: Harper, 1973.

Carter, Kathryn, and Carole Spitzack. *Doing Research on Women's Communication: Perspectives on Theory and Method*. Norwood, New Jersey: Ablex, 1989.

Colbert, Kent, and Thompson Biggers. "Why Should We Support Debate?" *Journal of the American Forensics Association* 21 (Spring 1985): 237-40.

Dudczak, Craig A. "On the Dilemma of Ad Hoc Argument Fields: The Inadequacy of Field-Dependent Argument Standards." *Argument and Social Practice: Proceedings of the Fourth SCA/AFA Conference on Argumentation*. Eds. J. Robert Cox, Malcolm O. Sillars, and Gregg B.

Walker. Annandale, VA: Speech Communication Association, 1985. 886-96.

Ehninger, Douglas and Wayne Brockriede. *Decision by Debate*. New York: Dodd, Mead and Company, 1963.

Foss, Sonja K. *Rhetorical Criticism: Exploration and Practice*. Prospect Heights: Waveland P, 1989.

Harris, Scott L., and Robert Rowland. "Post-Modernism, Argumentation, and Praxis: A Case Study of Academic Debate." *Argument and the Postmodern Challenge: Proceedings of the Eighth SCA/AFA Conference on Argumentation*. Ed. Raymie E. McKerrow. Annandale, VA: Speech Communication Association, 1993. 31-35.

Herbeck, Dale. "Debate Scholarship: A Needs Assessment." *National Forensic Journal* 8 (Spring 1990): 1-16.

Hill, Bill. "The Value of Competitive Debate as a Vehicle for Promoting Development of Critical Thinking Ability." *CEDA Yearbook* 14 (1993): 1-22.

Hill, Bill, and Richard W. Leeman. "On Not Using Intrinsic Justification in Debate." *Argumentation and Advocacy* 26 (Spring 1990): 133-44.

—. "The Impracticality of Intrinsic Justification: Response to Bahm." *Argumentation and Advocacy* 30 (Summer, 1993): 50-57.

Hollihan, Thomas A., and Patricia Riley. "Academic Debate and Democracy: A Clash of Ideologies." *Argument and Critical Practices: Proceedings of the Fifth SCA/AFA Conference on Argumentation*. Ed. Joseph W. Wenzel. Annandale, VA: Speech Communication Association, 1987. 3

Jaggar, Allison. *Feminist Politics and Human Nature*. Totowa, New Jersey: Rowman and Allanheld, 1983.

Kay, Jack. "Research and Scholarship in Forensics as Viewed by an Administrator and Former Coach." *National Forensic Journal* 8 (Spring 1990): 61-68

Klumpp, James F. "Beyond the Social Engineering Paradigm: Public Policy Decision-Making—Fifteen Years Later." Argument and Critical Practices: Proceedings of the Fifth SCA/AFA Conference on Argumentation. Ed. Joseph W. Wenzel. Annandale, VA: Speech Communication Association, 1987. 395-98

Lake, Randall A., and Brooks Haynie. "Debate Against Itself: Post-Modernism, Academic Debate, and the Public Sphere." *Argument and the Postmodern Challenge: Proceedings of the Eighth SCA/AFA Conference on Argumentation*. Ed. Raymie E. McKerrow. Annandale, VA: Speech Communication Association, 1993. 17-24.

Madsen, Arnie, and Robert C. Chandler. "When the Whole Becomes a Black Hole: Implications of the Holistic Perspective." *CEDA Yearbook* 9 (1988): 30-37.

Marcus, Jane. "Storming the Toolshed." *Feminist Theory: A Critique of Ideology*. Eds. Nannerl 0. Keohane, Michelle Z. Rosaldo, and Barbara C. Gelpi. Chicago: U of Chicago P, 1986.

McKerrow, Ray E. "On Fields and Rational Enterprises: A Reply to Willard." Proceedings oft he [First] Summer Conference on Argumentation. Eds. Jack Rhodes and Sarah Newell. Falls Church, VA: Speech Communication Association, 1980. 403-13.

Panetta, Edward M., and Dale A. Herbeck. "Argument in a Technical Sphere: Incommensurate Rhetorical Visions." *Argument and the Postmodern Challenge: Proceedings of the Eighth SCA/AFA Conference on Argumentation*. Ed. Raymie E. McKerrow. Annandale, VA: Speech Communication Association, 1993. 25-30.

Rowland, Robert. "Argument Fields." *Dimensions of Argument: Proceedings of the Second Summer Conference on Argumentation*. Eds. George Ziegelmueller and Jack Rhodes. Annandale, VA: Speech Communication Association, 1981. 56-60.

Rowland, Robert C. and Scott Deatherage. "The Crisis in Policy Debate." *Journal of the American Forensic Association* 24 (Spring 1988): 246-50.

Showalter, Elaine. "Introduction: The Feminist Critical Revolution." The New Feminist Criticism: Essays on Women, Literature, and Theory. New York: Pantheon, 1985.

Sillars, Malcolm and David Zarefsky. "Future Goals and Roles of Forensics." *Forensics as Communication: The Argumentative Perspective*. Ed. James H. McBath. Skokie, IL: National Textbook, 1975. 83-100

Spitzack, Carole, and Kathryn Carter. "Women in Communication Studies: A Typology for Revision." *Quarterly Journal of Speech* 73 (1987): 401-23.

Sproule, J. Michael. "Constructing, Implementing, and Evaluating Objectives for Contest Debate." *Journal of the American Forensic Association* 11 (1974): 8-15.

Toulmin, Stephen. *The Uses of Argument*. Cambridge: Cambridge UP, 1969.

Trapp, Robert. "The Need for an Argumentative Perspective for Academic Debate." *CEDA Yearbook* 14 (1993): 23-33.

Tucker, Robert E. "An Archaeology of Argument: Post-Structuralism and

Intercollegiate Debate." *Argument and the Postmodern Challenge: Proceedings of the Eighth SCA/AFA Conference on Argumentation.* Ed. Raymie E. McKerrow. Annandale, VA: Speech Communication Association, 1993. 36-42.

Tuman, Joseph S. "A Response to Crenshaw's Dominant Form and Marginalized Voices: Argumentation about Feminism(s)." *CEDA Yearbook* 14 (1993): 84-91.

Warren, Helen B. "'The Truth Lies Somewhere Between the Two': Feminist Formulations on Critical Theory and Practice." *Argument and Critical Practices: Proceedings of the Fifth SCA/AFA Conference on Argumentation.* Ed. Joseph W. Wenzel. Annandale, VA: Speech Communication Association, 1987.103-12.

Willard, Charles Arthur. "Argument Fields." *Advances in Argumentation Theory and Research.* Eds. J. Robert Cox and Charles Arthur Willard. Carbondale and Edwardsville: Southern Illinois UP, 1982. 24-77.

Zarefsky, David. "Persistent Questions in the Theory of Argument Fields." *Journal of the American Forensic Association* 18 (Spring 1982): 191-203.

Carrie Crenshaw (Ph.D., University of Southern California) is a writer living in Birmingham, Alabama and formerly a tenured professor and President of the Cross Examination Debate Association. His essay was originally published in volume 15 (1994) of *CEDA Yearbook* (now known as *Contemporary Argumentation and Debate*), pp.76-85.

PART TWO:
THE QUESTION OF CRITICAL THINKING

To those outside the competitive academic debate community, the activity is often assumed to primarily emphasize skills in public speaking. To those who practice or teach research-oriented formats of debate though, the emphasis is often placed on critical thinking: the ability to understand, apply and evaluate ideas. While it is clearly central to the educational mission of debate, this concept is not easy to research and the results of the research that has been conducted thus far cannot be considered unambiguous. While research has continued following the original publication of these essays,[i] the included works by Hill and Colbert represent comprehensive attempts to address the issue of whether contemporary research on the critical thinking effects of debate training permits the conclusion that debate has tangible benefits. **Bill Hill** in *The Value of Competitive Debate as a Vehicle for Promoting Development of Critical Thinking Ability* urges a more critical attitude toward the claim that debate produces an increase in critical thinking. He concludes that, "the debate community has not generated sufficient research to demonstrate that participating in competitive debate promotes development of critical thinking ability to any significant degree." He notes that future research in this area should impart more precision to the concept of critical thinking, employ more diverse research methods, and demonstrate more applicability to different models of competitive debate team organization. **Kent Colbert** in *Enhancing Critical Thinking Ability Through Academic Debate* directly responds to Hill's central claim that current research is insufficient to permit a positive conclusion. Colbert argues that Hill calls for too direct and too deterministic a model and that his critique of current research reflects a hypercritical attitude about the debate activity. He concludes that there is "presumptive proof" for the existence of a relationship between debate training and critical thinking. This exchange provides an example of a focused debate on an essential and still very timely question.

[i] See for example Allen, M., Berkowitz, S., Hunt, S., & Louden, A. (1999). A meta-analysis of the impact of forensics and communication education on critical thinking. *Communication Education, 48:1*, 18-30.

THE VALUE OF COMPETITIVE DEBATE AS A VEHICLE FOR PROMOTING DEVELOPMENT OF CRITICAL THINKING ABILITY
Bill Hill

Demands for educational accountability have become increasingly widespread in higher education (Conrad and Wilson). Accountability demands may emerge from campus administrators, from within academic disciplines, or from students (Hill; Bogue and Saunders). University systems and state governments also have begun to impose accountability demands (Bogue and Saunders). Although accountability demands may be motivated by educational, political, or ethical concerns (Bogue and Saunders), financial concerns which have imposed an era of "unprecedented austerity" on education will remain a primary impetus for educational accountability (Zemsky and Massey). Failure to meet accountability demands can result in serious programmatic consequences; it can prevent implementation of new programs or force existing programs to be significantly cut back, restructured, or terminated (Barak; Conrad and Wilson).

Meeting educational accountability demands remains a significant concern for the debate community. As Sillars and Zarefsky explain, because of the immense pressures for educational account-ability, we no longer can assume our programs will "survive as ends in themselves or simply through the force of tradition" (84). Rather, they say, "[a]s programs are evaluated, it legitimately will be asked to what extent they advance educational goals" (84).[1] Additionally, some have persistently questioned the educational value of debate (Sproule; Herbeck), while others more emphatically suggest our activity has lost touch with any sense of a basic educational mission (Kay).[2] Not only is it reasonable that, as educators, we be expected to address those questions seriously,[3] it may well be imperative to the existence of our programs. As Russell Church so aptly stated, "if we do not do things to save and promote the activity, it may not sur-vive the current budgetary and political climates in higher educa-tion" (2).[4]

One way we have attempted to explain and justify our education-al mission has been to argue that participating in debate promotes development of critical thinking ability. Although most writers do not claim that developing critical thinking ability is our only educational goal, there is little doubt that many have assumed it to be our most important. Developing critical thinking ability is argued to be central to the educational mission of debate (Ehninger and Brockriede; Freeley), it has become one of the most frequently cited educational justifications for debate (Colbert), and more research has explored how debate promotes development of critical thinking ability than any of our other possible educational values. Forensic directors have rated developing critical thinking as our highest educational goal (Rieke),[5] and debaters have suggested that it should be (Matlon and Keele). Some have suggested that developing critical thinking ability should be the "overriding concern of academic debate" (Hill 23).

I contend that, despite its presumed importance, we are ill-pre-pared to use development of critical thinking ability to meet educa-tional accountability demands. In order to substantiate that con-tention, I will: 1) review the relevant research and explain why it is insufficient to convincingly demonstrate that participating in com-petitive debate promotes development of critical thinking ability; and 2) argue that future research in this area needs to consider two gen-eral principles—clarification and diversification—in order to gather the data necessary to meet educational accountability demands. Ultimately, my purpose is to demonstrate that we need additional research about this possible educational outcome and to suggest some ways to make that research more productive.

CURRENT RESEARCH ON PROMOTING CRITICAL THINKING ABILITY

Prior to 1983, six experimental studies were conducted to test the degree to which training in argumentation and debate promotes development of critical thinking ability. Howell tested debaters in 24 different high schools before and after completion of a 6 month debate season. In 12 schools, the debaters outgained the non-debaters on the critical thinking test instrument, while in 11 schools the non-debaters outgained the debaters.[6] Although the results suggest that there might be a relationship between training in debate and development of critical thinking abiity, Howell was not able to demonstrate that the relationship was significant. Brembeck studied students in argumentation classes at 11 different institutions and found that in 8 of the institutions, the students in the argumentation class outgained the control students. Although the gains within the sub-samples were not statistically significant, Brembeck was able to demonstrate a significant overall effect by adding scores across these sub-samples. He also found that the argumentation students in 10 of the 11 sub-samples had a higher average pre-test score than the students in the control sample, which he suggested made the findings even more significant. Williams compared college debaters and non-debaters in a pre-test/post-test design on a critical thinking test. Like Howell, Williams found gains in the direction of the improved critical thinking ability for those with debate experience but could not demonstrate that the gains were statistically significant. Beckman tested students in argumentation courses and students in discussion courses in 8 different colleges and universities. Beckman did not report significant differences between experimental and control groups within the same college or university but did find that differences in mean gain between colleges were significant. Jackson tested debaters at 9 different colleges and found that in 5 colleges, debaters made significantly higher gains in critical thinking than non-debaters, while in 4 colleges the non-debaters out-gained the debaters. Cross studied high school students across their first semester of debate and found that on two of the sub-tests of the critical thinking instrument, those debaters classified as "high participators" registered statistically significant gains in developing critical thinking ability when compared to a control group of non-debaters. He did not report statistically significant results for either low or non-participators.

While these studies suggest that there may be a relationship, they do not convincingly demonstrate that participating in debate, significantly promotes develop of critical thinking ability. Each study used the Watson-Glaser Test of Critical Thinking as its measurement instrument. However, no study reported that in each of its sub-samples training in debate promoted development of critical thinking skills. In fact, all studies reported that in some of the sub-samples, no effect or the opposite effect occurred. Although Howell, Williams, and Cross report an overall effect which suggests that training in debate promotes development of critical thinking ability, they were not able to demonstrate that it was significant.

Both Brembeck and Beckman report statistically significant gains, but they were able to achieve significance only by adding scores across all sub-samples. In Brembeck's study, 11 total sub-samples were analyzed and the experimental students outgained the control students in 8 of those sub-samples. However, in 6 of those 8 sub-samples, difference in mean gain was not significant. In Beckman's study, the experimental group did not achieve significant gains in any of the sub-samples. It is also the case that neither Brembeck nor Beckman made an effort to control the instructional methods nor content across sub-samples of students in the argumentation and discussion classes. However, the way an instructor teaches may be an important factor in promoting development of critical thinking ability (McMillan), and the content of a course might reasonably be expected to influence the skills students developed. Thus, one cannot assume that the sub-samples were functionally equivalent. Finally, it is problematic to assume that instruction received in either a semester-long argumentation or discussion class approximates the training and experience on receives by participating in competitive debate. Thus, the results of both of these studies must be interpreted cautiously.

Cross did find that students with high levels of participation in debate significantly outgained non-debaters; however, his results are tenuous. Cross reported gains for students with high participation in debate on two of the five sub-tests of the Watson-Glaser Critical Thinking Appraisal. Follert and Colbert convincingly argue that the results of this study are "equivocal" at best (7), since the two sub-tests of the Watson-Glaser Critical thinking instrument cannot be considered independently stable. Their argument is legitimate. Modjeski and Michael argue that the stability of test scores is a significant concern with the Watson-Glaser test.[7] Berger has also noted that the test authors do not encourage using part-scores on the test to evaluate sub-skills.[8]

Jackson's results also must be interpreted cautiously. While Jackson reports a statistically significant gain for experimental students in 5 of the 9 sub-samples he analyzed, he also reports that in the 4 other sub-samples, the control students outgained the experimental students. Additionally, Jackson was not able to demonstrate either that the amount of debate competition a student had or that the competitive success the student achieved contributed to the development of critical thinking ability.

Follert and Colbert performed a meta-analysis of the results of the studies by Howell, Brembeck, Williams, Beckman, and Jackson and concluded that the reported results were not sufficient to demonstrate with any degree of certainty that debate training promotes development of critical thinking ability.[9] Follett and Colbert analyzed the 47 paired comparisons (experimental group versus control group) reported across these studies. In 28 of the comparisons, the researchers reported that, to varying degrees, the experimental subjects (debaters or those in argumentation and debate classes) gained more on the critical thinking test (measured by pre-post test comparison) than did the control subjects (non-debaters and students not in the argumentation and debate course). However, in 19 of the comparisons, the control subjects gained more than the experimental subjects. Follert's and Colbert's statistical analysis of these paired comparisons indicated that there is "an 88% chance that these results could be accounted for by chance" (8). According to Follert and Colbert, "This research cast substantial doubt on the claimed relationship between debate training and critical thinking skill improvement" (8). They went on to explain the implication their research has on the educational mission of debate. They write:

> While this research may not prove that there is not a relationship between critical thinking skills and debate training, it shakes the foundation upon which this long-standing assumption has existed. If this relationship is not firmly established, a radical re-evaluation of our purpose is required. This is not to say that the debate activity does not offer many educational benefits and skills to individual participants. However, additional research which statistically demonstrates critical thinking benefits is clearly warranted (10-11).

When Follert's and Colbert's findings are considered with the mixed results reported in the studies they analyzed, their conclusion seems abundantly justified: until we generate more conclusive evidence, we have insufficient data to demonstrate that debate training significantly promotes development of critical thinking ability.

Since Follert and Colbert "shook our foundation," only two studies which investigated the presumed relationship between debate training and development of critical thinking ability have been reported. Colbert, using samples of both NDT and CEDA debaters, found that the combined debater samples (CEDA plus NDT) significantly outgained non-debaters on the critical thinking test. He also found that NDT and CEDA debaters differ significantly in terms of gains in development of critical thinking ability but concluded that his data did not justify identifying which group (NDT or CEDA) was significantly better.[10] Whalen compared students in an argumentation course with a co-curricular requirement of participating in debate, students in an argumentation course with no such requirement, and students in a basic speech class. Whalen was not able to demonstrate that students in an argumentation course with a co-curricular debate requirement made any significant gains in critical thinking ability. In fact, Whalen reported precisely the opposite; the students in the argumentation course with the co-curricular debate requirement actually achieved lower scores on the post-test than they had on the pre-test.[11]

Considered jointly, the results of these two studies do not provide the evidence Follert and Colbert so clearly demonstrated that we need. First, taken at face value, the results of the studies are contradictory; while Colbert finds debate training does result in significant gains in critical thinking ability, Whalen found that a decrease occurred.[12]   Second, both researchers suggest that additional research is necessary to demonstrate that participating in debate promotes development of critical thinking ability. Colbert, for example, reports that although his results are statistically significant, they offer only "preliminary proof" about the relationship.[13] He further suggests: "Replication of these results with larger samples are later needed to firmly establish a case for contemporary debate practices." Whalen makes the point more emphatically. Writes Whalen,

> many authors have suggested educational benefits other than critical thinking enhancement resulting from participation in intercollegiate debate (Colbert and Biggers, 1985). The data in this study begin to suggest that support for such a justification for a co-curricular requirement might be better sought through research into some of these other benefits (396).

While not attempting to argue that the results are conclusive, Whalen is apparently convinced that the prospect of convincingly demonstrating that participating in debate promotes development of critical thinking ability is remote.

We have not substantially improved our position since Follert and Colbert sounded the first notice that the results of our research are, at best, inconclusive. Taken as a whole, the available evidence neither demonstrates that debate does not affect development of critical thinking ability, nor that it does. Even though some evidence suggests that there is a relationship between debate training and development of critical thinking ability, we are not able to demonstrate convincingly that the relationship is significant. As a result, it is clear that we are ill-prepared to meet educational accountability demands by claiming that our activity promotes development of critical thinking ability.

SUGGESTIONS FOR FUTURE RESEARCH

Developing critical thinking ability is widely regarded to be an important educational goal. Developing critical thinking ability is argued to be important for adults in their personal relationships, the workplace, and in public decision-making (Brookfield). The importance of critical thinking ability is also thought to increase as technology and information increase (Cierzniak). McMillan cites a number of factors which suggest there is a national movement to promote development of critical thinking ability.[14] Understandably, Colbert argues that developing critical thinking ability is central to the goals of higher education generally,[15] and Katula and Martin argue that developing critical thinking ability is one of the major contributions speech communication can make to a student's education. As a result, if we can demonstrate that competitive debate significantly contributes to the development of critical thinking ability, we can forge a very compelling educational justification for our activity. Future research might productively utilize two important principles-clarification and diversification.

CLARIFICATION

Clarification is important in future research in two very different ways. First, we need to define more clearly the construct we propose to teach and to study. "Critical thinking" is not a precise concept. Ennis and Landis and Martin suggest that scholars have very diverse views about how to conceptualize "critical thinking ability." McPeck characterized these differences as "very real" (19).[16] Thompson and Melancon note that the diverse ways in which the construct is defined "pose serious impediments" (1224) to research about critical thinking ability.

As a field, we have not attempted to define with any precision what the construct means. Some of our writers speak of "critical thinking ability" without making any effort to specify what the construct means. For example, Freeley identifies developing critical thinking ability as one of the educational outcomes debate is "specifically designed to achieve" (21), but offers no explanation of what critical thinking involves other than referring to some unspecified "principles of critical thinking" those participating in debate can expect to enhance. Perhaps in response to the imprecise nature of this construct, or perhaps partly due to methodological expediency, researchers in our field (Howell; Brembeck; Williams; Beckman; Jackson; Cross; Huseman, Ware, and Gruner; Follert and Colbert; Colbert; Whalen) have consistently used the operational definition of "critical thinking" contained in the Watson-Glaser Test to explain the construct.[17]

The Watson-Glaser Critical Thinking Appraisal presumes that critical thinking is a composite of five abilities. They include: 1) the ability to define a problem; 2) the ability to select pertinent information for the solution of the problem; 3) the ability to recognize stated and unstated assumptions; 4) the ability to formulate and select relevant and promising hypotheses; and 5) the ability to draw valid conclusions and judge the validity of inferences (McPeck). While these appear to be abilities we might reasonably associate with critical thinking, there are two potential problems with this operational conception. One problem is that these abilities have not been demonstrated to be the constituents of critical thinking. Writes McPeck:

> How do Watson and Glaser know that there are true "abilities" at work here? Answer: because they took them from a list provided by Dressel and Mayhew in a government document. But how do Dressel and Mayhew know that there are "abilities" corresponding to these descriptions? Answer: because they *appear* to be related to the concept of critical thinking." Thus, we have one person's "appearance" serving as the next person's "reality," which has subsequently served as the basis for hundreds of empirical studies in the area. We have here in microcosm the chronology of how a casual phrase ("critical thinking abilities") can become a recurrent piece of educational jargon, which is eventually *reified* into a cognitive ability – in this case, a latent trait (57).

Similarly, Helmstader noted "disappointment" that "the construct validity of this trait and its measure [as used in the

Watson- Glaser test] has not been explored more thoroughly and systematically" (1693).

The other, and more serious, problem is that, even assuming it is well-grounded, Watson's and Glaser's operational definition does not provide a sufficient basis to explain our education mission with respect to critical thinking. In order to meet educational accountability demands, we must identify the general educational outcomes we attempt to achieve and specific abilities our students must develop en route to achieving those outcomes (Andersen; Sproule; Sillars and Zarefsky; McMillan). Specificity is necessary because the more clearly we can define the construct, the more fully we will understand what we seek to do, the more capable we will be to explain that mission to others, and the better suited we will be to develop research which provides a meaningful measure of the degree to which we accomplish the objectives we have established. However, Watson and Glaser do not identify the specific skills our students must develop in order to increase their critical thinking ability. Watson and Glaser treat the abilities they identify as though they are unidimensional.[18] However, the abilities they identify may, themselves, actually be multidimensional or composites of a number of additional sub-abilities. For example, the "ability to define a problem" is a composite of a number of sub-abilities such as the ability to identify a controversy, the ability to ascertain the scope of the controversy, the ability to characterize the nature of the controversy, and the ability to determine causal relationships, as is the ability to "select pertinent information for the solution of a problem, " which includes the ability to identify issues relevant to the resolution of a controversy, the ability to ascertain general types of information that may shed light on the controversy, and the ability to determine what specific types of information are preferable to resolve the controversy. Thus, for our purposes, Watson's and Glaser's list of "abilities"[19] is incomplete; it oversimplifies both the scope and complexity of what we might consider "critical thinking" to be.[20]

The second way we can incorporate clarification is to more clearly understand our research objective. In order to meet educational accountability demands we must be able to explain and justify the educational mission of *competitive debate programs.*

There are many operational models of "competitive debate programs." Although virtually all competitive debate programs share some general characteristics, each model also offers students a potentially different educational focus and type of experience. Colbert correctly differentiated between major models of competitive debate programs (NDT versus CEDA). To be meaningful, future research on critical thinking ability must account for the specific educational and experiential characteristics of the particular model(s) studied (CEDA model X versus CEDA model Y versus CEDA model Z, or NDT model N versus NDT model M versus NDT model O). Put simply, it is problematic to assume that students in all competitive debate programs experience the same educational outcomes to the same degree,

Research also must clearly distinguish the educational outcomes produced through competitive debate from those generated through regular classroom instruction. Although that point seems obvious, we have assumed that the educational experience of students in an argumentation course is analogous to that of students in a competitive debate program and thus, have included within our "body of research about critical thinking" those studies which tested students in argumentation classes.[21]

However, the educational experience a student gets in an argumentation course does not necessarily replicate the educational experience a student gets in a competitive debate program. One important difference is the nature of the student-teacher interaction. Students in a competitive debate program are likely to interact more closely and intensely with their instructor (coach) than would students in a traditional classroom setting. As a result, the instructional strategies used by the coach might be more influential with the student than would those of a classroom teacher with which the student had less frequent and prolonged interactions. This difference is important because research seems to suggest that the instructor and instructional strategies interact with the development of critical thinking ability (McMillan).

Research also seems to suggests that students in a competitive debate program and students in an argumentation class do not necessarily make gains on the same types of skills presumed to be related to critical thinking. Howell found that high school debaters improved most on Tests C and F of the Watson-Glaser Critical Thinking Appraisal, while Brembeck found that argumentation classes also improved on Test F, but actually showed a negative gain on Test C. In addition, argumentation students registered their second greatest gain on test B-SP which Howell found debaters did not improve upon.[22] Nor does research support the conventional wisdom which suggests that if a semester-long argumentation class could be shown to improve critical thinking ability, then surely one could expect even more development through participation in a combined argumentation course-competitive debate program, or even in a competitive debate program without additional training in an argumentation course. Whalen's research suggests there is no significant increase in development of critical thinking skills for students involved in *both* an argumentation course and competitive debate when compared to students involved only in the argumentation course. Brembeck's research at least indirectly supports this finding because it demonstrates that gains in critical thinking ability for students with prior debate training who were enrolled in an argumentation course and students with no prior debate training who were enrolled in an argumentation course were not significant.[23] Jackson's research is also at least partially relevant because it casts doubt on the implicit assumption that "if a little training is good, more training is better." Jackson did not find that the amount of debate experience a student had contributed significantly to development of critical thinking ability.

Although tentative, these research findings suggest a number of important issues which should help us clarify the focus of our research. I will mention two here. First, we should not presume that an argumentation course and a competitive debate program promote development of the same sorts of critical thinking skills (Howell; Brembeck). Doing so compromises our ability to justify the resources expended to support competitive debate programs and undermines the degree to which our research can accurately assess the unique educational outcomes achieved by participating in competitive debate. Rather, we should attempt to delineate the unique educational experiences each offers. Ultimately, if we know enough about their differences, we may be able to fully explain and productively utilize their similarities. Second, we should not assume that the more training one has in debate/argumentation, the greater one's critical thinking ability will become (Jackson; Whalen). Meeting educational accountability demands requires a reasonable assessment of the educational outcomes we achieve. Knowing when participating in our activity no longer contributes to particular educational outcomes is part of a *reasonable* assessment. It is also vital information our community needs to ensure that students who make a long-term commitment to our activity achieve educational rewards commensurate with that commitment.[24]

DIVERSIFICATION

The second major principle we need to incorporate in future research is diversification. We need diversification in both the empirical methodologies used and the types of research we conduct. Researchers in this area have utilized very similar designs and methodologies; generally, experimental studies intended to measure the degree to which debate training produces gains in critical-thinking ability as measured by pre and post scores on the Watson-Glaser Critical Thinking Appraisal.[25] While using similar approaches across studies enhances the possibility of replication, it may be advisable to incorporate more diverse approaches in two particular respects.

First, researchers should consider utilizing other tests to measure gains in critical thinking ability. Although across disciplines the Watson-Glaser Critical Thinking Appraisal is the most widely used test (McPeck), some question its validity and reliability. The test is argued to measure the same general ability as an IQ test (Kurfiss; McPeck; Helmstader) and to measure little more than reading comprehension (McPeck). The latter concern is particularly important for researchers in our field to consider because much of the critical thinking presumably involved in debate occurs about information that is presented orally. Assuming that critical thinking through reading and critical thinking through listening are the same is problematic. Berger notes it is not clear "as to whether people taking a similar test of critical thinking through listening would obtain a score comparable to the one obtained through reading" (1692). Limiting our research methodologies to instruments which tap only written communication is inconsistent with the fundamental importance our discipline attributes to listening skills (Rosenfeld and Berko).

Modjeski and Michael also shed light on the validity and reliability of the Watson-Glaser Critical Thinking Appraisal. They had a panel of twelve psychologists who actively study critical thinking evaluate both the Watson-Glaser and Cornell critical thinking tests on 10 essential validity standards and 5 essential reliability standards established for educational and psychological tests. Although the Watson-Glaser was generally rated higher in both validity and reliability,[26] Modjeski and Michael concluded that, "it would appear that a considerable amount of research and developmental effort needs to be expended to improve the reliability and validity of the Cornell and Watson-Glaser. It is recommended that consideration be given to revising both scales in the near future" (1196).[27]

My point is not to "nitpick" the Watson-Glaser Critical Thinking Appraisal, because it may be unrealistic to expect to find a better instrument (Follert and Colbert). However, I suggest that it is precisely because no perfect instrument is available that it does not make sense to rely exclusively on any single measurement. Additionally, using other instruments could help us better understand the construct. No two critical thinking tests purport to measure exactly the same thing. Critical thinking instruments are generally composed of a series of sub-tests. Across instruments there is certainly some overlap among sub-tests: however, there are also noticeable differences in degree of specificity, if not in complete subject matter.[28] Because the results obtained by any instrument are necessarily limited to the particular sub-tests of the instrument, each difference becomes a potential "unique" component of critical thinking which the particular instrument with that sub-test "uniquely" measures. Landis and Michael performed a factorial validity comparison and found that both the Watson-Glaser and Curry tests loaded on at least one factor unique to the particular sub-tests. As they explain, "each critical thinking measure generated its own instrument-specific factor from sub-tests of that measure" (1165). Thus, by using a range of test instruments we can better understand which of the "unique" components of particular instruments should be included within our conception of critical thinking (Thompson and Melacon).[29]

Second, we should use more diverse types of research to examine critical thinking. We have relied almost exclusively on experimental studies to examine critical thinking. While results from these types of studies are surely necessary to meet educational accountability demands, they are not sufficient. Qualitative/descriptive analyses of the relationship between debate training and critical thinking ability are also important.[30] Such analyses are important in one sense because they can help generate better quantitative research. By attempting to describe how the learning experiences in debate might relate to development of critical thinking ability, we would be able to better develop and test theoretical explanations for why particular types of learning experiences debaters have *should* contribute to development of critical thinking ability. As McMillan writes: "Such descriptions would help to improve the construct and external validity of the research" (14). Qualitative/descriptive research is important in another sense because it can help improve pedagogy. We have not adequately explored the pedagogical implications of attempting to promote development of critical thinking ability (Follert and Colbert). Porter posed an interesting question to our community when she asked, "How can we claim to be educators until we know what objectives, if any, we are meeting as we currently practice our discipline?" (98) I suggest that question has an equally interesting and relevant corollary: "Can we claim to be educators if we are unable to explain *HOW* we propose to achieve those objectives we seek?" Qualitative/descriptive research might help us better understand the "how's" related to this immensely important educational outcome. Ultimately, insight gleaned from such research can help us understand how our instructional methods might be better used to promote development of critical thinking ability.

CONCLUSION

Developing critical thinking ability has long been assumed to be one of the primary educational outcomes a student might receive by participating in competitive debate. While that outcome is presumptively important, the debate community has not generated sufficient research to demonstrate that participating in competitive debate promotes development of critical thinking ability to any significant degree. Future research about the relationship between debate training and development of critical thinking ability might productively incorporate two major principles – clarification and diversification.

There are many significant education benefits students can derive from participating in competitive debate. The CEDA debate community needs to develop an educational mission which reflects the diverse range of educational benefits participating in our activity potentially offers to students. We can no longer assume that our educational mission is apparent to those outside our community, or that others value its importance. Nor can we assume that our history and traditions are sufficient to ensure a prosperous future. Educational accountability is a very real demand the debate community will face. As we prepare to meet educational accountability demands, we should keep in mind one fundamental principle we try to teach our students: "They who assert must prove." We have the burden of proof to demonstrate the educational value of our activity.

WORKS CITED

Andersen, Kenneth. "A Critical Review of Behavioral Research in Argumentation and Forensics." *Journal of the American Forensic Association 10 (1974):* 147-55.

Barak, Robert J. *Program Review in Higher Education.* Boulder, Colorado: National Center for Higher Education Management Systems, 1982.

Beckman, Vernon E. "An Investigation of the Contribution to Critical Thinking Made by Courses in Argumentation and Discussion in Selected Colleges." Diss. U of Minnesota, 1956.

Berger, Allen. "Review of the Watson-Glaser Critical Thinking Appraisal." *The Ninth Mental Measurements Yearbook* (1985): 1692-93.

Bogue, E. Grady, and Robert L. Saunders. *The Evidence for Quality: Strengthening the Tests of Academic and Administrative Effectiveness.*

San Francisco: Jossey-Bass, 1992.

Brembeck, Winston. "The Effects of a Course in Argumentation on Critical Thinking Ability." *Speech Monographs* 16 (1949): 177-89.

Brookfield, Stephen. *Developing Critical Thinkers: Challenging Adults to Explore.* San Francisco: Jossey-Bass, 1987.

Church, Russell. "The State of CEDA Debate." *CEDA Executive Secretary's Report.* (1992).

Cierzniak, Suzanne L. *The Question of Critical Thinking: An Annotated Bibliography.* South Bend, IN: Indiana University, 1985. ERIC ED 260 069.

Colbert, Kent. "The Effects of CEDA and NDT Debate Training on Critical Thinking Ability." *Journal of The American Forensic Association* 23 (1987): 194-201.

Colbert, Kent, and Thompson Biggers. "Why Should We Support Debate?" *Journal of the American Forensic Association* 21 (1985): 237-40.

Conrad, Clifton F., and Richard F. Wilson. *Academic Program Reviews: Institutional Approaches, Expectations, and Controversies.* Washington, D.C.: Association for the Study of Higher Education, 1995.

Cross, Gary P. "The Effects of Belief Systems and the Amount of Debate Experience on the Acquisition of Critical Thinking." Diss. U of Utah, 197 1.

Ehninger, Douglas, and Wayne Brockriede. *Decision By Debate.* New York: Harper and Row, 1978.

Ennis, Robert H. "A Concept of Critical Thinking. " *Harvard Education Review 32* (Winter, 1962): 81-110.

Follert, Vincent F., and Kent Colbert. *An Analysis of the Research Concerning Debate Training and Critical Thinking Improvements.* Valdosta, GA: Valdosta State College, 1983. ERIC ED 238 058.

Freeley, Austin J. *Argumentation and Debate: Reasoned Decision Making.* Belmont, CA: Wadsworth, 1981.

Helmstader, Gerald C. "Review of the Watson-Glaser Critical Thinking Appraisal." *The Ninth Mental Measurements Yearbook,* (1985): 1693-94.

Herbeck, Dale. "Debate Scholarship: A Needs Assessment." *National Forensic Journal* 9 (Spring, 1990): 1-16.

Hill, Bill. "The Educational Goals of CEDA: Clarification and Reformulation." *The Forensic of Pi Kappa Delta* 73 (October, 1987): 17-27.

Howell, Wilbur S. "'The Effects of High School Debating on Critical

Thinking. " *Speech Monographs 10* (1943): 96-103.

Huseman, Richard, Glenn Ware, and Charles Gruner. "Critical Thinking, Reflective Thinking, and The Ability to Organize Ideas: A Multi-Variate Approach. " *Journal of the American Forensic Association* 9 (Summer, 1972): 261-65.

Jackson, Teddy R. "The Effects of Intercollegiate Debating on Critical Thinking Ability." Diss. U of Wisconsin, 1961.

Katula, Richard, and Celest Martin. "Teaching Critical Thinking in the Speech Communication Classroom." *Communication Education* 33 (April, 1984): 160-67.

Kay, Jack. "Research and Scholarship in Forensics as Viewed By an Administrator and Former Coach." *National Forensic Journal* 8 (Spring, 1990): 61-68.

Kurfiss, Joanne Gainen. *Critical Thinking: Theory Research, Practice, and Possibilities.* Washington, D.C.: Association for the Study of Higher Education, 1999.

Landis, Richard E., and William B. Michael. "The Factorial Validity of Three Measures of Critical Thinking Within the Context of Guilford's Structure of Intellect Model for a Sample of Ninth Grade Students." *Educational and Psychological Measurement* 41 (1981): 1147-66.

Leeman, Richard W. "Taking Perspectives: Teaching Critical Thinking in Argumentation Class." Speech Communication Association Convention. Boston, November, 1987.

Matlon, Ronald J., and Lucy M. Keele. "A Survey of Participants in the National Debate Tournament, 1947-1980." *Journal of the American Forensic Association* 20 (1994): 194-205.

McMillan, James H. "Enhancing College Students' Critical Thinking: A Review of Studies." *Research in Higher Education* 26 (1987): 3-29.

McPeck, John E. *Teaching Critical Thinking: Dialogue and Dialectic.* New York: Routledge, 1990.

Modjeski, Richard B., and William Michael. "An Evaluation by a Panel of Psychologists of the Reliability and Validity of Two Tests of Critical Thinking." *Educational and Psychological Measurement* 43 (1983): 1197-97.

Perry, William G. *Forms of Intellectual and Ethical Development in College Years.* New York: Holt, Rinehart and Winston, 1968.

Porter, Sharon. "Forensic Research: A Call for Action." *National Forensic*

Journal 8 (Spring, 1990): 95-103.

Rieke, Richard R. "College Forensics in the United States-1973." *Journal of the American Forensic Association* 10 (1974) 121-33.

Sillars, Malcolm, and David Zarefsky. "Future Goals and Roles of Forensics." *Forensics as Communication.- The Argumentative Perspective.* Ed. James H. McBath. Skokie, IL: National Textbook, 1975: 83-100.

Sproule, J. Michael. "Constructing, Implementing, and Evaluating Objectives for Contest Debate. " Journal *of the American Forensic Association* 11 (1974): 8-15.

Tame, Ellwood R, "An Analytical Study of the Relationship Between Ability in Critical Thinking and Ability in Contest Debate and Discussion." Diss. U of Denver, 1958.

Thompson, Bruce, and Janet Malacon. "Validity of a Measure of Critical Thinking *Skills. " Psychological Reports 60* (1987): 1223-30.

Whalen, Shawn. "Intercollegiate Debate as a Co-Curricular Activity: Effects on Critical Thinking." *Argument in Controversy.- Proceedings of the Seventh SCA/AFA Conference on Argumentation.* Ed. Donn W. Parson. Annandale, VA: Speech Communication Association, 1991. 391-97.

Williams, David. "The Effects of Training in College Debating on Critical Thinking Ability." Th. Purdue U, 1951.

Zemsky, Robert, and Walter Massey. "Cost Containment: Committing to a New Economic Reality." Policy *Perspectives.* Pew Higher Education Research Program, (Feb. 1991): 1-2.

FOOTNOTES:

[1] Sillars and Zarefsky were certainly not the first to raise the concern about our ability to meet educational accountability demands. Kenneth Andersen prophetically noted eighteen years ago that the educational mission of debate programs would come under closer scrutiny because of the "age of educational accountability," and others have, in various ways, echoed the spirit of this warning. Sillars and Zarefsky expanded upon Andersen's warning. Similarly, I have argued (Hill) that the CEDA debate community needs to develop a well-defined educational agenda in order to meet educational accountability demands.

[2] Herbeck states that "a growing body of evidence reveals that a disparity may he developing between our educational objectives and the forensics experiences we are -providing to debaters" (4). He supports this conclusion with the following footnote: "Any number of sources could be cited to substantiate this claim. See, for

example, Michael McGough, 'The Decline of Debate: Pull It Across Your Flow,' *The New Republic 10* Oct. 1988: 17-19; Karen McGlashen, 'On the State of Debate,' *California Speech Bulletin* 23 (1990): 4, fn. 12."

3 I have previously argued (Hill) that as the largest national debate organization and as an organization founded on the hopes of providing an educationally distinctive approach to debate (Howe, 198 1; Tomlinson, 199 1; Swanson, 199 1; Louden and Austin, 1993), CEDA bears a special responsibility to develop a clearly defined and defensible educational mission. Although many now argue that CEDA no longer offers a "distinctive" approach to debate, our status as the largest national debate organization continues to demand that we address the educational value of the activity we promote.

4 Colbert and Biggers note that debate programs have been forced to respond to accountability demands. More recently, persistent economic problems have result-ed in significant cutbacks and/or discontinuation of some debate programs. Accountability demands accelerate as programs are forced to compete more direct-ly for increasingly scarce resources.

5 80.4% of the respondents rated improving critical thinking skills as "very impor-tant" and 12.2 rated it as "important."

6 Only 23 schools are counted in the results because there was no control group in one of the schools.

7 According to their study, 10 of the 12 panel members suggested that the stabil-ity of test scores had not been demonstrated.

8 Berger states, "The authors rightly point out that 'they do not encourage efforts to utilize the part-scores on the test to evaluate individual attainment in the sub-skills, since the part-scores are based upon a relatively small number of items and therefore lack sufficient reliability for this purpose. It is feasible, however, to uti-lize these part-scores to analyze the critical thinking abilities of a class or larger group and to determine in light of such analysis the types of critical thinking training most needed by the group"' (1692).

9 Follett and Colbert did not include the results of Beckman's study in their meta-analysis. As I will argue later, however, we cannot presume in our research that the educational outcomes in an argumentation and debate course are equivalent to those in competitive debate. Thus, Beckman's study should be omitted because the evidence it provides bears no necessarily direct relationship to meeting educational accountability demands for competitive debate programs.

10 The NDT sample outscored the control group by a 7.95 mean difference, while the CEDA group outscored the control group by a 4.39 mean difference.

11 The pretest mean for those in the class with the debate requirement was 60.3 and the post-test mean was 59.82. Whalen concluded: "The mean, having slightly declined in this group, made any further analysis unnecessary as no significant

increase was made" (395).

¹² I am not assuming that the studies are methodologically equivalent. Colbert has more clearly defined samples, larger samples, and employed different versions of the Watson-Glaser Test of Critical Thinking to account for differences in the difficulty level between versions.

¹³ Colbert also notes limitations of his study that further emphasize the preliminary nature of this conclusion. In particular he notes that the experimental and control groups were not randomly assigned, many of the CEDA debaters had previous NDT experience and could not be used in the comparison between NDT and CEDA groups, no evidence is offered to distinguish between the selection phenomena-those with better critical thinking skills choose to debate-and the actual effect debate training had on critical thinking skills (200).

¹⁴ These factors include recent nationally funded reports on critical thinking, university graduation requirements, and the attention the issue has received in major scholarly and educational journals.

¹⁵ Colbert cites the following works to support his claim: Linda Arinis, and David Annis, "ne Impact of Philosophy On Students' Critical Thinking Ability," *ContemPorary Educational Psychology 4* (1979): 219-26; Paul A. Fritz, and Richard Weaver, *Teaching Critical 7thinking Skills in Public Speaking Courses: A Liberal Arts Perspective.* ERIC ED 249 556; and Richard A. Katula, and Celest A. Martin, "Teaching Critical Thinking in the Speech Communication Classroom," *Communication Education* 33 (1984): 160-67.

¹⁶ An interesting explanation of these various points of concern can be found in John E. MePeck, *Teaching Critical Thinking.- Dialogue and Dialectic,* New York: Routledge, Chapman and Hall, 1990. McPeck identifies at least three major perspectives on what critical thinking is. Particular issues about which theorists disagree are: whether the ability to make value judgments should be included within the critical thinking construct whether critical thinking can be considered as a general ability or as a set of specific skills; to what degree critical thinking should be dependent upon formal logic versus more informal notions of "good reasons; " and whether critical thinking should be viewed as content free or content specific. Additional sources which touch on portions of these issues include: Robert H. Ennis, "A Concept of Critical Thinking, " Harvard *Education Review* 32 (1962): 81-110; Mary M. Barabeck, "The Relationship Between Critical Thinking Skills and Development of Reflective Judgment," *DAI,* 41 (May, 198 1); Tony W. Johnson, "Philosophy for Children: An Antidote to Declining Literacy," *Educational* Forum 48 (1984A): 435-41.

¹⁷ My intention is not to singularly indict those in our field who have conducted studies which simply borrowed the Watson-Glaser definition. Certainly, this has also been a tendency with researchers in other fields. See for example, David Annis and Linda Annis, "Does Philosophy Improve Critical Thinking?" *Teaching Philosophy 3* (Fall 1979): 2; and Robert E. Young, "Editor's notes: Critical Thinking-a Renewed

Interest," Ed. Robert E. Young, *New Directions for Teaching and Learning: Fostering Critical 7thinking,* San Francisco: Jossey-Bass, 1980.

18 McPeck says these "abilities" are not "unitary."

19 McPeck presents an interesting analysis which suggests that defining a problem, selecting pertinent information for the solution of the problem, recognizing stated and unstated assumptions, formulating and selecting relevant and promising hypotheses, and drawing valid conclusions and judging the validity of inferences are not "abilities," but rather are "achievements." He explains that the abilities "are all descriptions of *achievements-in each* case something has been successfully accomplished. Notice, further that achievements do not necessarily *describe* corresponding abilities. For example, the statements 'He reached the summit of the mountain' and 'He crossed the finish line' both describe achievements, but in neither case do you know *how* it was done" (58, emphasis his).

20 One could argue that each of the "sub-abilities" I have identified are, in fact, "composits" of additional sub-sub-abilities, and that is probably the case. My intention. however, is not to suggest that we must identify every sub-ability until we can identify no more. Rather, my argument is that we need to be able to explain *how* we accomplish our objectives and that requires that we more clearly define the abilities we which *we propose* to be the constituents of "critical thinking. "

21 Freeley, Follert and Colbert, Colbert, and Whalen are illustrative of such inclusion.

22 Brembeck explains the four sub-tests: "(1) Test B-SP, a test of logical reasoning in the area of social problems, which measures ability to recognize whether conclusions drawn are soundly deduced from the premises which are given, regardless of personal bias for or against the conclusions themselves; (2) Test C, an inference test, is designed to measure ability to judge the probable truth or falsity and the relevancy of inferences drawn from given statements of fact. Students are asked to judge whether the inference drawn is true, false, probably true, probably false, or whether it should be labeled insufficient data; (3) Test E, a discrimination of arguments test, asks students to judge whether the arguments presented on opposing sides of ten questions are weak or strong; (4) Test F, an evaluation of arguments test, attempts to measure appreciation of the following four principles relating to proof in argument: (a) If certain premises are accepted, then valid inferences which follow from those premises must be accepted; (b) Crucial words or phrases must be precisely defined, and a change definition will produce a changed conclusion, although argument from each definition is logical; (c) The validity of an indirect argument depends upon whether all the possibilities have been considered; (d) A logical argument cannot be disproved by ridiculing the arguer, or his arguments, or by attacking his motives" (178).

23 Brembeck concludes that "debate training does not help in the study of those principles in the argumentation course which are covered by the tests any more than other factors-i.e., maturation, other college experiences, etc" (183). Brembeck does qualify this conclusion by noting that because debaters scored higher on the

pre-test they did not have as much "range for improvement" as did the non-debaters who scored lower of the pre-test (183).

24 The obvious implication of this point is that we must have a broadly based educational agenda which includes significant components other than developing critical thinking ability.

25 Tame, and Huseman, Ware, and Gruner also study critical thinking. Tame, however, looks at the relationship between critical thinking scores and contest debate performance while Huseman, Ware, and Gruner look at the predictive function critical thinking scores might have about debate ability. As a result, neither study is directly related to the issue discussed here.

26 The Watson-Glaser test was favorably evaluated on 5 of the 10 measures of validity while the Cornell test was favorably evaluated on 2. The Watson-Glaser was favorably evaluated on 4 of 5 standards for reliability and the Cornell was favorably evaluated on 2.

27 They raise the same concern about the Cornell (CCTf) test.

28 For example, the Watson-Glaser Critical Thinking Appraisal and the Curry Test of Critical Thinking each contain five sub-tests, and one of those sub-tests is related to recognizing or making an assumption. However, the remaining four sub-tests of the Watson-Glaser instrument include inference, deduction, interpretation, and evaluation of arguments, while the remaining sub-tests on the Curry Test of Critical Thinking include fact and opinion, false authority, inadequate data, and improper analogy. Thompson and Melacon provide a complete enumeration of the sub-tests. They also identify the basic sub-areas of the Cornell Critical Thinking Test, whether a generalization is warranted, whether a hypothesis is justified, whether a reason is relevant, the ability to judge reliability of authority, whether a statement follows from premises, the ability to identify assumptions, and the relevance of information in deduction. Clearly, differences between the Cornell Test and both the Watson-Glaser and Curry test are apparent. Thompson and Melacon also provide preliminary support for the construct validity of a new test composed of six sub-tests: identification of information relevant to testing a given hypothesis; discrimination between fact versus opinion; discrimination between primary and secondary source; inference skills; detecting assumptions implicit in statements; and deduction skills (1225). Again, a test with noticeable differences compared to the other tests.

29 They also argue that because it "remains somewhat ambiguous," additional measurement instruments may help define the critical thinking construct.

30 One example of such an analysis is that done by Leeman. Leeman uses Perry's nine stages of intellectual development to describe how a course in debate and argumentation can promote development of critical thinking ability.

Bill Hill (Ph.D., Florida State University) is Professor of Communication Studies and Associate Dean of the College of Arts and Sciences at the University of North Carolina in Charlotte, North Carolina. This essay was originally published in volume 14 (1993) of *CEDA Yearbook* (now known as *Contemporary Argumentation and Debate)*, pp.1-22.

ENHANCING CRITICAL THINKING ABILITY THROUGH ACADEMIC DEBATE
Kent R. Colbert

In a recent issue of the CEDA Yearbook, Hill (1993) reviewed debate-critical thinking research. He suggested data are insufficient to demonstrate a debate-critical thinking relationship, concluding the literature does not "demonstrate that participating in competitive debate promotes the development of critical thinking ability to any significant degree" (p. 18). Certainly additional research to consummate sound educational objectives and critical thinking is well advised. The research exploring the debate-critical thinking relationship is not complete. It does, however, establish a relationship. Like other social sciences, debate-critical thinking research operates on the basis of probability, not a deterministic model asserting causation. Hill's (1993) claim suggested forensic educators are "ill-prepared to use development of critical thinking ability to meet educational accountability demands" (p. 3) may be attributed to misunderstanding social science research, specifically debate-critical thinking research, and the nature of psycho-metric instruments.

Underlying Hill's (1993) assessment is what Johnson (1943) termed a "hypercritical attitude" or the "tendency to reject all conclusions based upon probabilities; an unwillingness to make a tentative choice; a tendency to demand 'all' the evidence... to the point of intellectual fence-sitting" (p. 86). This hypercritical attitude driven by a crisis mentality is reflected by some members of the forensics community who are troubled by (what they see) as a groundswell of unfounded panic about the basic worth of intercollegiate debate. Unfortunately, the resulting economic-survival rationale attempts to influence the direction of future research. Contrary to this crisis mentality, debate-critical thinking research establishes presumption favoring positive results. Objective analyses of the defendable studies indicate academic debating consistently enhances participant critical thinking abilities. And under certain conditions and instructional approaches, debating can significantly increase critical thinking abilities.

This paper will: 1) classify and review debate-critical thinking research; 2) evaluate the Watson-Glaser Critical Thinking Appraisal (WGCTA) with respect to Hill's (1993) recommendation of clarification and diversification; and finally 3) contend future debate-critical thinking researchers should concentrate their efforts using the principles of replication and cooperation.

It is important to initially examine the complexity of the critical thinking process before rejecting previous attempts to conceptualize and measure it. Critical thinking remains a difficult and challenging construct to define, operationalize, measure, learn, and teach. As Meyers (1986) explained, "The process of modifying old, or creating new, mental structures is often uncomfortable and at times even painful...Teaching critical thinking involves intentionally creating an atmosphere of disequilibrium, so that students can change, rework, or reconstruct their thinking processes" (p. 13-4). The interactive experience of the debating process appears to present a catalyst creating the disequilibrium, motivation, and framework needed to facilitate the acquisition of critical thinking abilities.

The ability to think critically has been an imperative of scholars for many years. From Plato's rationale analysis, and Aristotle's empiricism, to Guilford's (1967) intellectual operations of information, and Piaget's (1972) writings on primary structures, educators have long deliberated about critical thinking. The origin of measuring critical thinking can be traced to Dewey's (1910) formation of "reflective thinking" that inspired a permutation of scientific inquiry concerning the thought process. The need to move beyond elocution was subsequently articulated by Johnson (1942). She stated, "Experimental studies in discussion, debate, and persuasion, though numerous and valuable, have been confined to largely rhetorical considerations..." (p. 84). The early debate-critical thinking ability researchers acknowledged Johnson's call by attempting to *measure* the effects of debating, an activity sharing many similar elements associated with the process of critical thought.

The major studies of a debate-critical thinking relationship (Howell, 1943; Brembeck, 1949; Williams, 1951; Beckman, 1954; Jackson, 1961; Cross, 1971; Colbert, 1987) have provided valuable pedagogical data for researchers looking beyond the acceptance or rejection of a null hypothesis. However, other studies display several fatal methodological flaws making their conclusions ill-suited for earnest comparisons. (Luck & Gruner, 1970; Huseman, Ware, and Gruner, 1971l Gruner, Huseman, & Luck, 1971; Follert & Colbert, 1983; and Whalen, 1991). A superior explanation of debate-critical thinking research is possible by critically examining the specific experimental treatments, rather than simply reporting their results in chronological order. The three categories that will be used to explain the debate-critical thinking relationship are: 1) Classroom Training Studies; 2) Competitive Experience Studies; and 3) Incidental Studies.

CLASSROOM TRAINING STUDIES

In 1947, Winston L. Brembeck attempted to determine if a semester's course in argumentation improves critical thinking. He had these conclusions:

> 1) The argumentation students as a whole out gained control students in critical thinking scores over a one semester experimental period. The critical ratio of the difference in battery mean gains between the two groups was found to be 2.56. There is approximately only one time in a hundred that this difference could occur by chance. Therefore, it may be concluded that, on the whole, the argumentation courses studies in this experiment improved critical thinking ability... 2) In all but one of the schools the experimental students had an average test

score higher than the control students. This may mean that the students taking argumentation were more capable. Even though this pretest advantage served to narrow the range for improvement, the experimental groups still out gained the controls...3) The participating schools differed widely in terms of changes in critical thinking ability...4) Experimental students with one or more years of debate training (high school and/or college) made critical thinking pretest scores which are significantly higher than scores made by those with no previous debate training.

The second major study of classroom debate training and critical thinking was conducted by Vernon E. Beckman during the 1954-5 school year at five colleges or universities. He concluded:

1) It cannot be concluded from the present study that there is a significant difference in critical thinking ability, as measured by the WGCTA, between students in college argumentation courses, discussion courses, and other courses of the type used as controls in this investigation. Analysis of variance of gain scores and of covariances of adjusted post test scores showed an F ratio that was below the five per cent level of significance...2) The conclusion can be drawn that there are statistically significant differences in gins between schools...3) Students who score high on the pretest make relatively smaller gains than those with lower pretest scores...

Both studies (Howell, 1947 and Beckman, 1954) comparing traditional classroom debate training reported an overall increase in critical thinking scores. Beckman's critical thinking differences between the debate and control groups were not significant, although the direction favored the experimental group. Does this mean, as Hill (1993) speculated, that one study cancels the other? Given the methodologies were not as closely replicated as Hill (1993) presumed, cross comparisons are severely limited. First, the specific training methods were not reported or manipulated by either researcher. Both studies reported significantly different critical thinking scores between schools. Beckman's (1954) lack of significance likely reflects differences in instruction and course design. Course content, instructors, teaching methods, curriculum requirements, and other factors suggest argumentation courses (the experimental treatment) were not equivalent.

Second, despite the positive direction favoring the potential of classroom training to enhance critical thinking, it is unlikely any single course can completely isolate an effect on students also exposed to a variety of courses and experiences related to critical thinking. Meyers (1983) explained, "teachers must be realistic about what can be accomplished in the way of critical thinking development in a typical ten-week college course. Most students' previous thinking processes are not going to be radically altered in this length of time" (p. 23). Researchers in several disciples agree. Frank's (1969) research revealed only certain speech communication courses improve critical thinking (p. 296-302). Similar claims are reported in other fields. Henkel (1968), Yoesting and Renner (1969), Seymour and Sutman (1973), George (1968), Brakken (1965), and Ness (1967) all found a particular course topic is not a sufficient guarantee of critical thinking improvement. Annis and Annis (1979) concluded, "This study provides some initial evidence regarding the impact of philosophy on critical thinking. Future research should...[determine] the effects of specific kinds of course goals, content, organization, and teaching strategies have on critical thinking" (p. 225). Debate-critical thinking researchers should also pursue investigations documenting and manipulating the precise experimental treatment (course), especially since different programs consistently produce statistically different results.

COMPETITIVE DEBATING STUDIES

The second category of debate-critical thinking research encompasses competitive tournament debating. William S. Howell, whose 1943 dissertation founded this specific locus of research concluded:

> 1) Considering the entire experimental and control groups, the debaters out gained non-debaters in critical thinking scores over the experimental period of six months. The critical ratio of the difference in mean gains is 1.04. Since a minimum criti-

cal ratio of 2 is required for significance, we cannot conclude that high school debaters are certain to out gain non-debaters. There are 85 chances in 100 that this difference is real...2) When the experimental and control groups are equated on I.Q. scores the debaters again out gain the non-debaters, but not significantly...3) Both debaters and non debaters show significant gains in critical thinking scores over one debate season of approximately six months...4) Even though the debaters and non-debaters are closely matched on I.Q. scores, the debaters show significant superiority on both pretest and post test of critical thinking...5) The high school debater's advantage in scores on the WG tests carries over to the college level. The evidence included on this point is not conclusive, but it indicates that college students with high school debate experience score consistently higher on these critical thinking tests than do those who have not debated...6) Great differences in mean gains of debaters over non-debaters were found among participating schools...

The second major study is a master's thesis of Donald E. Williams at Purdue University during the 1950-51 debate season and involved competing college debaters. Williams concluded:

1) Debaters did make significant gains in critical thinking, as measured by the WGCTA, but that their gains were not significantly greater than the gains of similar group of non-debaters...2) There was a slight suggestion that those college students who have previous experience in debating in high school and in college may have greater critical thinking ability as measured by this test than those who had one year or less of such experience...3) Those students who have more than one year of experience in debating did not have greater critical thinking ability as measured by this test than those students who had one year or less of such experience...4) There was some indication that those students who are rated as better debaters by their coaches will have greater critical thinking ability than those who are rated as having less skill in debating.

In 1961, Jackson, under the supervision of Brembeck, tested the debate-critical thinking relationship observing 100 debaters and 147 non-debaters from nine colleges and universities. Jackson reported:

> The difference between gains was statistically significant between the .05 and .01 level of confidence. An analysis of the variance yielded an F ratio of 8.20...2) There were considerable differences among schools in the sample. Pretest total sample means ranged from 66.82 to 79.29 (99 maximums). Debater pretests ranged from 70.64 to 81.50. All of the schools, with one exception, had debater pretest mean advantage over the non-debaters. Posttest means for the debaters at all schools were higher...3) Previous debating experience gave the students in this study a definite advantage. Those with previous debating experience, either in high school and/or college, had a mean pretest advantage of 5.43. A X^2 of 13.86 was significant at the .001 level. 4) There was no significant relationship between success at winning debate contests and gain I critical thinking ability. Those who won over 80 percent of their debates have a slightly higher gain, but it was not statistically significant. 5) There was significant relationship between the amount of participation during the experimental period and gain in critical thinking ability. Those who participated in over 20 debates registered a slightly higher mean, but it was not statistically significant.

In 1971, Cross studied 136 students at nine high schools to investigate the attainment of a "specific educational goal" believed to be related to competitive debating. An analysis of covariance (ANCOVA) produced significant F values using the WGCTA. He concluded:

> 1) Those who are drawn to competitive debate, low and high participants, and continue for one academic year have greater thinking facilities than those who are not attracted to debate...2) High participation in competitive debate accelerates debaters' capacity in critical thinking while low participation may not enhance critical thinking beyond the normal improvement in an academic year...3) Debaters with abstract

belief systems significantly out gained debaters with concrete belief systems in critical thinking...4) Abstract subjects with higher belief systems significantly out gained others in critical thinking while concrete subjects with debater experience only out gained non-debaters...

The most recent major study of the competitive debate-critical thinking relationship was reported by Colbert (1987) who investigated 275 CEDA and NDT debaters and non-debaters at nine universities for one complete academic year. Unlike previous research, his study design and use of the pretest as a covariant better controlled for extraneous variables, institutional differences, the instrument's ceiling effect, and self-selection. He reported a sample size estimate calculated with a moderate (.5 sd.) to large (.8 sd.) effect size illustrating the magnitude of the differences found. The data represented several geographical regions, small and large institutions, and private and publicly funded universities. He reported that:

1) CEDA and NDT debaters scored 61.18 on the WGCTA pretest, 64.53 on the posttest, and a mean difference between the pre and posttest of 3.35. Non debaters had a pretest score of 52.67 on the WGCTA, 49.14 on the posttest, and a negative mean difference of –3.53. CEDA, NDT, and high school debaters outscored non-debaters on the WGCTA on the pretest, posttest, and the gain from pretest to post test. An analysis of covariance was made to test for significant differences between debaters and non debaters...2) CEDA debaters scored 62.67 on the pretest of the WGCTA, 63.53 on the post test, and scored 62.67 on the pretest, 49.14 on the post test, and a mean difference of –3.53. CEDA debaters out scored non-debaters by a mean of 10 on the pretest, 14.39 on the posttest, and scored a mean difference of 4.39. ANCOVA produced an F value of 5.368 significant at the .005 levels...4) NDT debaters scored 63.49 on the pretest on the WGCTA, 67.91 on the post test, and scored a mean increase of 4.42. The control group scored 52.67 on the pretest, 49.14 on the posttest, and a negative mean difference of –3.53. NDT debaters outscored the controls by a mean of 10.82 on the pretest and 18.77 on the post

test for a mean difference form the pretest to the posttest of 7.95. ANCOVA found differences between NDT debaters and non-debaters produced and F value of 31.77 significant at the .001 level.

While the competitive debate-critical thinking studies had similarities, variations in the version and modification of the WGCTA, sampling, population differences, length of experimental treatment, and statistical procedures were substantially different. These differences likely explain why some debate-critical thinking studies report significant findings, while others do not. For example, the WGCTA was administered in each study; however, it was revised by Watson and Glaser (1980) several times during this period. Howell (1947) independently modified the WGCTA in his study. Generalizations equating Howell's self-modified WGCTA with studies using the original and the subsequently refined WGCTA instrument make any comparisons inappropriate.

Sampling procedures also differed across studies. Howell (1943) randomly assigned students to debate and control groups. Williams (1951) and Jackson (1961) stratified their control groups. They matched a control group with the experimental group on differing dimensions including age, sex, educational background, and educational performance. In addition, Jackson (1961) stratified for college major and matched the groups IQs. Cross (1971) randomly selected the members of his control group. Colbert (1987) matched non-debating controls at each experimental group's institution. Some of these studies routinely engaged speech courses as control groups and research indicates speech courses also develop critical thinking abilities (Smith, 1942; Ness, 1967; and Frank, 1969). Claims that debating produces small positive or regressive effects on critical thinking (Whalen, 1991; Hill 1993) are based on studies using no control groups, ones receiving similar experience (treatment) as the debaters, and small unrepresentative samples.

The population samples for each of the competitive debate studies were dissimilar. There were differences between college and high school students, instructors, and quality of instruction, and competition level. Teachers used the instructional methods they deemed appropriate. Thus, no attempt was made to control or manipulate the instructional method, content, or conduct of instruction because the researchers were more interested in testing the way debating was being taught. Obtaining institutional and individual support to participate in time consuming research, the inability to administer an appraisal instrument at tournaments (40 minutes to an hour and a half), and the need for long term training and experience makes it unusually impractical for individual researchers to conduct this type of research alone.

The length of exposure to the experimental treatment also varied in the debate-critical thinking research. Howell's (1943) experiment was conducted over six months. Williams (1951) observed on semester of debate competition. Jackson's (1961) experimental period lasted six to seven months. Cross (1971) waited for one school year to pass, as did Colbert (1987). It appears one full year of competitive debate experience consistently produces significantly higher critical thinking scores. Perhaps a period of "Reflective Thinking" (Dewey, 1910) is needed before measurable differences surface. Findings that students with prior debate experience consistently out gained controls also suggest a minimum threshold of training and experience may be required over time for researchers to detect the debate-critical thinking relationship. Consequently, more experience compressed into shorter durations of time may not simulate exposure to debating over longer periods of time. Attending three tournaments a semester in four years, for example, is not comparable to debating in twenty-four tournaments in one year. The time needed to learn, think, discover, reflect, mature, interact with others, and consider several different topics may require more than a semester or two of debating.

The different statistical procedures each researcher chose should also be considered. In analyzing the results of the research, critical ratios (Howell, 1943), t-test (Jackson, 1961), ANCOVA and Scheffe's post comparison statistics (Cross, 1971), and ANCOVA (Colbert, 1987) were used. More robust statistical procedures could account for different results. Given the nature of the instrument and the need to control for extraneous variances, the ANCOVA appears most appropriate. Studies using ANCOVA in a pretest posttest design consistently rejected the null and supported the alternative hypothesis that debate training significantly promotes critical thinking scores.

Another issues involves the purported "attraction" or "self-selection" effect. Basically, the theory suggests those with greater critical thinking abilities seek out debate activities. Howell (1948), Williams (1951), and Cross (1971) found debaters with previous experience had higher critical thinking scores on their pretest. Jackson (1961) and Colbert (1987) reported the same relationship among college students. Why would critical thinkers be attracted to debating? It is likely debating stimulates critical thinking. If competitive debating was not a critical thinking activity, it is unlikely critical thinkers would elect or continue to participate. Those with prior debate experience indeed test higher on the pretest, but research also shows experienced debaters can and often do improve during the experimental period. If individuals with greater critical thinking abilities are attracted, they could benefit more from debate than novice participants (Howell, 1948). Additionally, there is no reason to believe critical thinkers would gain, develop, or maintain critical thinking without activities like debating that exercise and hone them. The key issue is not whether debating causes critical thinking, but to discover how debating can cultivate it for those with varying levels of critical thinking ability.

Of the five major competitive debate-critical thinking studies, only Howell (1948) and Williams (1951) failed to reject the null hypothesis. At least three explanations are available for studies without significant differences between experimental and comparison groups. First, Howell (1948) modified an early version of the WGCTA to suit his research interest. Second, Howell (1948) randomly assigned students to debate and non-debate conditions. While randomization reduces the risk of motivational side effects, it also increases the probability that reactance effects will undermine the research efforts. Students forced to engage in the activity may not be receptive to the stimulus being offered. Similarly, coaches with unwilling subjects may also exhibit reactance effects. Reactance effects could diminish the benefits derived from the debating. Thus, studies randomly assigning students to debate groups were testing debating in a way that doesn't accurately reflect reality. Third, those with previous debate students had higher critical thinking scores to begin with. The ceiling effect identified by Crites (1965) could have compressed the gains made by the debaters, diminishing the measured effects. If the students begin high on the scale, they will have less room for improvement. This factor could explain why debaters consistently gain in critical thinking, but not always significantly more than control groups. One study (Lucas, 1972) suggested individuals with low scores systematically improve more than high scoring students (p. 381-7). Despite limited range of improvement, debater WGCTA scores were consistently in the predicted (positive) side.

Another important finding was the significant differences observed between schools participating in the debate-critical thinking studies. Howell (1948) and Jackson (1961) both reported significant (WGCTA) differences between debate groups attending different institutions. Their findings implied instructional techniques, methods, and/or content probably influenced the acquisition of critical thinking skills. If some teaching methods fail to produce significant results, we should not presume it cancels out methods that are successful. Williams' (1951) thesis, for example, only studied one institution despite the knowledge that most previous research suggested significant differences between schools existed. The inability of this study to observe significant results is likely from observing one atypical competitive debate program.

The preponderance of defendable evidence suggests competitive debate experience can indeed improve critical thinking skills. The lack of significance in some studies is reflected in design limitations, instrument ceiling, sampling, teaching methods, or statistical procedures. Rationalizing that one insignificant study cancels a significant one is parsimonious. There are no compelling reasons why competitive debating, when properly taught, is unlikely to improve critical thinking skills. Some convincingly argue that debating practiced correctly is a method of critical thinking (Perella, 1988). All of the major debate critical-thinking researchers generally concluded debating improved critical thinking scores.

INCIDENTAL STUDIES

Three studies (Luck & Gruner, 1970; Gruner, Huseman, and Luck, 1971: and Huseman, Ware, and Gruner, 1972) measured high school debaters at a summer workshop, administering the WGCTA (Form

YM), and the California F scale (authoritarianism). Luck and Gruner (1970) made no claim of a debate critical thinking relationship, only that critical thinking and authoritarianism have a "negative r of -.322 (p<.01)" (p. 380). While Gruner, Huseman, and Luck (1971) concluded, "debate ability has been shown once again to be related to critical thinking ability," they did not predict a positive increase in critical thinking as a result of debating (p.65). Their data suggested a negative relationship between authoritarianism and critical thinking in the best-rated debaters. Presumably, better debaters have higher critical thinking scores, and are less authoritative. Huseman, Ware, and Gruner (1972) concluded, debate "director[s] can best improve their charges' debating performance by attempting to develop in them the abilities measured by the tests in this study [WGCTA]" (p. 265). All three studies (Luck and Gruner, 1970; Grunder, Huseman, and Luck, 1971; and Huseman, Ware, and Gruner, 1972) suffer serious methodological flaws making their conclusions little more than speculation. First, the studies were one-shot design measures. Second, no control or comparison groups were used to isolate the experimental treatment from a host of extraneous variables (Campbell and Stanley, 1963). Third, the researchers admittedly used "crude" methods of having "coach-critic-judges" rate debaters into "debate ability quartiles" without measuring the reliability or validity of their methods (Holsti, 1969). Although Luck and Gruner (1970); Gruner, Huseman, and Luck (1971); and Huseman, Ware and Gruner, (1971) provided interesting questions about debating and authoritarianism, data are insufficient to support or deny a debate-critical thinking relationship.

A meta-analytic study by Follert and Colbert (1983) attempted to analyze debate-critical thinking research collectively. Admittedly, their study suffered methodological shortcomings. The methodological differences of previous studies severely limited statistical generalizations. The "shaking of the educational foundation" did not suggest the foundation does not exist. It sounded a call for additional research. They stated, "since there are some problems with score stabilities and [WGCTA] form compatibility, the more powerful meta-analytic techniques were rejected" (p. 8). The authors further cautioned that using dichotomous binomial distribution estimates would sacrifice part of the variance. These and other limitations prevented using Follert and Colbert's (1983) results to reject the findings of Howell (1948), Jackson (1961), Williams (1951), and Cross (1971). The heuristic value of Follert and Colbert (1983) was to provide future scholars an alternative procedure to examine debate-critical thinking research and stimulate interest for the additional study of contemporary competitive debate practices. What is most important, the authors cautioned others against making cross comparisons and generalizations using various debate-critical thinking studies.

More recently, Whalen (1991) attempted to study the self-selection supposition, the amount, and type of debate experience and its effect on critical thinking. The focus on isolating debate and specific treatments raised interesting questions about debate-critical thinking research. However, several fatal laws make any conclusion from the conference paper untenable. First, he sampled one institution ignoring previous research reporting significant difference in critical thinking scores between schools. Second, the sample size was inadequate. The author reported the "average subject size for these tests was approximately 12 per group." Third, the author did not provide a sample size estimate or rationale to justify an extremely small N. Fourth, only one form of the WGCTA was employed in a pretest posttest design, clearly against the recommendations of Watson-Glaser (1980). Fifth, many speech courses also contain the critical thinking components taught in debate, so there is no way to determine if the comparison (speech) group was receiving similar stimuli as the control group. Finally, the author claimed to control for self-selection, but never reported if students registering for the debate courses were aware of the course requirements before doing so. Whether the course was a curriculum requirement, or how systematically excluding those with previous debate experience produced valid conclusions about those being "attracted was not addressed." Concluding with the debate course group without competitive experience out gained the debate course group with a debate requirement was significant at the .10 alpha levels. This level of significance is not consistent with the .05 alpha levels used by previous researchers. If the aforementioned researchers raised their acceptable error level, virtually all of them could have claimed debaters significantly out gained non-debaters on the WGCTA.

Ironically, Hill (1993) quoted Whalen's (1991) conclusion because it was stated "more emphatically" (p. 7). Given the many deficiencies of Whalen's (1991) study, any comparison or conclusion based on it is meaningless.

THE WATSON-GLASER CRITICAL THINKING APPRAISAL

Hill (1993) offered two recommendations for future debate-critical thinking research—clarification and diversification. The basic proposition underlying Hill's (1993) general principle of "clarification" relies on criticism of the WGCTA. While a superior measuring instrument is always desirable, many of Hill's (1993) indictments concerning the WGCTA are not supported by the preponderance of empirical research. The following section briefly describes the WGCTA and discusses reliability and validity of the instrument as it relates to the "clarification" principle.

The WGCTA measures five dimensions of critical thinking: 1) Inference; 2) Recognition of Assumption; 3) Deduction; 4) Interpretation; and 5) Evaluation of Arguments. Sixteen questions (Forms *A* and *B*) are used in each scale to explore the five "subabilities" (Watson and Glaser, 1980). Together the composite score reflects a sampling of overall critical thinking ability, as it measures various ability domains of the critical thinking process. While other definitions of critical thinking are possible, they are "likely [to produce] considerable overlap among alternative lists of component abilities" (Watson and Glaser, 1980, p. 1). The WGCTA provides an operational definition to measure the critical thinking construct and appears the most promising to satisfy the educational accountability demands Hill (1993) contended "may be imperative to the existence of our [debate] programs" (p. 2).

The individuals demanding "program accountability" require the most reliable and valid instrument available, especially when comparisons are made with competing programs that empirically assess their outcomes. The WGCTA is the most reliable measure of critical thinking that exists. The reliability of the total test score is adequate. Annis and Annis (1979) observed, "In critical reviews the Watson-Glaser [Critical Thinking Appraisal] generally has been evaluated as an effective test instrument" (p. 221). Crites (1965) supported the WGCTA stating, "Watson-Glaser represents an approach to the measurement of ability which is novel, as far as item content and format are concerned, and is a laudable approach. It is also one which data on the test justify as empirically useful...[and] its internal consistency is high..." (p. 785).

In 1980 the WGCTA changed from Ym and Zm to the currently used A and B forms. In a review of the A and B forms Helmstadter (1983) writes in a review of the Watson-Glaser Critical Thinking Appraisal:

> A wide variety of reliability indexes have been computed using different groups and different method for assessing this characteristic of tests...[I]n suggesting uses of the test, proper professional restraint and scientific caution have been used. All of the above contributes to a feeling of confidence that this test is a good, solid measure of adequate—but not outstanding—reliability" (p. 1692-3).

Keyser and Sweetland (1985 reported:

> In a recent survey of a panel of psychologists, Mofjeski and Michael (1983) found the WGCTA to meet more of the criteria for a psychological test than did its only competitor, the Cornell Critical Thinking Test (Ennis, Millman, and Tomko, 1979)... [T]he WGCTA was rated more highly with respect to having clearly defined the universe of situations and how it was sampled. Overall, the WGCTA rated as superior to the Cornell in terms of the test criteria described as 'essential' in the Standards for Educational and Psychological Test (American Psychological Association, 1974) (p. 685).

Berger (1983) concurred, "This is a well-constructed test...This reviewer knows of no similar test that is on a par with the WGCTA" Woehlke (1985) concluded, "this reviewer recommends the WGCTA as the best available instrument for measuring critical thinking ability" (p. 685). In short, the WGCTA is reliable for group comparisons of total test scores of critical thinking in educational settings, so long as the subscales are not generalized as independent measures.

The majority of Hill's (1993) "clarification" issues related to specific validity concerns. For example, he quoted McPeak (1990) who accused Watson-Glaser of taking their definitions from a "list in a government document" (p. 10). This content validity challenge deserves further explanation. Watson-Glaser spent more than forty years developing and enhancing their definition of critical thinking. In constructing the original WGCTA, thirty-five scholars from a wide variety of disciplines and universities contributed to constructing test items to enhance content validity. The five abilities as measured by the WGCTA are consistent with, though not exhaustive, most definitions of critical thinking. The assertion that Watson-Glaser's definitions "have not been demonstrated to be the constituents of critical thinking" (Hill, 1993 p. 10) is not supported by any convincing empirical research. Anastasi (1982) observed, "content validation involves essentially the systematic examination of the test content to determine whether it covers a representative sample of the behavior domain to be measured" (p. 131). Hill (1970) explained:

> The five subtests [of the WGCTA] ...are clearly pertinent to most definitions of 'critical thinking'... The WGCTA is one of the most useful instruments to understand and appraise critical thinking. (p.796-7).

Comparisons between the conceptual definitions of Dewey (1910), Dressell and Mayhew (1954), Brembeck (1949), Follman, Brown, and Burg (1970), Ennis (1969), Drake (1976), and the WGCTA subscales correspond to a great degree. The composite of abilities as measured by the WGCTA is a fair representation of overall critical thinking ability, even though it may not include every conceivable rudiment of the critical thinking process.

The ensuing admonishment of the WGCTA pertains to the issue of construct validity. The "more serious problem" is the WGCTA does not "provide a sufficient basis to explain our [debate community] educational mission" (Hill, 1993, p. 11). The abilities of the WGCTA are consistent with the objectives of many forensic educators. The ability to define a problem directly relates to the issues of topicality. The ability to select pertinent information for the solution of a problem is reflected in the burden of proof requirements and solvency issues frequently argued in debates. The ability to recognize stated and unstated assumption is found in the practice of debaters analyzing published authoritative proof in support of claims. The ability to formulate and select relevant hypotheses are depicted through interpreting resolutions, writing plans and criteria, and developing cases of advocacy. The ability to draw valid conclusions and judge the validity of inferences are intrinsic components in all debating. The reasons why measuring these five abilities fail to generate a numerical benchmark of overall debater-critical thinking are unclear. The problem-solving framework operationalized by the WGCTA and mastering these abilities is a reasonable representation of critical thinking goals of debating. Hills' (1993) criticism of the WGCTA would be applicable to most psychological measures. Do IQ tests measure every aspect of intelligence? Do ACT, SAT, or GRE tests measure every ability gained or needed representing a student's education? They do not and cannot. However, their utility in providing information about thinking abilities remains important and influential. Given no measuring device can capture every element of complex though processes like intelligence, aptitude, or critical thinking, instruments like the WGCTA are preferred because they are far more precise than the "qualitative research alternatives."

Another validity contention of Hill (1993) concerned the correlation of the WGCTA with measures of intelligence. He referenced McPeak (1990), Kurfiss (1988), and Helmstader (1985) contending the WGCTA measures the same ability as IQ tests. McPeak (1990), Kurfiss (1988), and Helmstader (1985) support their conclusion with anecdotal claims about the WGCTA without empirical support. It is inconsistent for Hill (1993) to challenge the debate-critical thinking studies on the basis of "unconvincing empirical proof" and then make factual conclusions without a similar burden. Factor analysis has revealed the WGCTA correlates with general intelligence, but its overlap as a construct is not complete. For example, Landis (1976) factor analyzed the WGCTA with measures drawn from the Guilford Structure of Intellect Model. The WGCTA reflected a dimension of intellectual functioning that is independent of that tapped by the measures of intellect system. Follman, Miller and Herandez (1969) also reported high loadings on a single factor, when analyzed along with achievement and ability measures. Follman, Brown, and Burg (1970) reported a factor analysis of the WGCTA:

> It appears that the basic structure of the interrelations of the (WGCTA) is not a general ability but a composite of different groups and specific factors each accounting for a relatively small percent of the variance (p. 16).

Combining the WGCTA with the personality and aptitude scales have produced two factors, (Westbrook and Seller, 1967) five factors, (Singer and Roby, 1967) and even more (Hunt and Randhawa, 1973). Their factor analyses supported the claims of Watson and Glaser that their test overlaps with intelligence, while retaining an unidimensional quality. Certainly, some intelligence level seems necessary to develop higher level thought processes like critical thinking, but this does not imply the WGCTA only measures intelligence.

Similarly, Hill (1993) also referenced McPeak's (1990) assertion the WGCTA measures "little more than reading comprehension" (p. 15). The A and B forms of "the WGCTA w[ere] carefully examined for reading difficulty using three indices: the Dale-Chall, the Fry, and the Flesch. Sections of the test that exceeded a ninth-grade reading level were either modified or eliminated" (Watson and Glaser, 1980, p. 1). The test would therefore be appropriate for those having a ninth grade level or above. After postulating the WGCTA simply measures reading comprehension, Hill (1993) reasoned, "much of the critical thinking presumably involved in debate occurs about information that is presented orally" (p. 15). Although speeches during debates are presented orally, much critical thinking occurs when reading, marking, selecting, and processing information into briefs that debaters use to support their claims. This is not to say that critical thinking does not occur during debates, but successful debaters prepare and develop arguments well in advance of the actual presentation. Critical thinking is also likely developed through discovery, information processing, hypothesis testing, interaction, and reflective processes, not exclusively from the oral component of the activity. A compelling logical nexus between the debate process and critical thinking development can be made directly relating to the activities of processing written information.

Overall, the WGCTA represents a reliable, valid, and appropriate measure to quantify the critical thinking abilities of debaters. It is the best available measure of critical thinking ability. According to the American Psychological Corporation, a more refined version is scheduled for release in 1996. While experimenting with other methods of inquiry is interesting and qualitative assessment has been reported in the literature since classical rhetoric, the debate community would be well served at this time to continue to develop the foundation of empirical research based on the WGCTA.

FUTURE RESEARCH

Do critical thinkers migrate toward academic debating or does academic debating enhance critical thinking? The two seem intrinsically related. Whether the chicken or the egg came first may not be as important as considering whether one could develop without the other. Few scholars challenge the importance of developing critical thinking skills and that students participating in debate generally have a higher level of critical thinking than their non-debating counterparts. In this regard, debate educators have a tremendous opportunity and obligation to maximize a unique educational interaction for these highly talented students. Therefore, how should the forensics community proceed with future critical thinking research?

While Hill's (1993) suggestion for "diversification" in debate-critical thinking research is interesting, it does not address his premise of producing defensible data in the age of educational accountability. First, no other empirical measure is equal or superior to the WGCTA and the vast majority of educational researchers in many domains utilize it. Second, the use of qualitative explanations of "how" argument enhances thinking has been explored throughout history dating back to classical rhetoric. Third, it appears unlikely individual researchers will abandon training and research skills taking many years to acquire. Conducting both types of research does not appear mutually exclusive. The danger in advocating a shift to only one was articulated by Anderson (1897):

> Method becomes ideology because it is useful to control membership (you cannot be one of us unless you know our meth-

ods); to distinguish nonmembers (you cannot be one of us because you do not use our methods); and to distribute power and resources (you must use our methods to eat at our table) (p. 17).

Qualitative and descriptive research concerning debate-critical thinking research should *not* be discouraged. However, it should *not* be considered a substitute for or in place of well-designed empirical study.

Improving debate-critical thinking research will require longitudinal trend, cohort, and panel studies. Empirical replications should explicate the precise methods, instructional content, and practices found to be most effective. These studies should report the specific components of the debate experience resulting in optimal critical thinking development. Advancing a debate curriculum based on cumulative empirical research offers greater potential benefits than adopting a "crisis mentality" and starting over. In this regard, two principles should be considered by future researchers—replication and cooperation.

REPLICATION

Previous debate-critical thinking research focused on epistemology. It has consistently shown some methods of debate training and competitive experience can elevate critical thinking, while others have not. The ontology and praxiology issues in the debate-critical thinking relationship remain unexplored. Some instructors, for example, may approach the task by teaching debaters game strategies. Others emphasize classical argumentation and rhetorical theories, or subscribe to problem solving, hypothesis testing, judicial, and legislative paradigms. There are many different perspectives available for teaching competitive debate, but little or no research to discern which method(s) works best regarding critical thinking ability development. The specific characteristics, methods, and practices of tournament debating need additional investigation.

Replication of debate-critical thinking research should focus on the specific nature of the debating process. Classroom studies need to collect and report specific course characteristics. Some courses may have the goal of obtaining critical thinking, while others may not. What teaching methods are being used? Lecture formats may not be as effective as mastery learning strategies or those promoting interactive learning. Teaching philosophies may also play a significant role in the outcomes of a debate course. Instructional content, performance activities, evaluation procedures, course organization, and requirements can all play a role in developing critical thinking. The availability and affordability of video recording can make subsequent analysis of the treatment far more precise and meaningful. Replicating classroom debate-critical thinking studies could provide valuable information about "how to" teach critical thinking using debate. Replicating studies with better control, reporting, and observation of various strategies could provide guidance for debate educators in developing their programs. As Babbie (1995) observed, "replication can be a general solution to problems of validity in social research" (p. 326).

Beyond teaching methods and strategies, the process or framework used by debaters needs examination. As Meyers (1986) stated, "no matter what specific approach is used, a teacher must present some explicit perspective or framework for disciplinary analysis—a structure for making sense of the materials, issues, and methodologies of the discipline being taught" (p. 6). The debate activity through its framework for analysis may be a catalyst and motivator for critical thinking, rather than a specific cause of it. Meyers (1986) continued, "teaching a framework for analysis will be in vain unless students have the motivation to engage in critical thinking" (p. 8). Research should isolate the demand characteristics of preparing to debate (research) and the optimal amount of debating (number of rounds, tournaments, topics, years, etc...) enhancing critical thinking short of diminishing returns. Is it beneficial to hold tournament competitions lasting ten to twelve hours a day over three to four days? Should students attend five, ten, fifteen, or more tournaments during an academic year? Past research supports a debate-critical thinking relationship, the challenge now is to discover why some programs produce significant positive outcomes and others do not. Building on existing data appears more productive, than reinventing the wheel or focusing on less defendable methodology.

Improvising the replication of debate-critical thinking research requires greater precision. Researchers should follow the recommendations and instructions of those designing measuring instruments. Inferring from subscales, using one nonequivalent form, unrepresentative sampling, not reporting effect size, and inappropriate instrument administration practices reduce detecting valid findings using the WGCTA or any measuring instrument. Building on past designs by using the pretest as a covariant is an effective method to control for extraneous variations (i.e., self-selection, IQ, past experience, differing experimental treatments...) that otherwise complicate interpreting results. Multiple classification analyses can also be used to determine the extent of extraneous variation. Moreover, researchers using the WGCTA should carefully read and follow the instructions found in the appraisal manual. And before embarking on new, untested, and underdeveloped instruments, debate-critical thinking researchers should continue using the WGCTA until a better instrument is available. Many other educational domains use the WGCTA to justify their pedagogical methods. If accountability becomes relevant to program existence, forensic educators would want to report the "best" available measuring device was used to demonstrate its results. As Anderson (1987) observed, "the proof of the method is its utility in solving the problem" (p. 17). In short, abandoning this genre of research would strengthen the anecdotal criticism about the debate-critical thinking relationship making educational accountability more difficult.

COOPERATION

Few educators in the forensic community deny the advantages of additional debate-critical thinking research. However, few have been willing or able to volunteer the time, effort, and expense needed to conduct long term studies producing incontrovertible data. All of the major studies reported with adequate sample size were doctoral dissertations and most were subsequently published in academic journals. Given the apparent pragmatic difficulties inherent in debate-critical thinking research, it is understandable why few of these researchers reported subsequent studies. Forensic educators often have similar teaching, research, and service responsibilities as their colleagues. In addition, travel to debate tournaments typically consumes anywhere from five to twenty weekends out of town, significant practice and preparation time, and substantial administrative tasks. In short, even the most dedicated forensics scholars have insufficient resources to individually conduct well-designed research projects measuring the effects of debating on critical thinking.

The debate community needs cooperation and its organizations (NDT, CEDA, NFL, ADA...) to coordinate, finance, support, and sponsor longitudinal studies. Debate-critical thinking research is expensive, time consuming, and dependent on highly specialized experts. Stronger research designs requiring many subjects contend with high attrition rates. The administration of the WGCTA requires between forty minutes and an hour making administration between debate rounds impractical at tournaments. The pragmatic difficulties of test administration, data collection, and processing are generally too difficult for individuals traveling as coaches, while also serving as full time faculty.

Debate-critical thinking research requires debate organizations to sponsor, coordinate, and support ongoing longitudinal research programs to determine not only the effects of debate on critical thinking, but the effects of debating on a variety of behavioral outcomes believed to be associated with participating in debate. As the academic debate community continues to evolve and its debate organizations establish and perpetuate their educational philosophies, they should follow a course proven to accommodate important educational outcomes like critical thinking. Debate organizations adopting value orientations had no empirical proof that discarding the problem solving framework practiced by policy debaters would be equal to or accelerate critical thinking skill development. Despite the organizational implications, forensic educators should promote and embrace research that identifies the best educational experience for participants. The fragmentation of the academic debate community necessitates cooperation to advance comprehensive critical thinking longitudinal studies.

In summary, the research spanning five decades supporting a debate-critical thinking relationship is under attack. Hill (1993) has suggested a radical shift in debate-critical thinking and essentially advocated redefining the concept itself. While clarification and diversity should be considered, the data and methods of measurements of existing studies should not be abandoned. A preponderance of defendable research already suggests debating, when properly taught, can enhance the critical thinking abilities as measured by the WGCTA. Critical thinking is difficult to measure, but these difficulties should not discourage scholars from developing an important field of research. The collective efforts of the forensics community could strengthen empirical investigations and contribute to maximizing critical thinking improvement.

This paper has responded to recent criticism regarding debate-critical thinking research. The appropriate classification and critical review of these studies reveal a wealth of information. Investigating complex thought constructs that apparently interact with behavioral activities present a difficult and interesting challenge. The instruments to measure critical thinking continue to improve and the WGCTA remains the best available measuring device. The academic debate communities innovating this genre of study should further replicate, extend, and develop empirical debate-critical thinking research. Cooperation among and between the many fragmented debate organizations' memberships is needed for long term longitudinal studies assessing, measuring, and reporting the specific characteristics of methods of different forms of academic debating.

Despite many limitations, the collective body of debate-critical thinking research supports at least three important inferences: 1) extended periods of training and experience in academic debating enhance critical thinking abilities as measured by the WGCTA; 2) specific educational strategies and certain academic debating experiences significantly increase critical thinking as measured by the WGCTA; and finally, 3) the debate-critical thinking literature provides presumptive proof favoring a positive debate-critical thinking relationship. Admittedly, not every form of, instruction in, strategy used or tournament experience in competitive academic debate assures critical thinking abilities for every individual. Research suggests some debate programs develop critical thinking abilities better than others. Cooperation and support by a collective debate community for long-term replicated longitudinal studies offer the best opportunity for educational accountability and improving academic debate.

WORKS CITED

Agnes and Blick, D (1972). A comparison of earth science classes taught by using original data in a research approach technique versus classes taught by conventional approaches not using such data. *Journal of Research in Science Teaching*, 9, 83-89.

Anatasti, A. (1987). *Psychological testing*. New York: MacMillan.

Anderson, J. A. (1987). *Communication research: Issues and Methods*. New York: McGraw-Hill.

Annis, L. and Annis, D. (1979). The impact of philosophy on students' critical thinking ability. *Contemporary Educational Psychology*, 4, 219-226.

Babbie, E. (1995). *The practice of social research*. (7th ed.) Belmont, CA: Wadsworth.

Bartanen, M. and Frank, D. (1994). *Nonpolicy debate*. Scottsdale, AZ: Gorsuch Scarisbrick.

Beckman, V. (1955). *An investigation of the contributions to critical thinking made by courses in argumentation and discussion in selected colleges*. Unpublished doctoral dissertation. University of Minnesota, Minneapolis, Minnesota.

Berger, A. (1983). Review of the Watson-Glaser Critical Thinking Appraisal. *Eighth Mental Measurement Yearbook*, p. 1347.

Brakken, E. (1993). Intellectual factors in PSSC and conventional high school physics. *The Journal of Research and Science Teaching*, 3, 19-25.

Brembeck, W. (1947). *The effects of a course in argumentation on critical thinking ability*. Doctoral dissertation, University of Wisconsin, Madison, Wisconsin.

Brembeck, W. (1949). The effects of a course in argumentation on critical thinking. *Speech Monographs*, 16, 172-89.

Brewer, K. (1984). *Introductory statistics for researchers*. Minneapolis, MN: Burgess.

Burns, R. (1974). The testing of a model of critical thinking ontogeny among Central Connecticut State College undergraduates. (Doctoral dissertation, Central Connecticut State College, 1973) *Dissertation Abstracts*, 5467-A.

Campbell, D. and Stanley, J. (1963). *Experimental and quasi-experimental designs for research*. American Educational Research Association.

Colbert, K. R. (1987). The effects of CEDA and NDT debating on critical thinking ability. *The Journal of the American Forensics Association*, 23, 194-201.

Colbert, K. and Biggers, T. (1985). Why should we debate? *The Journal of the American Forensics Association*, 21, 237-240.

Cohen, J. (1969). *Statistical power analysis for the behavioral sciences.* New York: Academic Press.

Crites, J. (1965). Test reviews. *Journal of Counseling Psychological*, 12, 328-30.

Cross, G. (1971). *The effects on belief systems and the amount of debate experience on the acquisition of critical thinking.* Unpublished doctoral dissertation, University of Utah, Salt Lake City.

Dewey, J. (1910). *How we think.* New York: D.C. Health and Co.

Drake, J. (1976). *Teaching critical thinking.* Dansville, IL: The Interstate Printers and Publishers.

Dressel, P. and Mayhew, L. (1954). General education: Exploration in evaluation. *Final Report of the Cooperative Study of Evaluation in General Education.* Washington, D.C.: American Council on Education.

Fogg, C. and Calia, V. (1967). The comparative influence on two testing techniques on achievement in science and critical thinking ability. *The Journal of Experimental Education*, 35, 1-14.

Follert, V. and Colbert, K. (1983). *An analysis of the research concerning debate training and critical thinking improvements.* (ERIC Document Reproduction Service No. ED 238 058).

Follman, J., Brown, L. and Burg, E. (1970). Factor analysis of achievement scholastic aptitude, and critical thinking subtests. *The Journal of Experimental Education*, 38, 11-16.

Follman, J., Miller W. and Hernandez, D. (1969). Factor analysis of achievement scholastic aptitude, critical thinking subtests. *The Journal of Experimental Education*, 38, 48-53.

Frank, D. (1969). Teaching high school speech to improve critical thinking. *The Speech Teacher*, 18, 296-302.

Fritz, P. and Weaver, R. (1984). Teaching critical thinking skills in public speaking courses: A liberal arts perspective. Paper presented at the *Annual Meeting of the Speech Communication Association.* (70th, Chicago, IL., November 1-4, 1984). (ERIC Document Reproduction Service No. ED 249 556).

George, K. (1968). The effects of critical thinking ability upon course grades in biology. *Science Education*, 52, 421-6.

Gruner, C. R., Huseman, R. C., and Luck, J. I. (1971). Debating ability, critical thinking ability, and authoritarianism. *Speaker and Gavel*, 8, 63-4.

Helmstader, G. (1965). Review of the Watson-Glaser Critical Thinking Appraisal. *The Seventh Mental Measurement Yearbook*, p. 784.

Helmstader, G. (1983). Review of the Watson-Glaser Critical Thinking Appraisal. *The Eighth Mental Measurement Yearbook*, p. 1347.

Henkel, T. (1968). Undergraduate physics instruction and critical thinking ability. *The Journal of Research and Science Teaching*, 5, 89-94.

Hill, B. (1993). The value of competitive debate as a vehicle for promoting the development of critical thinking ability. *CEDA Yearbook*, 13, 1-22.

Hill, W. (1970). Review of the Watson-Glaser Critical Thinking Appraisal. *The Fifth Mental Measurement Yearbook*. New Brunswick: Turgers.

Huseman, C. I. (1970). Review of the Watson-Glaser Critical Thinking Appraisal. *The Fifth Mental Measurement Yearbook*, 5.

Hovland, C. I. (1970). Review of the Watson-Glaser Critical Thinking Appraisal. *The Fifth Mental Measurement Yearbook*, 5.

Howell, W. (1943). The effects of high school debating on critical thinking. *Speech Monographs*, 10, 96-103.

Hunt, D. and Randhawa, B. (1973). Relationship between and among cognitive variables and achievement in computer science. *Education and Psychological Reports*, 36, 380.

Jackson, T. (1961). *The effects of intercollegiate debate on critical thinking*. Unpublished doctoral dissertation, University of Wisconsin.

Johnson, A. (1943). An experimental study in the analysis and measurement of reflective thinking. *Speech Monographs*, 10, 83-96.

Katula, R. and Martin, C. (1984). Teaching critical thinking in the speech communication classroom. *Communication Education*, 33, 160-167.

Keyser, D. and Sweetland, R. (1985). *Test Critiques*. Vol. III.

Kirk, R. (1968). *Experimental Design: Procedures for the behavioral sciences*. Belmont, CA: Brooks/Cole.

Kurfiss, J. G. (1988). *Critical thinking: Theory, practice, and possibilities*. Washington, D.C.: Association for the Study of Higher Education.

Landis, R. (1976). The psychological dimensions of three measures of critical thinking and twenty-four structures of intellect tests for a sample of ninth-grade students. *Dissertation Abstracts International*, 5705-A.

Lucas, A. (1972). Inflated posttest scores seven months after the pretest. *Science Education*, 56, 381-7.

Luck, J. L. and Gruner, C. R. (1970). Note on authoritarianism and critical thinking ability. *Psychological Reports*, 27, 380.

McPeak, J. (1990). *Teaching critical thinking: Dialogue and dialectic.* New York: Routledge.

Modjeski, R. and Michael, W. (1983). An evaluation by a panel of psychologists of the reliability and validity of two tests of critical thinking. *Educational and Psychological Measurement*, 43, 1187-1197.

Meyers, C. (1986). *Teaching students to think critically.* San Francisco: Jossey-Bass.

Ness, J. (1967). The effects of a beginning speech course on critical thinking ability. (Doctoral dissertation, University of Minnesota, Minneapolis, Minnesota). *Dissertation Abstract International, 28,* 4826A.

Nie, N., Hull, C., Jenkins, J., Steinbenner, K. and Brent, D. (1975). *Statistical package for the social sciences.* (2nd ed.). McGraw-Hill.

Perella, J. (1983). The debate method of critical thinking. Dubuque, IA; Kendall Hunt.

Rust, V. (1962). A factor-analytic study of critical thinking. *The Journal of Educational Research*, 55, 253-9.

Seymour, L. and Sutman, F. (1973). Critical thinking ability, open-mindedness, and knowledge of the process of science of chemistry and on chemistry students. *The Journal of Science Teaching*, 10, 159-63.

Smith, D. (1977). College classroom interactions and critical thinking. *Journal of Educational Psychology*, 69, 180-190.

Sorenson, L. (1966). Watson-Glaser Critical Thinking Appraisal: Changes in critical thinking associated with two methods of teaching high school biology. *Test Data Report No. 51.* New York: Harcourt Brace and World.

Trank, D. (1977). *Secondary forensics programs: Can they survive current pressures?* (ERIC Document Reproduction Service No. 170 824).

Trank, D. (1978). *Back to basics: A case for teaching forensics.* (ERIC Document Reproduction Service No. 170 824).

Watson, G. and Glaser, E. (1980). *Critical thinking appraisal manual for forms A and B.* New York: Harcourt Brace Jovanvich.

Watson, G. and Glaser, E. (1964). *Critical thinking appraisal manual for forms YM and ZM.* New York: Harcourt Brace Jovanvich.

Westbrook, B. and Seller, J. (1967). Critical thinking, intelligence, and vocabulary. *Education and Psychology*, 27, 443-6.

Whalen, S. (1991). Intercollegiate debate as a co-curricular activity: Effects on critical thinking skills. In Donn W. Parson (ed), *Arguments in Controversy: Proceedings of the Seventh SCA/AFA Conference on Argumentation*, (pp. 391-97). Annandale, VA: Speech Communication Association.

Williams, D. (1951). *The Effects of Training in College Debating on Critical Thinking Ability*. Unpublished Master's Thesis, Purdue University.

Wilson, D. and Wagner, E. (1981). The Watson-Glaser Critical Thinking Appraisal as a predictor of performance in a critical thinking course. *Educational and Psychological Measurement*, 41, 1319-1323.

Kent R. Colbert (Ph.D., The Florida State University) is President of Atlanta's Music Machine, Inc. and a Communication Consultant in Atlanta, GA. He was formerly a Director of Forensics and Associate Professor of Communication. This essay was originally published in volume 16 (1995) of *Contemporary Argumentation and Debate*, pp.52-72

PART THREE
VERSIONS OF CAUSE

The articulation of a causal relationship is at the heart of evaluation and advocacy: we pursue actions to bring about good results and we avoid actions which bring about bad results. To know the difference, we need to draw and test conclusions about causal relationships. This section illustrates the rich variety of approaches that can be brought to bear on the question of causality.

Irwin Mallin in *The Application of Proximate Cause to CEDA Debate,* notes that something meets the legal test of proximate cause when it is a direct and substantial factor in brining about a given result. He advocates proximate cause as a way to address the practice of offering overly "generic" arguments which rely on broad and encompassing links to a wide variety of case areas but which lack causal rigor. Employing the concept of proximate cause would lead to a better understanding of real life constraints and serve as a better analog of political decision-making. In *Dominant Form and Marginalized Voices: Argumentation about Feminism(s)* **Carrie Crenshaw** uses the frame of feminist argumentation in debate to criticize causal reductionism and "the assumption that there is such a thing as a direct and sole causal link to monolithic impacts." **David Berube** focuses his criticism on low-probability high-consequence arguments in *Debunking Mini-Max Reasoning: The Limits of Extended Causal Chains in Contest Debating.* Assigning a high consequence to a very small probability argument, known as mini-max reasoning, is uneconomical in training contest debaters, Berube notes. After detailing several limits to this type of reasoning and suggesting several ways of testing, he concludes by calling for the understanding and application of minimal standards of likelihood.

Finally, in *Counterfactual Possibilities: Constructing Counter-to-Fact Causal Claims*, **Ken Broda-Bahm** approaches causal statements as counterfactual claims, or statements about what the world would have been like if things had been different. Ways of addressing counterfactual claims in philosophy literatures offer methods of analyzing non-policy resolutions and provide a number of ways of conceiving of causal relationships. Taken together, these four essays can be seen as an argument for an expanded role for analysis in articulating and evaluating causal relationships.

THE APPLICATION OF PROXIMATE CAUSE TO CEDA DEBATE

Irwin Mallin

One of the most common problems in academic debate today is the use of arguments dependent on tenuous causal links. These so-called "generic" or "meatball" arguments deprive students of the educational benefits of studying issues of current public significance in a meaningful way. This problem has led authors (Hollihan, 1983, p. 9; Parson and Bart, 1987, p. 138; Walker, 1983, p. 17) to call for standards by which the reasonableness of debate arguments may be measured. This paper proposes importing the concept of proximate cause from the law of torts to CEDA debate as a means of deriving such standards. Proximate cause analysis in CEDA would help insure that generic arguments are subjected to a rigorous causal standard, provide debate with a real-world context, and aid debaters in developing inherency arguments.

JUSTIFICATION FOR APPLYING LEGAL CONCEPTS TO CEDA

A legal paradigm is particularly appropriate in CEDA. Issues of fact and issues of judgment are central both to CEDA debate and legal argumentation. The resolution of the issues of fact provide the "building blocks" upon which the issues of judgment are resolved. For example, several rounds on the Spring 1990 topic, "Resolved: That the trend toward increasing foreign investment in the United States is detrimental to this nation," focused on the question of fact of whether such trend is necessary to keep interest rates low. This is analogous to the questions of fact that permeate civil and criminal trials.

Issues of "judgment" are also central to both legal and CEDA debate arguments. For example, CEDA debaters argue which of competing values is greater. Similarly, cases decided in appellate courts of law often also involve weighing of values. Consider the recent U.S. Supreme Court decision that police sobriety-check roadblocks do not violate the Fourth Amendment's ban on unreasonable police seizures. In his majority opinion, Chief Justice Rehnquist wrote that "the balance of the State's interest in preventing drunken driving . . . and the degree of intrusion upon motorists who are briefly stopped, weighs in favor of the state program" (*Michigan State Police v. Sitz*, 1990, p. 2448). The balancing Rehnquist speaks of is similar to that called for by CEDA resolutions. For example, the Fall 1990 resolution "Resolved: that government censorship of public artistic expression in the United States is an undesirable infringement on individual rights," asks for a balancing of rights of artistic expression against the governmental interests (such as morality, or whatever else a negative team may reasonably choose to argue) that lead to censorship. The Spring 1990 topic asks for a balancing of the positive and negative attributes of foreign investment in the U.S., and for the judge to thereupon decide whether that trend is "detrimental."

Because CEDA debate operates at this evaluative pre-policy level, policy implications of CEDA debate arguments need to be examined in terms of their likelihood[1]. For example, if a negative team argues that a value objection to what affirmative proposes is that it would result in nuclear war, affirmative should begin its response in terms of the likelihood of nuclear war occurring as a result of their proposal. Should they conclude that nuclear war is not likely, the value objection becomes moot.

There is much precedent for the application of legal concepts to argumentation. Toulmin (1958, p. 7) and Perelman (1980) suggest jurisprudence as the model for argument theory. With regard to academic debate, Thompson (1962) has presented a judicial model of a counterplan. More recently, Ulrich (1982) argued that "the best model of debate is one that is drawn from legal reasoning" (p. 1). One reason for this is that a judicial approach provides a context for debate to occur. Ulrich notes that

> if debate is a totally isolated field of argument, then learning about debate would not train our students in any other field. It does mean that seeking universal rules for argument may be futile. Rather, we should seek to draw rules from debate that are similar in terms of goals, format, etc., and to deviate from those fields only if the unique characteristics of debate justify the deviation (p. 3).

As Ulrich argues, law is the field that best meets that criterion as

> legal argument (especially appellate argument) has many similar characteristics of academic debate. Legal argumentation is bilateral. The judge is external to the deliberation. The judge is expected to refrain from deciding a case based upon any issues other than those raised by the litigants. The Supreme Court even limits legal arguments before it to one hour. Legal reasoning has even developed standards for assigning presumption, determining the wording of a policy, and defining terms. If there is a genus/species relationship between argumentation and debate, then law is the species closest to debate (p. 4).

Another advantage to adopting a judicial paradigm is that as legal rules develop out of necessity, so do equivalent argument rules outside of law. Ulrich notes that the standards of presumption used in civil and criminal courts

> were developed not because of any abstract sense of the nature of presumption, but because the goals of the judicial system required such a presumption. The presumption of innocence, for example, is based upon society's view that it is better to let guilty people free than to convict innocent people. Other judicial systems that value liberty less might reverse this presumption, arguing that any risk of guilt is enough to convict a person. The implication is that legal presumptions are based either upon values that should be pro-

tected, or due to procedures that require the presuming of a fact to be true (p. 7).

While Ulrich concludes against adopting the judicial model of presumption because the reasons for its existence in law are not present in debate, the reasons for the existence of the judicial model of causation are present in debate. The key element of the judicial model of causation is proximate cause, which *Black's Law Dictionary* (1979, p. 1103) defines as "that which, in a natural and continuous sequence, unbroken by any efficient intervening cause [i.e., with no alternate causation], produces injury, and without which the result would not have occurred."[2]

The concept of *proximate cause* developed out of need. Society would not likely tolerate a judicial system that allowed advocates to make outrageous claims on behalf of their clients. Imagine a jury's reaction if an attorney argued that if the jury did not allow his clients to recover money from a corporate defendant, the corporation's shareholders would have more money, would spend the money on beef, and run a greater risk of heart disease. As Sheckels (1984, p. 189) argues, the public reaction to such an argument by a legislator would be equally unfavorable. Moreover, allowing an actor to be held liable for remote consequences of her actions violates our society's sense of fairness, as would a presumption of guilt in criminal trials. As Courtade et al. (1989) note, holding someone liable for losses that remotely flow from his acts "would be both impractical and unjust" (p. 420). This is because

> consequences may usually be traced to the proximate cause with some degree of assurance, but beyond that is the field of conjecture, where uncertainty renders the attempt at exact conditions futile. Causes of injury which are mere incidents of the operating cause, although in a sense factors, are so insignificant that the law cannot fasten responsibility on the one who may have set them in motion (Courtade, et al., 1989, p. 420).

Fairness with regard to imputing liability is also a concern in debate. Dudczak (1980) contends that the assumptions of fact in an argument "are subject to challenges of verification before any consideration of effects can be made" (p. 232) and "as the complexity of the causal model increases, it becomes more susceptible to indictment as each element of the model must be sustained to make the claim" (Dudczak, 1988, p. 18).

THE NATURE OF PROXIMATE CAUSE

In the law of torts, an actor is not liable for harm to another unless the actor's conduct was both the *cause-in-fact* (i.e., the "cause" as that word is typically used) and the proximate cause of the harm (*Restatement of the Law – Torts (Second)* Sec. 430 (1965))[3]. The issue of whether the conduct was the proximate cause of the harm is not reached until after it is determined that the conduct was the cause-in-fact of the harm.

The term *proximate cause* originally did mean nearest cause (Prosser, 1971, p. 244). Speiser, Krause and Gans (1986) attribute the phrase to Lord Bacon's maxim, "In law not the remote cause, but the nearest is looked to" (p. 383). Under modern law, however, proximate cause is not necessarily the nearest in the chain of events. As a result, some courts suggest that the synonymous phrases *efficient cause* (*Riddle v. Exxon Transportation*, 1977, p. 1116) or *legal cause* (*Derdiarian v. Felix Contracting*, 1980, p. 670) would be preferable. Although *legal cause* has been adopted by the American Law Institute (Restatement, Ch. 16) and is probably the most descriptive phrase, courts and commentators continue to commonly use *proximate cause*. It shall therefore be used in this paper[4].

Numerous formulations of the test for proximate cause have been developed. This paper will focus on one, the *substantial factor* test. First formulated by Smith (1911-12), the substantial factor test has been adopted by the American Law Institute (Restatement, Ch. 16) and by the courts of New York (*Derdiarian*, 1980, p. 670) and many other states. Restatement Sec. 431 provides that

> The actor's negligent conduct is a legal cause of harm to another if (a) his conduct is a substantial factor in bringing about the harm, and (b) there is no rule of law relieving the actor from liability because of the manner in which his negligence resulted in the harm.

Comment *e* to Sec. 431 notes that although the rule is stated in terms of negligent conduct, it is equally applicable where the conduct is intended to cause harm.

Restatement Sec. 432(1) provides that the actor's conduct is not a "substantial factor" (and therefore not a proximate cause) if the harm would have been sustained absent the actor's conduct. In debate jargon, the harm must have been "unique." The only exception to this rule is when either of two independent causes are each sufficient to bring about the harm. Then, either cause may be found to be a substantial factor (i.e., sufficient cause) in bringing it about (Restatement Sec. 432(2)). For example, if two fires are set by different actors, either or both of the actions may be found to be substantial factors in bringing about the resulting harm (Restatement Sec. 432(2), Illustration 4).

To demonstrate how proximate cause would apply in a debate setting, consider the following example of a "generic" argument as reported by Belkin (1985): a negative team argued that an affirmative proposal that

> would create several thousand jobs would lead to economic growth, which would lead to a rise in population, which would in turn increase carbon dioxide in the atmosphere, melt the polar ice caps and lead to nuclear war.

The team arguing this negative disadvantage would have to demonstrate that sufficient growth to cause the problems complained of would not happen absent adoption of the affirmative proposal. Otherwise, adoption of the affirmative proposal cannot be considered a proximate cause of the harms.

Three examples may help illustrate the concept of proximate cause and the rules that have emanated from it which are most applicable to debate. The first example illustrates that an event need not literally be the nearest cause of harm to be the proximate cause. The second illustrates the application of rules regarding the failure of third persons to prevent harm. The third example demonstrates the application of proximate cause to so-called "linear" arguments.

EXAMPLE 1: AN EVENT NEED NOT BE THE NEAREST CAUSE TO BE THE PROXIMATE CAUSE

In this example, a policeman shot his wife with the gun the police department issued him (*Bonsignore v. City of New York*, 1982). The wife sued the city, arguing that the city's failure to identify officers who are unfit to carry guns was a substantial factor in her injury. In legal jargon, the policeman's action here was an *intervening force* (Restatement, Sec. 441(1)). That is, after the city failed to screen out the officer (the negligent act), he shot his wife (the intervening force). The fact that there was an intervening force does not relieve the negligent actor of liability. Although it is not clear from the published opinion, it appears that the city argued that the officer's actions were a *superseding cause* of his wife's injuries. A superseding cause is an intervening force that *does* relieve the negligent actor of liability (Restatement Sec. 440).

The appellate court in this case held that a jury could reasonably find the city liable for the injury even though the acts of the officer were the immediate cause of the injury (*Bonsignore*, pp. 637-638, 1982). That is because of the rule that "an intervening act may not serve as a superseding cause, and relieve an actor of liability, where the risk of the intervening act occurring is the very same risk which renders the actor negligent" (*Derdiarian*, 1980, p. 671; Restatement Sec. 442B). In this case, the very risk the city took by not identifying officers who are unfit to carry guns was that an unfit officer might injure someone with the gun he is issued.

This example illustrates that an event need not literally be the nearest cause to be the proximate cause of harm. Thus if the affirmative proposal to create jobs would necessarily result in increased carbon dioxide emissions, the negative could properly charge the affirmative with whatever harm results from the emissions caused by the creation of *those jobs only*, which is not likely to include the melting of the polar ice caps.

EXAMPLE 2: AN ACTOR ISN'T LIABLE FOR SOMEONE ELSE'S FAILURE TO PREVENT HARM IF THAT SOMEONE ELSE HAS FULL RESPONSIBILITY FOR PREVENTING THE HARM

In this example, which comes from Illustration 10 of Restatement Sec. 452, an automobile manufacturer becomes aware of a defect in a model of car and supplies all of its dealers with parts to remedy the defect. A dealer calls a purchaser of one of the cars, offers him the part, and warns him of the danger. The purchaser refuses to accept the part. One year later this purchaser sells the car to someone else, who is subsequently injured as a result of the lack of the part. The manufacturer is not liable to the subsequent purchaser.

This result is because of the operation of Restatement Sec. 452(2), which provides that a third person's failure to prevent harm relieves a negligent actor of liability if the duty is found to have passed from the negligent actor to the third person. One instance where this duty is found to have passed is when "the court finds that full responsibility for control of the situation and prevention of the threatened harm has passed to the third person" (Restatement Sec. 452, Comment f)[5]. In the illustration, such responsibility passed on to the original purchaser of the car when he was notified of the defect and the availability of the remedying part[6].

Generic debate argumentation usually presents analogous situations. For example, the Environmental Protection Agency is charged with the "full responsibility for . . . prevention of" carbon monoxide levels so high that they threaten the polar ice caps[7]. Indeed, it is the government, and not private industry, that is charged with preventing nuclear war. The very reason that a lay audience would not respond favorably to a generic argument in a legislative setting is that a rational, sophisticated government would not consciously take actions likely to result in catastrophic public harms, and, as a result, government agencies have been created to prevent those harms.

EXAMPLE 3: IN THE COURT OF LAW A LINEAR HARM CAN ONLY BE HELD LIABLE IF IT'S MORE LIKELY THAN NOT THAT IT WOULD CAUSE THE ULTIMATE HARM

Our final example comes from a medical malpractice case (*Mortensen v. Memorial Hospital*, 1984). A plaintiff suffered from a disease that caused the muscles in his left leg to atrophy. The leg eventually had to be amputated. He sued his doctor, claiming that but for the doctor's negligence, the leg would not need to have been amputated. The plaintiff also argued that he should recover if he could prove that the doctor's negligence "deprived him of the possibility, no matter how slight, of saving the leg" (p. 270). The court disagreed, holding that in order for the doctor's negligence to be a substantial factor in producing the injury, the plaintiff would have to prove that, given the condition which existed in his leg, "it is more probable than not that the loss of the limb was caused by the doctor's negligence." (p. 270).

The court noted that the substantial factor test does not require that the substantial factor be the only cause which produces the injury (p. 270; Restatement Sec. 433B, Comment *b*). If another possible cause concurs with the defendant's negligent act, the plaintiff is still liable if the plaintiff "shows facts and conditions from which the negligence of the defendant and the causation of the [injury] by that negligence may reasonably be inferred (p. 270, citing *Ingersoll*, 1938, p. 830). In other words, the negligent actor remains liable if the plaintiff shows that the negligence was one of multiple independent causes, each of which would be sufficient to cause the harm by itself. But where an injury is one which naturally might occur from causes other than a defendant's negligence, the inference of his negligence is not fair and reasonable (*Foltis, Inc. v. City of New York*, 1941, p. 460). If conflicting inferences may be drawn, choice of inference must be made by the jury (*Foltis*, 1941, p. 461; Restatement Sec. 434).

Therefore, a plaintiff cannot prove proximate cause by merely showing that the actor's conduct contributed in some small way to causing the harm alleged. Debaters who run generic arguments often argue that the harms they complain of are "linear," and therefore any actors who contribute in any small way to causing those harms should be held liable for the entire harm. Such arguments are not allowed under the judicial paradigm of causation unless it can be shown that it is more probable than not that the damage was caused by the actor. Consider the example provided by Belkin (1985). The debaters she cites link a modest increase in employment to an increase in carbon dioxide emissions, which in turn are linked to the melting of the polar ice caps. These debaters would likely argue that since any carbon dioxide emissions contribute to the total problem, it is not unreasonable to link the tiny increase in emissions caused by the new jobs affirmative calls for to the ultimate negative harm, the melting of the polar ice caps. However, proximate cause analysis would require these debaters to prove that it is more probable than not that the carbon dioxide emissions caused by the new jobs affirmative calls for are sufficient to melt the polar ice caps.

Although it would be impossible to present a comprehensive treatment of proximate cause in this limited space, the above is adequate to demonstrate the concept and its application to academic debate.

ADVANTAGES AND IMPLICATIONS

Subjecting debate argumentation to a rigorous causal standard would be advantageous for a variety of reasons, one of which is that it would compel debaters to argue the resolution in a meaningful way. CEDA debaters who debated in high school no doubt found generic arguments to be common, virtually prerequisites to success. Belkin (1985) reports that a debater from Bronx High School of Science told her that "in this game, if you can't prove that something will lead to nuclear war, you can't win." It is without question that high school debaters import these arguments to CEDA when they enter college. I judged a round on the Spring 1986 CEDA topic, "Resolved: That membership in the United Nations is no longer beneficial to the United States," in which the first affirmative speaker read one card alleging that a certain action of the United Nations causes economic growth and spent the remainder of his time reading evidence of the harms of economic growth, weaving a chain of causal links virtually identical to the one reported above. The first negative responded not with causation or topicality arguments, but rather with eight minutes of "growth is good." These debaters were able to complete their research on the topic upon the discovery of one card tenuously linking the topic to economic growth. They managed to defeat the aim of academic debate to give students an opportunity to research and discuss important issues in a meaningful way (Sheckels, 1984, p. 188). Ehninger and Brockriede (1963) claim that "the debater does not seek conviction regardless of the terms. He is more concerned that decision be reflective and that his method be correct than that any particular result be obtained by his appeals" (p. 18). But the debater who claims that he or she should earn a judge's ballot because of an argument with minimal causal relationship to the topic is clearly more concerned with the particular result than a correct, reflective decision[8]. Similarly, Dudczak (1988) contends that the lack of a rigorous standard of causation teaches debaters that "reason-governed choice is not relevant to argumentative discourse" (p. 20).

The desirability of proximate cause standards in debate is illustrated by comparison with another set of proposed standards. Pfau (1987, p. 63) cites Unger (1981) as having proposed a set of four standards to be used in evaluating generic arguments in policy debates: *internal context* (are all sources defining and implicating terms the same way?), *external context* (do the sources cited in the generic argument support the link between that argument and the opposing team's specific proposal?), *subject matter context* (is there one expert who agrees with the generic argument in its entirety?), and *historical context* (why hasn't the impact of the generic argument happened yet?).

While Unger's standards are doubtlessly valid, proximate cause analysis is also a legitimate means of analyzing generic arguments and is uniquely useful in CEDA rounds because, as noted above, legal and CEDA debates both focus on propositions of judgment. Additionally, Unger's standards are essentially evidence-dependent, while the underlying problem with bad generic arguments is related to causation, not evidence. For example, a team could meet Unger's standards by relying on evidence from a dubious source who claims horrendous harms unless a given event happens. This is not unlikely, as it has been said that some debaters "quote *World Marxist Review* as freely as *Foreign Affairs*" (McGough, 1988, p. 19). Conversely, it is possible for a generic argument to be legitimate without anything specific enough to meet Unger's criteria having been published on it. This is an important consideration, as the goals of CEDA include striking "a balance among analysis, delivery and evidence" (Constitution of the Cross Examination Debate Association, 1988, Art. II, Sec. 1) and "seek[ing] to be a full, free testing of ideas" (CEDA Ethics Committee, 1989, p. 6). So testing of arguments in CEDA may be as appropriate at the idea/analysis level as at the evidence level.

Some authors (Brownlee, 1987, p. 441; Dudczak, 1987; 1988; Freely; 1986, p. 173) propose that inherency arguments be part of CEDA debaters' arsenals. Those who heed this advice will find that proximate cause analysis is an excellent means of locating inherency arguments as "inherency is essentially causal in nature" (Cherwitz & Hikins, 1977, p. 83).

One may argue that a judicial paradigm is not appropriate in academic debate because while tort liability results in extreme, immediate harms (i.e., being compelled to pay a potentially large judgment), academic debate is "just a game." However, if as Colbert and Biggers (1987) contend, we should justify our expenditures on debate in terms of educational value, then we should not condone argumentation that has no validity in legal or legislative debate. Although Colbert and Biggers (1987) found that, generally, "the data suggesting that debate is valuable to the pre-law student is over-whelming" (p. 4), Fadely (1982) reports that "upon their arrival at law school [undergraduate debate alumni] often find that the debating done there . . . bears little resemblance . . . to the debating which they did at the undergraduate level" (p. 13).

The adoption of a judicial paradigm, particularly with regard to causation, would make undergraduate debate more beneficial to future lawyers[9].

CONCLUSION

Proximate cause analysis is used in the courtroom to determine the legitimacy and fairness of causal arguments. This paper contends that it would fulfill the same purpose if used in CEDA debate. It would also provide students with a better understanding of the constraints placed on debate in a real life context, and of the policy reasons for those constraints. This is beneficial for all students, not merely those who aspire to be lawyers. As Rowland (1984) notes, a principal justification for the study of argumentation is to teach students "to distinguish between strong arguments, which more often than not lead to accurate conclusions, and weak arguments, which do not" (p. 76).

REFERENCES

American Bar Association. (1984). *Annotated Model Rules of Professional Conduct*. Chicago: American Bar Association.

Belkin L. (1985, April 29). Teen-age debaters resolve who's best in New York State. *New York Times*, pp. A1, B4.

Black's Law Dictionary (5th ed.). (1979). St. Paul, MN: West.

Bonsignore v. City of New York, 683 F.2d 635 (2d Cir. 1982).

Brownlee, D. (1987). Advocacy and values. In D. A. Thomas & J. Hart (Eds.), *Advanced debate* (3rd ed., pp. 440-442). Lincolnwood, IL: National Textbook.

CEDA Ethics Committee. (1989, Dec. 27). *Statement of ethical principles (draft)*.

Cherwitz, R. A., Hikins, J.W. (1977). Inherency as a multidimensional construct: A rhetorical approach to the proof of causation. *Journal of the American Forensic Association, 14*, 82-90.

Colbert, K., & Biggers, T. (1987). Why should we support debate. In D. A. Thomas & J. Hart (Eds.), *Advanced debate* (3rd ed., pp. 2-6). Lincolnwood, IL: National Textbook.

Constitution of the Cross Examination Debate Association. (1988, July).

Courtade, C., et al. (1989). Negligence. In Van Knapp, D. P. (Ed.), *American Jurisprudence (second)* (rev. ed.). Vol 57A. Rochester, NY: Lawyers Co-Operative.

Derdiarian v. Felix Contracting, 414 N.E.2d 666 (N.Y. 1980).

Dudczak, C. A. (1980). Direct refutation in propositions of policy: A viable alternative. *Journal of the American Forensic Association, 16*, 232-235.

Dudczak, C. A. (1987). Inherency in non-policy propositions: Rediscovering the 'lost' issue. In J.W. Wenzel, et al. (Eds.), *Argument and critical practices: Proceedings of the Fifth SCA/AFA Conference on Argumentation* (pp. 371-378). Annandale, VA: Speech Communication Association.

Dudczak, C. A. (1988). Inherency as a stock issue in non-policy propositions. *CEDA Yearbook, 9*, 15-22.

Ehninger, D., & Brockriede, W. (1963). *Decision by debate*. New York: Dodd, Mead.

Fadely, D. (1982-83). The courts of reason and law: A comparative model. *Speaker and Gavel, 20*, 13-20.

Foltis, Inc. v. City of New York, 38 N.E. 2d 455 (N.Y. 1941).

Freely, A. J. (1986). *Argumentation and debate* (6th ed). Belmont, CA: Wadsworth.

Hollihan, T. A. (1983, April). *Generic argument: Contrivance of scoundrels or refuge for the unimaginative.* Paper presented at the meeting of the Central States Speech Association, Lincoln, NE.

Ingersoll v. Liberty Bank of Buffalo, 14 N.E. 2d 828 (N.Y. 1938).

McGough, M. (1988, October 10). Pull it across your flow. *The New Republic*, pp. 17-19.

Michigan State Police v. Sitz, 110 S.Ct. 2481 (1990).

Mortensen v. Memorial Hospital, 483 N.Y.S.2d 264 (1st Dept. 1984).

Parson, D. W., & Bart, J. (1987). On "being reasonable": The last refuge of scoundrels – Part II: The scoundrels strike back. In D. A. Thomas & J. Hart (Eds.), *Advanced debate* (3rd ed., pp. 130-138). Lincolnwood, IL: National Textbook.

Perelman, C. (1980). *Justice, law and argument.* Hingham, MA: Reidel-Kluwer.

Pfau, M. (1987). A reasonable approach to generic argument. In D. A. Thomas & J. Hart (Eds.), *Advanced debate* (3rd ed., pp. 56-65). Lincolnwood, IL: National Textbook.

Poretta v. Superior Dowel Co., 137 A.2d 361 (Me. 1957).

Prosser, W. L. (1971). *Handbook of the law of torts* (4th ed.). St. Paul, MN: West.

Restatement of the Law – Torts (Second). (1965). St. Paul, MN: American Law Institute Publishers.

Riddle v. Exxon Transportation, 563 F.2d 1103 (4th Cir. 1977).

Rock group not liable for deaths. (1990, September 10). *National Law Journal*, p. 33.

Rowland, R. C. (1984). Tabula rasa: the relevance of debate to argument theory. *Journal of the American Forensic Association, 21*, 76-88.

Sheckels, T. F., Jr. (1984). *Debating: Applied rhetorical theory.* New York: Longman.

Smith, J. (1911-12). Legal cause in actions of tort. *Harvard Law Review, 25*, 103-128, 223-252, 303-321.

Speiser, S. M., Krause, C. F., & Gabs, A. W. (1986). *The American Law of Torts.* Vol. 3. Rochester, NY: Lawyers Co-Operative.

Thompson, W. N. (1962). The effect of a counterplan upon the burden of proof. *Central States Speech Journal, 13*, 247-252.

Toulmin, S. E. (1958). *The uses of argument.* Cambridge, UK: Cambridge

University Press.

Ulrich, W. (1982, November). A judicial paradigm for the evaluation of debates. Paper presented at the meeting of the Speech Communication Association, Louisville, KY. (ERIC Document Reproduction Service No. ED 220 895).

Unger, J. J. (1981, November). *The words of a debate resolution and the subject matter: Friends or foes?* Paper presented at the meeting of the Speech Communication Association, Anaheim, CA.

United States Government Manual 1989/90. Washington: Government Printing Office.

Walker, G. (1983, April). *The appropriate use and inappropriate abuse of generic arguments in competitive debate.* Paper presented at the meeting of the Central States Speech Association, Lincoln, NE.

NOTES

[1]The author wishes to thank Craig Dudczak of Syracuse University for suggesting this concept and for his many other valuable suggestions upon reviewing the various drafts of the original version of this paper.

[2]Newspaper accounts suggest that this concept was the basis of the judge's decision in the recent Nevada case involving the "heavy metal" band Judas Priest. The Associated Press reports that the judge ruled that alleged subliminal messages on one of the band's albums did not cause the suicides of two people who listened to the album ("Rock Group Not Liable for Deaths," 1990).

[3]The Restatement, authored by the American Law Institute, is cited throughout this paper. While the Restatement is not the official code of any jurisdiction, courts have held that Restatements "may be regarded as both the product of expert opinion and as the expression of the law by the legal profession" (*Poretta v. Superior Dowel Co.*, 1957, p. 373).

[4]Additionally, argumentation scholars would confuse the legal use of "efficient cause" with the use given it by Cherwitz and Hikins (1977).

[5]Restatement Sec. 452(2) is an exception to the general rule in the law of torts that the failure of a third person to prevent harm to one threatened by a negligent actor's conduct does not relieve the negligent actor of liability (Restatement Sec. 452). For the reasons stated in the text, though, I contend that the exception stated in Sec. 452(2) is the rule that represents the situation more analogous to generic debate argumentation.

[6]A complete list of the rules that determine whether an intervening act is a super-

seding cause is found at Restatement Secs. 442-453.

[7] "The air activities of the [Environmental Protection] Agency include . . . emission standards for hazardous pollutants" (U.S. Government Manual 1989/90, p. 555).

[8] While in the judicial model, advocates are expected to "take whatever lawful and ethical measures are required to vindicate a client's cause or endeavor" (Comment, Rule 1.3, American Bar Association Model Rules of Professional Conduct, 1984), those measures are limited to the "lawful and ethical" to help insure correct, reflective, decisions.

[9] This is especially true in light of the recent tendency for courts to enact rules calling for sanctions to be imposed on lawyers who file frivolous lawsuits. See, for example, Rule 11, Federal Rules of Civil Procedure; N.Y. Civil Practice Law and Rules Sec, 8303-a; and 22 N.Y. Code of Rules and Regulations Sec. 130-1.1.

Irwin Mallin (Ph.D., Indiana University, J.D. Syracuse University) is an Assistant Professor of Communication at Indiana University-Purdue University Fort Wayne. An earlier version of this essay was published in volume 11 (1990) of *CEDA Yearbook* (now known as *Conemporary Argumentation and Debate*, pp. 44-56). At that time the author was an attorney practicing in Syracuse, New York.

DOMINANT FORM AND MARGINALIZED VOICES: ARGUMENTATION ABOUT FEMINISM(S)

Carrie Crenshaw

F eminism is not dead. It is alive and well in intercollegiate debate. Increasingly, students rely on feminist authors to inform their analysis of resolutions. While I applaud these initial efforts to explore feminist thought, I am concerned that such arguments only exemplify the general absence of sound causal reasoning in debate rounds. Poor causal reasoning results from a debate practice that privileges empirical proof over rhetorical proof, fostering ignorance of the subject matter being debated. To illustrate my point, I claim that debate arguments about feminists suffer from a reductionism that tends to marginalize the voices of significant feminist authors.

David Zarefsky made a persuasive case for the value of causal reasoning in intercollegiate debate as far back as 1979. He argued that causal arguments are desirable for four reasons. First, causal analysis increases the control of the arguer over events by promoting understanding of them. Second, the use of causal reasoning increases rigor of analysis and fairness in the decision-making process. Third, causal arguments promote understanding of the philosophical paradox that presumably good people tolerate the existence of evil. Finally, causal reasoning supplies good reasons for "commitments to policy choices or to systems of belief which transcend whim, caprice, or the non-reflexive 'claims of immediacy'" (117-9).

Rhetorical proof plays an important role in the analysis of causal relationships. This is true despite the common assumption that the identification of cause and effect relies solely upon empirical investigation. For Zarefsky, there are three types of causal reasoning. The first type of causal reasoning describes the application of a covering law to account for physical or material conditions that cause a resulting event. This type of causal reasoning requires empirical proof prominent in scientific investigation. A second type of causal reasoning requires the assignment of responsibility. Responsible human beings as agents cause certain events to happen; that is, causation resides in human beings (107-08). A third type of causal claim explains the existence of a causal relationship. It functions "to provide reasons to justify a belief that a causal connection exists" (108).

The second and third types of causal arguments rely on rhetorical proof, the provision of "good reasons" to substantiate arguments about human responsibility or explanations for the existence of a causal relationship (108). I contend that the practice of intercollegiate debate privileges the first type of causal analysis. It reduces questions of human motivation and explanation to a level of empiricism appropriate only for causal questions concerning physical or material conditions. Arguments about feminism clearly illustrate this phenomenon.

Substantive debates about feminism usually take one of two forms. First, on the affirmative, debaters argue that some aspect of the resolution is a manifestation of patriarchy. For example, given the spring 1992 resolution, "[r]esolved: That advertising degrades the quality of life," many affirmatives argued that the portrayal of women as beautiful objects for men's consumption is a manifestation of patriarchy that results in tangible harms to women such as rising rates of eating disorders. The fall 1992 topic, "[r]esolved: That the welfare system exacerbates the problems of the urban poor in the United States," also had its share of patriarchy cases. Affirmatives typically argued that women's dependence upon a patriarchal welfare system results in increasing rates of women's poverty. In addition to these concrete harms to individual women, most affirmatives on both topics, desiring "big impacts," argued that the effects of patriarchy include nightmarish totalitarianism and/or nuclear annihilation.

On the negative, many debaters countered with arguments that the some aspect of the resolution in some way sustains or energizes the feminist movement in resistance to patriarchal harms. For example, some negatives argued that sexist advertising provides an impetus for the reinvigoration of the feminist movement and/or feminist consciousness, ultimately solving the threat of patriarchal nuclear annihilation. Likewise, debaters negating the welfare topic argued that the state of the welfare system is the key issue around which the feminist movement is mobilizing or that the consequence of the welfare system – breakup of the patriarchal nuclear family – undermines patriarchy as a whole.

Such arguments seem to have two assumptions in common. First, there is a single feminism. As a result, feminists are transformed into *feminism*. Debaters speak of feminism as a single, monolithic, theoretical and pragmatic entity and feminists as women with identical motivations, methods, and goals. Second, these arguments assume that patriarchy is the single or root cause of all forms of oppression. Patriarchy not only is responsible for sexism and the consequent oppression of women, it also is the cause of totalitarianism, environmental degradation, nuclear war, racism, and capitalist exploitation. These reductionist arguments reflect an unwillingness to debate about the complexities of human motivation and explanation. They betray a reliance upon a framework of proof that can explain only material conditions and physical realities through empirical quantification.

The transformation of feminists into *feminism* and the identification of patriarchy as the *sole* cause of all oppression is related in part to the current form of intercollegiate debate practice. By "form," I refer to Kenneth Burke's notion of form, defined as the "creation of appetite in the mind of the auditor, and the adequate satisfying of that appetite" (*Counter-Statement* 31). Though the framework for this understanding of form is found in literary and artistic criticism, it is appropriate in this context; as Burke notes, literature can be "equipment for living" (*Philosophy* 293). He also suggests that form "is an arousing and fulfillment of desires. A work has form in so far as one part of it leads a reader to anticipate another part, to be gratified by the sequence" (*Counter-Statement* 124).

Burke observes that there are several aspects to the concept of form. One of these aspects, conventional form,

> involves to some degree the appeal of form *as form*. Progressive, repetitive, and minor forms, may be effective even though the reader has no awareness of their formality. But when a form appeals as form, we designate it as conventional form. Any form can become conventional, and be sought for itself – whether it be as complex as the Greek tragedy or as compact as the sonnet (*Counter-Statement* 126).

These concepts help to explain debaters' continuing reluctance to employ rhetorical proof in arguments about causality. Debaters practice the convention of poor causal reasoning as a result of judges' unexamined reliance upon conventional form. Convention is the *practice* of arguing single-cause links to monolithic impacts that arises out of custom or usage. Conventional form is the *expectation* of judges that an argument will take this form.

Common practice or convention dictates that a case or disadvantage with nefarious impacts causally related to a single link will "outweigh" opposing claims in the mind of the judge. In this sense, debate arguments themselves are conventional. Debaters practice the convention of establishing single-cause relationships to large monolithic impacts in order to conform to audience expectation. Debaters practice poor causal reasoning because they are rewarded for it by judges. The convention of arguing single-cause links leads the judge to anticipate the certainty of the impact and to be gratified by the sequence. I suspect that the sequence is gratifying for judges because it relieves us from the responsibility and difficulties of evaluating rhetorical proofs. We are caught between our responsibility to evaluate rhetorical proofs and our reluctance to succumb to complete relativism and subjectivity. To take responsibility for evaluating rhetorical proof is to admit that not every question has an empirical answer.

However, when we abandon our responsibility to rhetorical proofs, we sacrifice our students' understanding of causal reasoning. The sacrifice has consequences for our students' knowledge of the subject matter they are debating. For example, when feminism is defined as a single entity, not as a pluralized movement or theory, that single entity results in the identification of patriarchy as the sole cause of oppression. The result is ignorance of the subject position of the particular feminist author, for highlighting his or her subject position might draw attention to the incompleteness of the causal relationship between link and impact. Consequently, debaters do not challenge the basic assumptions of such argumentation and ignorance of feminists is perpetuated.

Feminists are not feminism. The topics of feminist inquiry are many and varied, as are the philosophical approaches to the study of these topics. Different authors have attempted categorization of various feminists in distinctive ways. For example, Alison Jaggar argues that feminists can be divided into four categories: liberal feminism, marxist feminism, radical feminism, and socialist feminism. While each of these feminists may share a common commitment to the improvement of women's situations, they differ from each other in very important ways and reflect divergent philosophical assumptions that make them each unique. Linda Alcoff presents an entirely different categorization of feminist theory based upon distinct understandings of the concept "woman," including cultural feminism and post-structural feminism. Karen Offen utilizes a comparative historical approach to examine two distinct modes of historical argumentation or discourse that have been used by women and their male allies on behalf of women's emancipation from male control in Western societies. These include relational feminism and individualist feminism. Elaine Marks and Isabelle de Courtivron describe a whole category of French feminists that contain many distinct versions of the feminist project by French authors. Women of color and third-world feminists have argued that even these broad categorizations of the various feminism have neglected the contributions of non-white, non-Western feminists (see, for example, hooks; Hull; Joseph and Lewis; Lorde; Moraga; Omolade; and Smith).

In this literature, the very definition of feminism is contested. Some feminists argue that "all feminists are united by a commitment to improving the situation of women" (Jaggar and Rothenberg xii), while others have resisted the notion of a single definition of feminism. bell hooks observes, "a central problem within feminist discourse has been our inability to either arrive at a consensus of opinion about what feminism is (or accept definitions) that could serve as points of unification" (*Feminist Theory* 17). The controversy over the very definition of feminism has political implications. The power to define is the power both to include and exclude people and ideas in and from that feminism. As a result,

> [b]ourgeois white women interested in women's rights issues have been satisfied with simple definitions for obvious reasons. Rhetorically placing themselves in the same social category as oppressed women, they were not anxious to call attention to race and class privilege (hooks, *Feminist Theory* 18).

Debate arguments that assume a singular conception of feminism include and empower the voices of race- and class-privileged women while excluding and silencing the voices of feminists marginalized by race and class status. This position becomes clearer when we examine the second assumption of arguments about feminism in intercollegiate debate – patriarchy is the *sole* cause of oppression.

Important feminist thought has resisted this assumption for good reason. Designating patriarchy as the sole cause of oppression allows the subjugation of resistance to other forms of oppression like racism and classism to the struggle against sexism. Such subjugation has the effect of denigrating the legitimacy of resistance to racism and classism as struggles of equal importance. "Within feminist movement in the West, this led to the assumption that resisting patriarchal domination is a more legitimate feminist action than resisting racism and other forms of domination" (hooks, *Talking Back* 19).

The relegation of struggles against racism and class exploitation to offspring status is not the only implication of the "sole cause" argument. In addition, identifying patriarchy as the single source of oppression obscures women's perpetration of other forms of subjugation and domination. bell hooks argues that we

> should not obscure the reality that women can and do partici-

pate in politics of domination, as perpetrators as well as victims – that we dominate, that we are dominated. If focus on patriarchal domination masks this reality or becomes the means by which women deflect attention from the real conditions and circumstances of our lives, then women cooperate in suppressing and promoting false consciousness, inhibiting our capacity to assume responsibility for transforming ourselves and society (hooks, *Talking Back* 20).

Characterizing patriarchy as the sole cause of oppression allows mainstream feminists to abdicate responsibility for the exercise of class and race privilege. It casts the struggle against class exploitation and racism as secondary concerns.

Current debate practice promotes ignorance of these issues because debaters appeal to conventional form, the expectation of judges that they will isolate a single link to a large impact. Feminists become feminism and patriarchy becomes the sole cause of all evil. Poor causal arguments arouse and fulfill the expectation of judges by allowing us to surrender our responsibility to evaluate rhetorical proof for complex causal relationships. The result is either the marginalization or colonization of certain feminist voices. Arguing feminism in debate rounds risks trivializing feminists. Privileging the act of speaking about feminism over the content of speech "often turns the voices and beings of non-white women into commodity, spectacle" (hooks, *Talking Back* 14). Teaching sophisticated causal reasoning enables our students to learn more concerning the subject matter about which they argue. In this case, students would learn more about the multiplicity of feminists instead of reproducing the marginalization of many feminist voices in the debate itself.

The content of the speech of feminists must be investigated to subvert the colonization of exploited women. To do so, we must explore alternatives to the formal expectation of single-cause links to enormous impacts for

appropriation of the marginal voice threatens the very core of self-determination and free self-expression for exploited and oppressed peoples. If the identified audience, those spoken to, is determined solely by ruling groups who control production and distribution, then it is easy for the marginal voice striving for a hearing to allow what is said to be overdetermined by the needs of that majority group who appears to be listening, to be tuned in (hooks, *Talking Back* 14).

At this point, arguments about feminism in intercollegiate debate seem to be overdetermined by the expectation of common practice, the "game" that we play in assuming there is such a thing as a direct and sole causal link to a monolithic impact. To play that game, we have gone along with the idea that there is a single feminism and the idea that patriarchal impacts can account for all oppression.

In making this critique, I am by no means discounting the importance of arguments about feminism in intercollegiate debate. In fact, feminists contain the possibility of a transformational politic for two reasons. First, feminist concerns affect each individual intimately. We are most likely to encounter patriarchal domination "in an ongoing way in everyday life. Unlike other forms of domination, sexism directly shapes and determines relations of power in our private lives, in familiar social spaces..." (hooks, *Talking Back* 21).

Second, the methodology of feminism, consciousness-raising, contains within it the possibility of real societal transformation. "[E]ducation for critical consciousness can be extended to include politicization of the self that focuses on creating understanding the ways sex, race, and class together determine our individual lot and our collective experience" (hooks, *Talking Back* 24). Observing the incongruity between advocacy of single-cause relationships and feminism does not discount the importance of feminists to individual or societal consciousness raising.

A large part of the problem of the mutation of feminists into feminism is conventional expectation on the part of judges. However, conventional expectation is not set in stone. Debaters can influence judges' perceptions by arguing about what conventional expectation should be. Debate is an educational laboratory in which everything is subject to a dialectical struggle, including what should constitute audience expectation. Debaters can argue about the appropriate decision-calculus of the judge. In addition, we can teach debaters how to articulate the limitations of reasoning that assumes direct and sole causal links to monolithic impacts. We can teach them the

role of rhetorical proof in debates about causality. Most importantly, we can refuse to abandon our responsibility for evaluating those
rhetorical proofs. If we achieve these goals, argumentation about
feminists would not reproduce the marginalization of women who do
not exercise race and class privilege found in mainstream feminist
movement. We can teach our students *how* to learn more about the
subject matter they debate. We can teach them more about argumentation than how to count the number of nuclear wars possible in
a one-hour-and-thirty-minute debate.

WORKS CITED

Alcoff, Linda. "Cultural Feminism vs. Post-Structuralism: The Identity
    Crisis in Feminist Theory. " *Signs* 13 (1988): 405-27.

Burke, Kenneth. *Counter-Statement*. Berkeley: U of California P, 1968.

—. *The Philosophy of Literary Form*. Berkeley: U of California P, 1973.

hooks, bell. "Feminism: A Transformational Politic." *Theoretical
    Perspectives on Sexual Difference*. Ed. Deborah L. Rhode. New Haven:
    Yale UP, 1990. 185-93.

—. *Feminist Theory: From Margin to Center*. Boston: South End, 1984.

—. *Talking Back: Thinking Feminist * Thinking Black*. Boston: South End,
    1989.

Hull, Gloria T., Patricia Bell Scott, and Barbara Smith, eds. *All the Women
    Are White, All the Blacks Are Men, But Some of Us Are Brave*. New York:
    City U of New York, Feminist P, 1982.

Jaggar, Alison, and Paula S. Rothenberg. *Feminist Frameworks*. New York:
    McGraw-
Hill, 1984.

Jaggar, Alison. *Feminist Politics and Human Nature*. Totowa, NJ: Rowman
    and Allanheld, 1983.

Joseph, Gloria I., and Jill Lewis. *Common Differences: Conflicts in Black and
    White Feminist Perspectives*. Boston: South End, 1981.

Lorde, Audre. *Sister Outsider*. Freedom, CA: Crossing, 1984.

Marks, Elaine, and Isabelle de Courtivron, eds. *New French Feminists*. New
    York: Schocken, 1981.

Moraga, Cherie. "From a Long Line of Vendidas: Chicanas and Feminism."
    Feminist Studies/Critical Studies. Ed. Teresa de Lauretis. Bloomington:
    Indiana UP, 1986. 173-90.

Offen, Karen. "Defining Feminism: A Comparative Historical Approach." *Signs* 14 (1988) 119-57.

Omolade, Barbara. "Black Women and Feminism." *The Future of Difference*. Ed. Hester Eisenstein and Alice Jardine. Boston: G.K. Hall, 1980. 247-57.

Smith, Barbara. *Toward a Black Feminist Criticism*. Freedom, CA: Crossing, 1977.

—, ed. *Home Girls: A Black Feminist Anthology*. New York: Kitchen Table, 1983.

Zarefsky, David. "The Role of Causal Argument in Policy Argumentation." *Advanced Debate*. Skokie, IL: National Textbook, 1979.

Carrie Crenshaw (Ph.D., University of Southern California) is a writer living in Birmingham, Alabama and formerly a tenured professor and President of the Cross Examination Debate Association. His essay was originally published in volume 14 (1993) of *CEDA Yearbook* (now known as *Contemporary Argumentation and Debate*), pp.72-79.

DEBUNKING MINI-MAX REASONING: THE LIMITS OF EXTENDED CAUSAL CHAINS IN CONTEST DEBATING

David M. Berube

To employ a mathematical analogy, we can say that although the risk of extinction may be fractional, the stake is, humanly speaking, infinite, and a fraction of infinity is still infinity.
– Jonathan Schell

The lifeblood of contemporary contest debating may be the extended argument. An extended argument is any argument requiring two or more distinct causal or correlational steps between initial data and ending claim. We find it associated with advantages to comparative advantage cases, with counterplan advantages, with disadvantages, permutation and impact turnarounds, some kritik implications, and even probabilistic topicality arguments. In practice, these often are not only extended arguments, they are causal arguments using mini-max reasoning. Mini-max reasoning is defined as an extended argument in which an infinitesimally probable event of high consequence is assumed to present a highly consequential risk. Such arguments, also known as low-probability high-consequence arguments, are commonly associated with "risk analysis." The opening statement from Schell represents a quintessential mini-max argument. Schell asked his readers to ignore probability assessment and focus exclusively on the impact of his claim. While Schell gave very specific reasons why probability is less important than impact in resolving this claim, his arguments are not impervious to rebuttal.

What was a knotty piece of evidence in the 1980s kick-started a practice in contest debating which currently is evident in the ubiquitous political capital disadvantage code-named "Clinton." Here is an example of the Clinton disadvantage. In theory, plan action causes some tradeoff (real or imaginary) that either increases or decreases the President's ability to execute a particular agenda. Debaters have argued the following: Clinton (soon to be Gore or Bush) needs to focus on foreign affairs. A recent agreement between Barak and Assad needs presidential stewardship. The affirmative plan shifts presidential focus to Nigeria that trades off with focus on the Middle East. As a result, the deal for the return of the Golan Heights to Syria fails. Violence and conflict ensues as Hizbollah terrorists launch guerrilla attacks into northern Israel from Lebanon. Israel strikes back. Hizbollah incursions increase. Chemical terrorism ensues and Israel attacks Hizbollah strongholds in southern Lebanon with tactical nuclear weapons. Iran launches chemical weapons against Tel Aviv. Iraq allies with Iran. The United States is drawn in. Superpower miscalculation results in all-out nuclear war culminating in a nuclear winter and the end of all life on the planet. This low-probability high-consequence event argument is an extended argument using mini-max reasoning.

The appeal of mini-max risk arguments has heightened with the onset of on-line text retrieval services and the World Wide Web, both of which allow debaters to search for particular words or word strings with relative ease. Extended arguments are fabricated by linking evidence in which a word or word string serves as the common denominator, much in the fashion of the sorities (stacked syllogism): A ◊ B, B ◊ C, C ◊ D, therefore A ◊ D. Prior to computerized search engines, a contest debater's search for segments that could be woven together into an extended argument was incredibly time consuming.

The dead ends checked the authenticity of the extended claims by debunking especially fanciful hypotheses. Text retrieval services may have changed that. While text retrieval services include some refereed published materials, they also incorporate transcripts and wire releases that are less vigilantly checked for accuracy. The World Wide Web allows virtually anyone to set up a site and post anything at that site regardless of its veracity. Sophisticated super search engines, such as Google® help contest debaters track down particular words and phrases. Searches on text retrieval services such as Lexis-Nexis Universe® and Congressional Universe® locate words and word strings within n words of each other. Search results are collated and loomed into an extended argument. Often, evidence collected in this manner is linked together to reach a conclusion of nearly infinite impact, such as the ever-present specter of global thermonuclear war.

Furthermore, too much evidence from online text retrieval services is unqualified or under-qualified. Since anyone can post a web page and since transcripts and releases are seldom checked as factual, pseudo-experts abound and are at the core of the most egregious claims in extended arguments using mini-max reasoning.

> In nearly every episode of fear mongering ... people with fancy titles appeared.... [F]or some species of scares ... secondary scholars are standard fixtures. ... Statements of alarm by newscasters and glorification of wannabe experts are two telltales tricks of the fear mongers' trade... : the use of poignant anecdotes in place of scientific evidence, the christening of isolated incidents as trends, depictions of entire categories of people as innately dangerous. ... (Glassner 206, 208)

Hence, any warrant by authority of this ilk further complicates probability estimates in extended arguments using mini-max reasoning. Often the link and internal link story is the machination of the debater making the claim rather than the sources cited in the linkage. The links in the chain may be claims with different, if not inconsistent, warrants. As a result, contextual considerations can be mostly moot.

Not only the information but also the way it is collated is suspect. All these engines use Boolean connectors (*and, or,* and *not*) and

Boolean connectors are dubious by nature.

> Boolean logic uses terms only to show relationships – of inclusion or exclusion – among the terms. It shows whether or not one drawer fits into another and ignores the question whether there is anything in the drawers. ... The Boolean search shows the characteristic way that we put questions to the world of information. When we pose a question to the Boolean world, we use keywords, buzzwords, and thought bits to scan the vast store of knowledge. Keeping an abstract, cybernetic distance from the source of knowledge, we set up tiny funnels. ... But even if we build our tunnels carefully, we still remain essentially tunnel dwellers. ... Thinking itself happens only when we suspend the inner musings of the mind long enough to favor a momentary precision, and even then thinking belongs to musing as a subset of our creative mind. ... The Boolean reader, on the contrary, knows in advance where the exits are, the on-ramps, and the well-marked rest stops. ... The pathways of thought, not to mention the logic of thoughts, disappear under a Boolean arrangement of freeways." (Heim 18, 22-25)

Heim worries that the Boolean search may encourage readers to link together nearly *empty* drawers of information, stifling imaginative, creative thinking and substituting *empty* ideas for *good reasons*. The problems worsen when researchers select word strings without reading its full context, a nearly universal practice among contest debaters. Using these computerized research services, debaters are easily able to build extended mini-max arguments ending in Armageddon.

Outsiders to contest debating have remarked simply that too many policy debate arguments end in all-out nuclear war; consequently, they categorize the activity as foolish. How many times have educators had contest debaters in a classroom discussion who strung out an extended mini-max argument to the jeers and guffaws of their classmates? They cannot all be wrong. Frighteningly enough, most of us agree. We should not ignore Charles Richet's adage: "The stupid man is not the one who does not understand something – but the man who understands it well enough yet acts as if he didn't" (Tabori 6).

Regrettably, mini-max arguments are not the exclusive domain of contest debating. "Policies driven by the consideration of low risk probabilities will, on the whole, lead to low investment strategies to prevent a hazard from being realized or to mitigate the hazard's consequences. By comparison, policies driven by the consideration of high consequences, despite low probabilities, will lead to high levels of public investment" (Nehnevajsa 521). Regardless of their persuasiveness, Bashor and others have discovered that mini-max claims are not useful in resolving complex issues. For example, in his assessment of low-probability, potentially high-consequence events such as terrorist use of weapons of mass destruction, Bashor found simple estimates of potential losses added little to contingency planning. While adding little to policy analysis, extended arguments using mini-max reasoning remain powerful determinants of resource allocation. As such, they need to be debunked.

Experts agree. For example, Slovic advocates a better understanding of all risk analysis since it drives much of our public policy. "Whoever controls the definition of risk controls the rational solution to the problem at hand. If risk is defined one way, then one option will rise to the top as the most cost-effective or the safest or the best. If it is defined another way, perhaps incorporating qualitative characteristics or other contextual factors, one will likely get a different ordering of action solutions. Defining risk is thus an exercise in power" (699). When probability assessments are eliminated from risk calculi, as is the case in mini-max risk arguments, it is a political act, and all political acts need to be scrutinized with a critical lens.

This essay intends to examine some of the problems associated with extended arguments using mini-max reasoning. First, extended arguments will be examined in respect to logical problems associated with causality, corroboration, and equivocation. Second, minimax reasoning will be examined in an attempt to debunk its persuasiveness. Finally, I will introduce three criteria for assessing the probative value of mini-max extended arguments.

THE LIMITS OF EXTENDED ARGUMENTS

The strength of the relationship between the claims in extended arguments rests on the probability of the causation between and among the simple claims. The relationship between each claim in an extended argument is moderated by its probability. Probability is challenging to define. Many scientists and members of the risk assessment community "have not as yet come to grips with the foundational issue about the meaning of probability and the various interpretations that can be attached to the term *probability*. This is extremely important, for it is how one views probability that determines one attitude toward a statistical procedure" (Singpurwalla 182)

> We employ the notion of probability when we do not know a thing with certainty. But our uncertainty is either purely subjective (we do not know what will take place, but someone else may know) or objective (no one knows, and no one can know). Subjective probability is a compass for an informational disability. ... Probability is, so to speak, a cane for a blind man; he uses it to feel his way. If he could see, he would not need the cane, and if I knew which horse was the fastest, I would not need probability theory. (Lem 142)

In simple arguments, "risks are simply the product of probability and consequence" (Thompson & Parkinson 552). Thompson and Parkinson found a difficulty in risk assessment associated with mini-max arguments that they identified as the problem of *risk tails*. "Risk tails are the segments of the standard risk curve which approach the probability and consequence axes. The tails represent high-consequence low-probability risk and low-consequence high-probability risk" (552). This region, especially the high-consequence low-probability tail, is the site of mini-max computation.

The complex probabilities of extended arguments are problematic. For example, too much reliance is given an extended link story when each step in the link exhibits a probability that is geometrically self-effacing. According to the traditional multiplication theorem, if a story is drawn from A ◊ B ◊ C ◊ D, the probabilities of A ◊ B and B ◊ C and C ◊ D are multiplied. "The probability that two subsequent events will both happen is a ratio compounded of the probability of the 1st, and the probability of the 2nd in the supposition the 1st happens" (Bayes 299). If the probability of A ◊ B is .10 and the probability of B ◊ C is also .10, then the probability of A ◊ C is .01. If the probability of C ◊ D is also .10, then the probability of A ◊ D is .001.

If all we had to do to determine probability involved multiplying fractions, calculating probabilities would be easy. Unfortunately, such is not the case. An interesting caveat involves conditional probability. "Its expositors hold that we should not concern ourselves with *absolute probabilities*, which have no relevance to things as they are, but with *conditional probabilities* – the chances that some event will occur when some set of previous conditions exists" (Krause 67). Conditional probabilities are most often associated with calculations involving variables that may be even remotely associated, such as phenomena in international relations.

> If one considers the probability of many separate events occurring, one must also consider whether or not they are correlated – that is, whether or not they are truly independent. If they are correlated, simply multiplying individual probabilities will not give you the correct estimate, and the final probability may actually be much larger than one will predict if one makes this error. For example, the probability that I will utter an obscenity at any given instance may be small (although it is certainly not zero). The probability that I will hit my funny bone at any given instant is also small. However, the probability that I will hit my funny bone and then utter an obscenity is not equal to the product of the probabilities, since the probability of swearing at a given instant is correlated to the probability of hurting myself at a given instant. (Krause 67)

Hence, "if we calculate *a priori* the probability of the occurred event and the probability of an event composed of that one and a second one which is expected, the second probability divided by the first will be the probability of the event expected, drawn from the observed event" (Laplace 15).

Another complication of extended causal chains is the corroboration principle. "There are cases in which each testimony seems unreliable (i.e., has less than 0.5 probability) on its own, even though the combination of the two testimonies is rather persuasive. ... [I]f both testimonies are genuinely independent and fully agree with one another, we are surely going to be inclined to accept them" (Cohen 72). When we are uncertain about a probability, we might try to engage multiple sources making the same or same-like claim. We feel it is less likely that two or more sources are incorrect than that a single source will be. While corroboration seems valid, it is a persuasive pipe-dream. If we use this calculus to draw our claims, errors are likely to be shared and replicated. Witness some of the problems associated with *realism* in international relations literature.

As such, the multiplication theorem has been subverted by conditional probabilities and undercut by corroboration, but contest debaters and policy makers have not risen to the challenge. While contest debating has borrowed heavily from policymaking and systems analysis, it has not resolved the causality issues any better than have policy studies experts. The grand calculus used in systems analysis is as simplistic as it is in contest debating. Lichtman and Rohrer described what happens to systems analysis in a contest debate two decades ago. "To determine the level of net benefits achieved by a policy system when multiple outcomes are considered, policy makers simply sum, for all anticipated results, the product of their probabilities and values" (238).

In contest debating, each critic will have her own threshold at which she is prepared to make a commitment. The critic tries to establish this threshold by examining the probabilities of the causal story in the argument. Zarefsky asserted that setting the threshold may be so challenging that most critics opt for rounding instead.

> The only alternative to probabilistic analysis in argumentation is a rounding-off process that either reduces probability measures to zeros or elevates them to one (100%). . . . Yet whatever the threshold chosen by a decision maker may be, the practical result is still a rounding-off of probability to zero or one with consequent errors, in the assessment of policy. (Qtd in Lichtman and Rohrer 239)

Zarefsky's observation is intriguing. Consider how often critics have voided disadvantages following a uniqueness response. For example, in response to a Presidential leadership internal link story, a contest debater may claim that recent Presidential behavior makes the claim not unique. However, uniqueness is not a threshold issue, it is a linear one, a probabilistic one. While the response reduces the likelihood of the internal link story, uniqueness responses only reduce the probability of the internal link story. The likeliness a uniqueness response is absolute is very low. Some uniqueness, or probability, remains after a uniqueness challenge, yet the critics round down and ignore the leadership disadvantage entirely. On the other hand, many judges round up as well, responding to contest debaters who have begged the risk question by a final rebuttal appeal to mini-max reasoning. Risk theorists find this false dualism troubling. For example, de Sousa warns:

> A pragmatic conception of probability needs something broad-
> er than mere *acceptance*, for acceptance is an on/off matter,
> and probability has degrees. . . . Because of the lottery para-
> dox, *high* probabilities can never be a sufficient condition of
> acceptance. And because of what I call the *Lem Paradox*[1], *low*
> probability can never be a sufficient condition of rejection."
> (261)

Tooley posed an even more intriguing question: "Does our world, then, simply contain an enormous number of highly unlikely accidents?" (105). The proponent of a mini-max disadvantage would want you to believe that such is true. Recently, we have learned highly unlikely accidents in a chaotic system are ordered (Bütz). If so, the extended mini-max argument might be one such ordering. Unfortunately for proponents of extended mini-max arguments, once any system is dominated by highly unlikely accidents, the logic of the extended argument corrodes. Predicting unpredictability is paradoxical.

We expect the critic in a contest debate to assess the strength of an extended argument and resolve its disposition. However, when the consequence is nearly infinite, it makes such a probability calculation thorny. Debaters seldom provide critics with a discussion of multiplicational versus correlational probability assessments, and often substitute simple corroboration for probability assessments.

While any claim made about a debate resolution by examining the plan might be deductive or inductive, the concoction of an extended argument is more akin to what C. S. Peirce called abduction. "Abduction merely suggests that something *might be*" (qtd. in Lanigan 50). As Schweder wrote, "Transcendent realities are of our own making, which sometimes succeed in binding us to the underlying reality that we imagine by giving us an intellectual tool – a metaphor, a premise, an analogy, a category – with which to live, to arrange our experience, and to interpret our experiences so arranged. In other words, the abductive faculty is the faculty of imagination" (361).

In the typical mini-max extended argument, a contest debater identifies a principle or rule, i.e., Presidential focus is limited and forces tradeoffs, then examines a result, i.e., the plan and its implications within a specific spatio-temporal political setting, and finally interpolates a case, i.e., the scenario and impact story. Such speculation is purely imaginative, especially when a debater uses multiple sources to create the argument.

Peirce proposes three rules for valid abduction: The hypothesis must explain the facts at hand. It must be capable of being subjected to experimental confirmation. It must be guided by economic considerations (Fann 59). What happens in contest debating? The contest debater hardly randomizes the observations drawn from research. While a research plan of any sort makes this unlikely, the Boolean search engines used for on-line text retrieval services, for example, make it wholly unlikely. That a contest debater might introduce exceptions within the extended mini-max argument is pure fancy. As such, even the extended mini-max argument as abduction is fallacious. As Peirce admitted, "From deduction to induction to abduction the security decreases greatly, while the uberty increases greatly" (qtd. in Fann 8). Unsurprisingly, the extended argument tends to have low validity and reliability whether deduced, induced, or abduced.

A final drawback of the extended argument is the likelihood of equivocation, particularly the term shift fallacy. Cedarbloom describes the problem.

> If an expression is used more than once in an argument, it must have the same meaning throughout the argument. When a word or expression shifts meaning from one occurrence in the

argument to the next, the argument commits the fallacy of equivocation.

Why do you doubt the miracles described in the Bible when you've witnessed miracles like man (sic) *landing on the moon?*

In the first occurrence, *miracle* means something that defies the laws of nature. In the second occurrence, *miracle* means something amazing, that you wouldn't have thought could be done. The fact that the second kind of miracle occurred doesn't make it more likely that the first kind occurred. (108)

The potential for term shifts in extended arguments is derived from the common practice of using terms distributed across several sources as a way of linking those sources in such a manner that they seem to construct a cohesive line of argument. The stringing together of out-of-context statements from multiple sources, each unaware of the new context into which their statements have been positioned, literally begs the question of equivocation.

THE LURE OF MINI-MAX REASONING

Vohra warned: "There are many inherent uncertainties in the quantitative assessment of accident probability. These uncertainties include lack of sufficient data, the basic limitations of the probabilistic methods used, and insufficient information about the physical phenomena . . . relating to the potential accident situation" (211). Why then, do we accept claims associated with these probability assessments? The answer lies in the seductiveness of the mini-max principle: Act to minimize the risk of maximum disaster.

According to Kavka, under the mini-max principle, "benefits and probabilities are disregarded, and that option is considered best which promises the least bad (or most good) outcome" (46-47). This is similar to what Kavka called the *disaster avoidance principle*: "When choosing between potential disasters under two-dimensional uncertainty, it is rational to select the alternative that minimizes the probability of disaster occurrence" (50), and what Luce and Raiffa called the *maximization-of-security-level theory* (278-281).

As a number of authors have noted, the mini-max principle is fraught with difficulties. I will recount four particular pitfalls in this article.

First mini-max reasoning is grounded in ultrapessimisim, or "disregarding a relevant experiment regardless of its cost" (Parmigiani 250). "The mini-max principle is founded on ultra-pessimism, [in] that it demands that the actor assume the world to be in the worst possible state" (Savage, "Statistical Decisions" 63). Savage concluded: "The mini-max rule based on negative income is ultrapessimistic and can lead to the ignoring of even extensive evidence and hence is utterly untenable for statistics" (*Foundations* 200). Furthermore, Parmigiani found that "no form of the mini-max principle is generally superior to the other in guarding against ultrapessimism. . . . [I]t is not possible to concoct a standardization method that makes the mini-max principle safe from ultrapessimism" (243, 249).

Second, mini-max reasoning is confounded by incorrect probability assessments. "Applying mini-max means ignoring the probabilities as various outcomes" (Finnis 221). One of the reasons for incorrect decisions is grounded in politics. Proponents of a mini-max claim may misrepresent the probabilities. "The group mini-max rule is also objectionable in some contexts, because, if one were to try to apply it in a real situation, the members of the group might well lie about their true probability judgments, in order to influence the decision generated by the mini-max rule in the direction each considers correct" (Savage, *Foundations* 175). This problem is worsened as proponents incorporate lay source material into their extended arguments.

> Several studies have noted that lay estimates of low probability hazards tend to be substantially higher than expert probability estimates. ... Is it that people sensitive to risk consequences, and unwilling to accept the risk or risk management or both strategies, might systematically exaggerate the magnitude of consequences while those in the *opposite* camp might systematically *underplay* the consequential danger involved? This implies the hypothesis that *acceptance* is an *a priori* condition, and becomes a driver of likelihood and consequence assessments, at least in some instances, while *threat probabilities* become the key causal factor in acceptance in still other instances. (Nehvevajsa 522)

The third fault with mini-max reasoning is that it is "flagrantly unde-mocratic. In particular, the influence of an opinion, under the group mini-max rule, is altogether independent of how many people in the group hold that opinion" (Savage, *Foundations* 175). In other words, singular experts make mini-max estimations. Quasi-experts or sec-ondary experts make some of the most bizarre extended arguments. In addition, there is an elitist sense to the process. The reasoning of the "expert" is presumptive over the opinion of individuals who are less educated, less affluent, or even less white. What happens when the elite are wrong? The arrogance of elitism is hardly more evident in any other setting. Deference to authority is an important co-requisite of extended mini-max claims in contest debates. There is an insipid maxim associated with it: "Don't understand? Don't worry. We do the thinking so you won't have to!" This problem is amplified when an exceptional source in a mini-max argument can-not be corroborated. Making a decision based on a sole opinion grossly inflates the qualifications of the source to make the claim. Consider how this issue worsens as well when the source is name-less or institutional, such as a press service.

The final pitfall of mini-max reasoning is that the persuasiveness of any such argument is a function of contingent variables, in partic-ular, its novelty. Consider this simple illustration: A single large out-come appears to pose a greater risk than does the sum of multiple small outcomes. "It is always observed that society is risk averse with respect to a single event of large consequence as opposed to several small events giving the same total number of fatalities in the same time period. Hence 10,000 deaths once in 10,000 years is per-ceived to be different from 1 death each year during 10,000 years" (Niehaus, de Leon & Cullingfort 93). Niehaus, de Leon, and Cullingford extended their analysis with a review of nuclear power plant safety. "The Reactor Safety Study similarly postulated that the public appears to accept more readily a much greater social impact from many small accidents than it does from the more severe, less frequent occurrences that have a similar society impact" (93). Theorists in many different settings have described this phenome-non. Wilson, for instance, devised a way to examine the impact of low-probability high-consequence events that more clearly por-trayed societal estimates of such events: "A risk involving N people simultaneously is N^2 (not N) times as important as an accident involving one person. Thus a bus or aeroplane accident involving 100 people is as serious as 10,000, not merely 100, automobile accidents killing one person" (274-275).

TESTING THE PROBITY OF MINI-MAX EXTENDED ARGUMENTS

If extended arguments using mini-max reasoning is so indefensible, what can we do? Surprisingly, the answer is quite a lot.

As a starting point, we need to reject the notion that contest debating would be impossible without them. We could demand a greater responsibility on the part of arguers making mini-max claims (a subject approached below). Debaters could use their plans and counterplans to stipulate the internal link and uniqueness stories for their extended arguments, consequently focusing the debate on probability assessment and away from exaggerated impacts. Alternatively, debaters may select to discuss ideas as we have seen in the recent trend toward kritik debating.

In addition, we need to understand that burdens of proof associated with extended arguments involving mini-max reasoning are not always extraordinary. Here is one rationale why it might be imprudent to reject all instances involving mini-max claims. Consider these two questions. Should we decide to forego a civil rights initiative in the U.S. because it may lead to a war in the Middle East? Should we refrain from building a plutonium reprocessing plant nearby to avoid the heightened incidence of cancer? We might accept the second more regularly than the first. The reason the second extended argument should be more presumptive is simply because interceding variables that might preclude the consequence are less reliable than in the first scenario because they would be derivative. In other words, the fix would need to be designed by agents similarly motivated. Just like "realist" foreign policy theorists may think too much alike, so do agents who are acting within the same agency. Unlike the second scenario, agents able to intercede between civil rights legislation and U.S.-Israeli foreign relations come from different disciplines and worldviews (different directions) and are less likely to share motivations which might prevent their capability to interpose end stops into a particular series of occurrences.

With these caveats out of the way and assuming some mini-max extended arguments are more reliable than others, I propose a number of tests by which the strength of particular mini-max extended arguments might be adduced. The tests fall into three general categories: probability and confidence, scenario construction, and perceptual bias. I offer these tests merely as suggestions and in full awareness of the fact that they hardly exhaust the potential checks on extended arguments using mini-max reasoning.

First, in addition to earlier remarks on general probability theory, we might want to learn about the source of a mini-max claim and her motivations. For example, we might want to discover whether estimates are intentional. In other words, did the journalist intend her rhetoric be linked into an argument of the sort being argued? Are the remarks actual or virtual? Did the journalist intend her rhetoric metaphorically or literally? She may have intended her remark as a rhetorical flourish rather than a causal claim. Are the explanations rational? Did the journalist intend the remark counterintuitively and is she equipped to make such a counterintuitive claim? Are the comments viable? Is the journalist's rhetoric related to the impact scenario? And, no less important, is the journalist motivated by truth or sales? Simply put, there is profit in fear. "A group that raises money for research into a particular disease is not likely to negate concerns about that disease. A company that sells alarm systems is not about to call attention to the fact that crime is down" (Glassner *xxiii*).

For the kritik aficionado, this hints at the political nature of risk. "When we speak of risk, however, we include a wide range of cognitive dimensions that extend well beyond the idea of risk as *quantitative* measures of hazard consequences expressed as conditional probabilities of experienced harm" (Slovic, Fischoff & Lichtenstein 91). Slovic came close to using the world paradigm to explain the political nature of risk estimation when he warned that "public views are influenced by worldviews, ideologies, and values; so are scientists' views, particularly when they are working at the limits of their expertise (1999). He provided a useful illustration.

One way in which subjectivity permeates risks assessments is in the dependence of such assessments on judgments at every stage of the process, from the initial structuring of a risk problem to deciding which endpoints or consequences to include in the analysis, identifying and estimating exposures, choosing does-response relationships, and so on. For example, even the apparently simple task of choosing a risk measure for a well-defined endpoint such as human fatalities is surprisingly complex and judgmental. ... Each way of summarizing death embodies its own set of value ... [e.g.,] reduction in life expectancy treats deaths of young people as more important than deaths of older people, who have less life expectancy to lose (690).

Researchers such as Earle and Cvetkovich have noted intercultural variations as well. "Risk is culturally constructed: individuals' expressions of concern about hazards are guided by the expected implications of those expressions for the individuals' preferred way of life. ... Cultural approaches to risk management also differ in their emphases on cultural stasis and cultural change. [For example,] since risk management conflicts are understood to be the products of cultural differences, the generation of (nonimposed) solutions to these conflicts depends on the emphasis that is placed on cultural change relative to cultural stasis" (55-56). While much research examines views across cultures separated by national boundaries, much of the research also deals with intranational cultural variations.

A second set of tests is associated with the narratives, or scenarios, constructed within the mini-max extended argument. Scenarios are imaginistic constructions abduced from rules and results.

> Prior to initiating interaction, interactants evaluate the goals that they have for the interaction in light of the information that they have about the situation (its norms, resources, and constraints) and the information that they have about their fellow interactants (expectancy information). In conducting this evaluation they generate scenarios concerning how the interaction is likely to unfold as a function of the tactics available to them. (Hilton, Darley & Fleming 46)

As Hilton, Darley, and Fleming suggest, "Situations create and possess resources that make certain kinds of strategic moves possible or impossible" (49). Doran warned about the incorporation of unlikely events as variables:

> In international relations at least, the problem is not that all forecasting is useless, but that forecasting that must contend with nonlinearities is useless. . . . When conditions are propitious and behavior over time is approximately linear, the linear forecast will fit that data tolerably well. But forecasts ultimately fail because no technique has been developed that allows the forecaster to predict, prior to the event itself, when a nonlinearity will occur. (34, 11)

Put more simply, before we can evaluate a scenario, we would need to learn who the actors are or would be. It is imprudent to predict the behavior of over generalized and unidentified participants; different people behave differently to similar stimuli and overgeneralization is an exercise in bigotry. We would need to ask the following questions as well: What would be predictable behavior? To borrow a term from counterfactuals, predicting behavior like behavior normally observed, hence from *nearest possible world*, would tend to avoid *noise*. Noise is the measurement of error reflected in the *variance* around a regression line fitted through a set of data points. As the behavior becomes more unusual and is less like the actual world, the noise will increase. "In general, there is an inverse relationship between the amount of noise around the trend-line of a prediction and the reliability of the forecast" (Doran 15). What would be a rational time frame? To borrow another term from counterfactuals, as a virtual world distances itself from the actual world, the breadth of *possible branching points* increases. "As one projects further and further into the future, the reliability of the forecast becomes less and less. This is expressed in the well-known aphorism, 'The best forecast is the last forecast.' As one attempts to forecast further and further into the future, the amount of error introduced into the forecast becomes greater and greater" (Doran 13). Moreover, is the scenario usable? "Model uncertainty is frequently important when the system involved is sufficiently complex that key influences have not been identified, or have been intentionally omitted or simplified to make the model computationally tractable" (Casman, Morgan &

Dowlatabadi 33-34). Some scenarios are purposefully simplified so they work. While including every conceivable variable "will not pass the laugh test in real-world policy circles . . . identifying some and getting part way to a full treatment is clearly better than simply ignoring the possibilities" (Casman, Morgan & Dowlatabadi 34, 41). Testing scenarios would solve more of the false persuasiveness of mini-max extended arguments.

A final set of tests deal with perceptual bias. Here are some fundamental observations about the psychology of risk analysis and communication. The research on bias is exceptionally dense and extensive. Here are four of the more prominent indictments of perceptual bias.

The first is overweighting. "Low probabilities are commonly overweighed but intermediate and high probabilities are usually underweighed relative to certainty. . . . The overweighting of small probabilities can give rise to risk seeking in the positive domain and risk aversion in the negative domain. . . . The inflated effect of small probabilities contributes to the appeal of lottery tickets and accident insurance" (Kahneman & Taversky 164). A probability closer to zero appears *more* greater than zero than do probabilities in the intermediate range of probability. The distance between .10 and .00 is .10. The distance between .40 and .30 is also .10. But the distance between.10 and .00 seems greater than the distance between .40 and .30. That is overweighting.

The second perceptual problem is framing bias. "Framing effects arise when the same objective alternatives are evaluated in relation to different points of reference" (Kahneman & Taversky 166). Risk is depressed and inflated depending on the frame. Kahneman and Taversky offer this illustration.

If Program *A* is adopted, 200 people will be saved. If Program *B* is adopted, there is a 1/3 probability that 600 people will be saved and a 2/3 probability that no people will be saved. Which of the two programs would you favor? The majority response to this problem is a risk-averse preference for Program *A* over Program *B*. Other respondents were presented with the same problem but a different formulation of programs: If Program *C* is adopted, 400 people will die. If Program *D* is adopted, there is a 1/3 probability that nobody will die and a 2/3 probability that 600 people will die. The majority choice in the problem is risk seeking. . . . The only difference is that in the first version the death of 600 people is the normal reference point and the outcomes are evaluated as gains, whereas in the second version no deaths is the normal reference point and the programs are evaluated in terms of lives lost (Kahneman & Taversky 166, 168).

The third is negative bias. In an interesting study by Stallen, Geerts, and Vrijling, the researchers examined different conceptions of quantified societal risk. "Results of the study showed a clear aversion to catastrophes . . . but no clear relationship of aversion with the number of fatalities was found" (642). This is a major problem because "just as individuals give greater weight and attention to negative events, so do the news media. . . . Adding fuel to the fire of asymmetry is yet another idiosyncrasy of human psychology – sources of bad news tend to be seen as more credible than sources of good news" (Slovic 698).

The final indictment of perception centers on deletion bias. Since the affirmative plan and the negative counterplan do not actually exist, canceling them does not seem to involve extirpation. All extirpations carry a tax. As Kahneman and Taversky put it:

> It is often easier to mentally delete an event from a chain of occurrences than it is to imagine the insertion of an event into the chain. Such a difference in imaginability could help to explain the observation that the regret associated with failures to act is often less intense than the regret associated with the failure of an action. . . . In general, the anticipation of regret is likely to favor inaction over action and routine behavior over innovative behavior. (173)

If the truth be told, debate critics are ill-prepared to evaluate mini-max arguments. While these arguments demand a systematic processing methodology, critics engage in something akin to a heuristic-systematic model. "Systematic processing is defined by effortful scrutiny and comparison of information, whereas heuristic processing is defined by the use of cues to arrive more easily at a judgment. ... This mode requires less effort and fewer resources" (Trumbo 391). Unfortunately, the cues are politically and culturally constructed and reflect the biases mentioned above.

CONCLUSIONS

It is difficult for me to suggest mini-max reasoning should go the way of should-would, counter-warrants, or intrinsicness arguments. That role seems too akin to Ayatollah Khomeini's *fatwa* on Salman Rushdie. Instead, my purpose has been to provide tests to challenge mini-max reasoned claims.

No contest debater can be expected to disprove all mini-max disadvantages. Without demanding some minimal level of likelihood, the debater would find her days and nights subverted, if not totally consumed, by on-line text-retrieval downloading by entering seemingly endless strings of search terms and Boolean connectors. It is simply uneconomical especially when contest debaters are also students and young adults.[2]

As an exercise in a logic classroom, mini-max claim making might be worthwhile. While mini-max reasoning may serve a productive function in some risk aversive situations, its role in contest debating seems uneconomical, hence a improper argument construction exercise. The nearly socio-pathological and paranoiac preoccupation with chasing improbable specters riding double behind apocalyptic horsemen is hardly productive training for undergraduate contest debaters. One of my primary concerns has been to reduce unwarranted fears and not add to them. As Glassner put it:

> We had better learn to doubt our inflated fears before they destroy us. Valid fears have their place; they cue us to danger. False and overdrawn fears only cause hardship. . . . The short answer to why Americans harbor so many misbegotten fears is that immense power and money await those who tap into our moral insecurities and supply us with symbolic substitutes. (xv, xxvii)

Teachers are not seducing our children. Urban crime is decreasing.

Planes are safe. Whites are many times safer than African-Americans are from African-American precipitated violence. Mothers seldom kill their own children. Moreover, schools are safe places.

You may think this case has been over made or worse that it describes a very low probability occurrence with an exaggerated consequence. If so, then rejecting my arguments compels you to reject extended arguments using mini-max reasoning as well. I believe I have not replaced one fear with another. But if rejecting one means rejecting both, I have succeeded. Hence, I end with this adage: We must avoid thinking that allows smoke to trump fire.

WORKS CITED

Bashor, Mark. "International Terrorism and Weapons of Mass Destruction." *Risk Analysis* 18:6. (August 1998): 675-678.

Bayes, Thomas. (1702-1761). An Essay Towards Solving a Problem in the Doctrine of Chances. *London Philosophical Transactions: 370-418.* (1763). Reprinted in *Biometrika* 45 (1958): 293-315.

Bütz, Michael R. *Chaos and Complexity: Implications for Psychological Theory and Practice.* Washington, DC: Taylor & Francis., Pub. 1997.

Casman, Elizabeth, M. Granger Morgan, and Hadi Dowlatabadi. "Mixed Levels of Uncertainty in Complex Policy Models. *Risk Analysis* 19:1 (January 1999): 33-42.

Cedarbloom, Jerry and David W. Paulsen. *Critical Reasoning: Understanding and Criticizing Arguments and Theories.* 2nd Ed. Belmont, CA: Wadsworth Co. 1986.

Cohen, L. Jonathan. "The Problem of Prior Probabilities in Forensic Proof." *Ratio* 24:1 (1982): 71-76.

de Sousa, Ronald. "Comments on Barbara S. Stengel: Thinking about Thinking: Wilfred Sellars' Theory on Induction." *Philosophy of Education: Proceedings of the Annual Meeting of the Philosophy of Education Society* 43 (1987): 259-262.

Doran, Charles. "Why Forecasts Fail: The Limits and Potential of Forecasting in International Relations and Economics." *International Studies* (1999): 11-41.

Earle, Timothy and George Cvetkovich. "Culture, Cosmopolitanism, and Risk Management." *Risk Analysis* 17:1 (January 1997): 55-65.

Fann, K. T. *Peirce's Theory of Abduction.* The Hague: Martinusnijhoff. 1970.

Finnis, John, Joseph M. Boyle, Jr. and Germain Grisez. *Nuclear Deterrence, Morality and Realism.* Oxford: Clarendon Press. 1987.

Glassner, Barry. *The Culture of Fear: Why Americans are Afraid of the Wrong Things.* NY: Basic Books. 1999.

Heim, Michael. *The Metaphysics of Virtual Reality* NY: Oxford UP. 1993.

Hilton, James L., John M. Darley, and John H. Fleming. "Self-Fulfilling Prophecies and Self-Defeating Behavior." *Self-Defeating Behaviors: Experimental Research, Clinical Impressions, and Practical Implications.* Ed. Rebecca C. Curtis. NY: Plenum Press. 1989: 41-65.

Kahneman, Daniel and Amos Tversky. "The Psychology of Preferences." *Scientific American* 256:1 (January 1982): 160-173.

Kavka, Gregory. "Deterrence, Utility and Rational Choice." *Theory and Decision* 12:1 (March 1980): 41-60.

Krause, Lawrence. *Beyond Star Trek: Physics from Alien Invasions to the End of Time.* NY: Basic Books. 1997.

Lanigan, R. L. "From Enthymeme to Abduction: The Classical Law of Logic and the Postmodern Rule of Rhetoric." *Recovering Pragmatism's Voice: The Classical Tradition, Rorty, and the Philosophy of Communication.* Eds. Lenore Langsdorf and Andrew R. Smith. Albany, NY: State University of New York Press. 1995: 49-70.

Laplace, Pierre. (1749-1827*). A Philosophical Essay on Probabilities.* Paris. 1814. Mineola, NY: Dover Press. 1951.

Lem, Stanislaw. "Cezar Kouska *De Impossibilitate Vitae* and *De Impossibilitate Prognoscendi,* (2 volumes Statni Nakladatelstvi N. Lit., Prague): A Review." *A Perfect Vacuum.* Trans. M. Kandel. NY: Harcourt Brace Jovanovich. 1979: 141-166.

Lichtman, Alan and Daniel Rohrer. "The Logic of Policy Dispute." *Journal of the American Forensic Association* 16 (Spring 1980): 236-247.

Luce, R. Duncan and Howard Raiffa. *Games and Decisions.* NY: John Wiley & Sons. 1957.

Nehnevajsa, Jiri. "Low-Probability/High-Consequence Risks: Issues in Credibility and Acceptance." *Low Probability High Consequence*

Risk Analysis: Issues, Methods, and Case Studies. Eds. Ray A. Waller and Vincent T. Covello. NY: Plenum Press. 1984: 521-529.

Niehaus, F., G. de Leon, and M. Cullingford. "The Trade-Off Between Expected Risk and the Potential for Large Disasters." *Low Probability High Consequence Risk Analysis: Issues, Methods, and Case Studies.* Eds. Ray A. Waller and Vincent T. Covello. NY: Plenum Press. 1984: 91-105.

Parmigiani, Giovanni. "Minimax, Information and Ultrapessimism." *Theory and Decision* 33:3 (November 1992): 241-252.

Richet, Charles. *L'homme Stupide.* Paris: E. Flammarion. 1919.

Savage, Leonard J. "The Theory of Statistical Decision." *Journal of the American Statistical Association* 46:253 (March 1951): 54-67.

_____. *The Foundations of Statistics.* NY: John Wiley & Sons, Inc. 1954.

Schell, Jonathan. *The Fate of the Earth.* NY: Alfred A. Knopf. 1982.

Schweder, Richard. *Thinking Through Cultures: Expeditions in Cultural Psychology.* Cambridge, MA: Harvard University Press. 1991.

Singpurwalla, N. "Statistics in Low-Probability/High-Consequence Risk Analysis. Introduction – Part 1." *Low Probability High Consequence Risk Analysis: Issues, Methods, and Case Studies.* Eds. Ray A. Waller and Vincent T. Covello. NY: Plenum Press. 1984: 181-182.

Slovic, Paul. "Trust, Emotion, Sex, Politics, and Science: Surveying the Risk-Assessment Battlefield." *Risks Analysis* 19:4 (August 1999): 689-701.

Slovic, Paul, Baruch Fischoff, and Sarah Lichtenstein. "Characterizing Perceived Risk." *Perilous progress: Managing the Hazards of Technology.* Eds. Robert W. Kates, Christoph Hohenemser and Jeanne X. asperson. Boulder, CO: Westview Press. 1985: 91-125.

Stallen, Pieter Jan, Rob Geerts and Han Vrijling. "Three Conceptions of Quantified Social Risk." *Risk Analysis* 16:5 (October 1997): 635-644.

Tabori, Paul. *The Natural History of Stupidity.* NY: Barnes and Noble Books. 1993.

Thompson, Paul T. and William J. Parkinson. "Situation Specific Indicators for Distinguishing between High Consequence/Low-Probability Risk and Low-Consequence/High-Probability Risk." *Low Probability High Consequence Risk Analysis: Issues, Methods, and Case Studies.* Eds. Ray A. Waller and Vincent T. Covello. NY: Plenum Press. 1984: 551-567.

Tooley, Michael. *Time, Tense, and Causation.* Oxford: Clarendon Press. 1997.

Trumbo, Craig. "Heuristic-Systematic Information Processing and Risk Judgment." *Risk Analysis* 19:3 (June 1999): 391-400.

U. S. Nuclear Regulatory Commission. *An Approach to Quantitative Safety Goals for Nuclear Power Plants.* NUREG-0739. October 1980.

Vohra, K. G. "Statistical Methods or Risk Assessment for Energy Technology." *Low Probability High Consequence Risk Analysis: Issues, Methods, and Case Studies.* Eds. Ray A. Waller and Vincent T. Covello. NY: Plenum Press. 1984: 201-215.

Wilson, Richard. "The Costs of Safety." *New Scientist* 68 (October 30, 1975): 274-275.

NOTES:

[1] Lem suggested, in effect, that you calculate the probability that *you yourself exist.* Allowing your father three or four ejaculations a week for fifty years, his lifetime output of spermatozoa is likely to have been in the region of one billion, only one of which could have been you. Multiply that by the number of ova in your mother's ovaries, preferably before birth when they too number in the tens of thousands. As the offspring of your parents, then, the chances against their child being *you* is far in excess of a trillion to one. Then consider the circumstance of your parents' more or less unlikely meeting. Repeat for each of your ancestors, multiplying each result with the last. In scarcely more generations than you can personally remember, the improbability of your existence is far greater than that of finding a single atom in the universe at random. If some level of improbability were sufficient for rejection, such a mediation should lead you to doubt your own existence (de Sousa 262). See Stanislaw Lem, "De Arte Prognosendi aut de Impossibilitate Vitae," in *A Perfect Vacuum: Imaginary Reviews of Non-Existent Books,* (NY: Harcourt, Brace and Jovanich, 1979).

[2] Another solution has been to hire card cutters (fifth year undergraduates), graduate assistants, or others to do the research to keep on the edge of the mini-max disadvantages. I will leave this issue for others to address.

David Berube (Ph.D., New York University) is an Associate Professor of Speech Communication and Director of Carolina Debate at the University of South Carolina in Columbia, South Carolina.This essay was originally published in volume 21 (2000) of *Contemporary Argumentation and Debate,* pp. 53-73.

COUNTERFACTUAL POSSIBILITIES: CONSTRUCTING COUNTER-TO-FACT CAUSAL CLAIMS
Kenneth T. Broda-Bahm

Advertising fosters consumption. If advertising was not as pervasive in this society, then the level of consumption would be much less than its current level.

The preceding is a counterfactual argument.[1] It asserts that certain results would obtain if conditions were different than they presently are. In the field of academic debate, such counterfactual claims recently have been the subject of increasing attention. Both inside and outside of the debate round, students and teachers of debate have confronted issues related to the validity and the meaning of such claims. Scholarship on counterfactual analysis in academic debate to date has focused on issues such as the paradigmatic validity of counterfactuals (Roskoski, 1992; 1994), their relationship to topicality and competition (Korcok, 1994), their applications within recent CEDA topics (Broda-Bahm, 1994; Hoe, 1994; Roskoski, 1994), problems associated with their use (Berube & Pray, 1994; Voight & Stanfield, 1992), and the issue of infinite regression (Broda-Bahm, 1994).

Without a doubt, many technical issues await resolution. These concerns can be most clearly addressed, however, in the context of a clear understanding of the possible meanings of counterfactual analysis and application. Accordingly, after first justifying the need for a schema for counterfactual analysis, the present essay will consider several such schemata, and ultimately advocate one as a consistent and relatively clear method of constructing counterfactual claims.[2] Such a focus on how we conceive of the counterfactual is not merely an exploration into a single "exotic" argument form. As the next section will show, the development of a coherent counterfactual schema is a helpful step in approaching basic and very practical questions of how we advance evaluative assessments, how we structure comparisons, and how we make causal claims.

THE NEED FOR A SCHEMA FOR COUNTERFACTUAL ANALYSIS IN ACADEMIC DEBATE

Counterfactual analysis is not new, nor is it removed from our current practice of argumentation and debate. As Matt Roskoski (1992) notes, clear parallels exist between the notions of causality and counterfactual analysis. Causation implies that an effect would be lessened in some alternative, counter-to-fact situation. To say "'a' causes 'b'" is often to say "absent 'a,' there would be no 'b.'"[3] As Kahneman and Varey (1990) note, "Causal attributions invoke counterfactual beliefs, for example, about what would have happened in the absence of a putative cause" (p. 1101). Similarly, David Lewis (1979) observes, "a causal chain is a certain kind of chain of counterfactual dependencies" (p. 459).[4] Beyond being a tool of the analysts, the counterfactual proposition has also shown itself to be a reliable description of the way ordinary people in ordinary situations evaluate causal claims (Dunning & Parpal, 1989; Hilton & Slugoski, 1986; Markovitz & Vachon, 1989; Wells, Taylor, & Turtle, 1987). To a large extent, we will recast the causal assertion (e.g., "buying that new car has caused me grief") into a counterfactual forms ("I would be happier if I hadn't bought that new car").

This relationship between the counterfactual statement and causality carries two implications. Initially, it suggests that counterfactual questions should be incorporated into debate at a basic level. The importance of counterfactual questions in debate parallels the importance of causality. Since debate on most questions (policy and non-policy) generally involves the evaluation of specific conditions and arrangements, the construction of causal argument seems inevitable. If such causal claims are to be evaluated (and not simply asserted in evidenced appeals) then a consideration of the form of the causal claim is an important precondition to analysis. As Roskoski (1992) notes:

> If causal analysis is actually the central issue upon which debates should turn, and counterfactual analysis is inextricably bound up with considerations of causality, then it follows syllogistically that counterfactual analysis ought to be central to academic debate. (p. 10)

A second implication of the connection between counterfactual analysis and causality relates to proposition type. A recent survey (Church, May, 1995) indicates that fully 58% of 125 responding Cross Examination Debate Association programs either agreed or strongly agreed with the statement, "No fact resolutions should be included on the [C.E.D.A. topic] ballot." While the survey did not make clear what was meant by "fact resolutions" it seems likely that several recent resolutions calling for the evaluation of an existing, 'factual,' circumstance or policy arrangement are actually the objects of concern.[5] While they are perhaps not technically resolutions of fact (containing as they do a clear evaluative word or phase) these resolutions are the ones most likely to be called "resolutions of fact" by debaters and claimed to be either true or false independent of their implied remedies. They are the resolutions that are perhaps least amenable to a conventional policy framework. It is arguably the lack of such a framework that accounts for the unpopularity of such resolutions. In the absence of a prospective dimension, debaters and coaches alike seem to lack a clear means of evaluating the proposition.

Counterfactual analysis could play a role in providing a means of evaluating propositions of this type. The proposition "Resolved: that the national news media in the United States impair the public's understanding of political issues," for example, identifies the national news media, or some manifestation thereof, as the *cause* of the impairment. To impair or "to lessen or make worse" is a comparative term and must be considered in relation to the *absence* of at least some form or trait of the national news media. To say that something impairs understanding is to say that understanding would have been better in some alternate, and hence counterfactual, situation. A similar analysis could be applied to any propositions which meets the previous description. In each case, the construction of causal arguments regarding an existing condition will require the consideration of a possible absence or alternate version of that condition.

Counterfactual analysis thus has the potential to play a role in resolutional analysis and more generally to assist in the evaluation of causal claims. Despite this utility, however, the presentation of counterfactual claims within a debate context is often met with confusion. It seems that we are capable of handling the implicit counterfactual arguments which are contained in all causal statements with little difficulty, but when the counterfactual components of those claims become explicit, they are treated as uniquely incomprehensible arguments. Clearly what is needed is a template for understanding counterfactual claims.

In order to present a consistent analysis, this essay will focus on propositions, like the ones discussed above, which entail a negative evaluation of an historical development, a present social condition, or a policy already enacted. It is important to note, however, that while it might apply most obviously to such "resolutions of fact," counterfactual analysis is not limited to such resolutions but also applies to arguments made within all proposition types. Value claims are frequently advanced by making causal arguments about the subject under evaluation. Similarly, policy claims are justified through recourse to causal arguments about present harms and future benefits. An advantage can be seen as a statement suggesting that "if the policy were currently in force (a counterfactual condition) then a benefit would accrue." To the extent that evaluations invoke causality, counterfactual analysis will be relevant.

POSSIBLE SCHEMATA FOR COUNTERFACTUAL CLAIMS

An extensive literature contains many avenues of advice on the construction of counterfactual claims. I will consider some of these ways of handling counterfactuals as well as some of the problems which they engender. Ultimately I will suggest a possible construct that, while retaining some ambiguity, has the potential to provide a relatively clear basis for constructing counterfactual claims.

IDEAL COMPARISON

A very common method of conceiving of counterfactual claims in academic debate up to this point has been to construct them in terms of ideals: An object, action, or condition is evaluated through a comparison to a superior or ideal form. Particularly when a resolution calls for a negative evaluation of its subject matter, that evaluation is often accomplished by contrasting the present-tense subject with a new or improved version, sometimes called a "plan." Advertising is shown to degrade the quality of life when an ideal or superior form of advertising can be demonstrated. Colleges and Universities are seen as inappropriately addressing issues of race or gender when ideal ways of addressing those issues are shown. The national news media is shown to impair understanding when better forms of media promotion of understanding can be said to have been possible. In each of these cases, the resolution's object of focus is indicted by contrasting that evaluatum with an ideal counterfactual version of itself (better advertising, better University attention to issues of race or gender, better news media promotion of understanding).

Evaluating objects or conditions in reference to their ideal counterfactual alternatives has some obvious weaknesses. Most basically, the existence of a superior alternative does not necessarily entail that the object under evaluation is causing harm. The introduction of the alternative, in fact, causes a shift of focus from the causal attributes of the resolution's evaluatum, to the benefits of the specified alternative. Writing about the "counterfactual" which he defines as "a line of reasoning based upon comparing something with an ideal" (p. 199), Charles Willard (1987) notes the disruptive effect of this shift of focus from the evaluated condition to the ideal alternative. As Willard asserts, "counterfactuals," in the sense described above, "are best seen as argumentative devices for blasting decision-making processes off course, for suddenly transfiguring argumentative conditions. They cause rather than settle disputes; they enhance opposition, introduce competition, and throw sand in the gears of what might otherwise be smoothly functioning decision-making" (p. 204).

Apart from causing an inappropriate shift in focus, the counterfactual based on ideal comparison also introduces a bias. Functionally, if a proposition is changed from "x has caused harm" to "x can be improved" then there is an obvious bias in favor of affirmation. In calling for an emphasis on causality, Zarefsky (1977) explains the effects of an ideal counterfactual focus on the process of fair debate:

> Not only does insistence upon causal argument improve the rigor of one's own analysis, but it also improves the fairness of argumentation as a means for decision-making. If one engages in a simple comparison of existing conditions with those imagined to accompany a new proposal [she or] he compares one system *as it actually exists* with another *as a theoretical ideal.* Such a double standard produces a pro-affirmative bias, a distortion in the instrument which predisposes one toward the acceptance of new proposals and against the reaffirmation of the existing order. By contrast, to search for causes is to initiate inquiry into why the existing order is as it is. (p. 190-91)

Regarding those propositions which call for a negative evaluation of a factual condition, it seems clear that showing a counterfactual improvement in that condition does not necessarily prove that the current condition causes harm. In addition to causing a shift in focus, proposed alternatives can also be seen as *non-sequitur* responses to resolutions which ask for an evaluation of an existing condition.

SIMPLE ABSENCE

The evaluation of an object or an event which actually exists may be accomplished by simply considering its counterfactual absence. If the effect of an event is being assessed, for example, we look at what would have happened if that event had not occurred. As Dunning and Parpal (1989) note, "Assessing the consequences of actions and events often requires comparing a mental simulation of the world in which the action is present to one in which the action is absent (p. 5)." This concept of absence, seems to apply quite well to the area of historical evaluation. As Rescher (1961) points out:

> Quite frequently the significance of a historical occurrence, the value of an invention or idea, or generally the contribution of some contributory cause in a composite causal chain can be assessed by carrying out a speculative thought experiment based upon the belief-contravening supposition that the events in question had not occurred. (p. 179)

Such a thought-experiment might simply remove the evaluated element in order to look at what would have happened in its absence. For example, on the national news media resolution the question would be, "what would be the state of the public's understanding in the absence of the national news media?" Given that the current media can be seen as playing an important role in *constituting* political issues (Graber, 1984), a simple absence of the national news media might arguably entail less understanding or even no understanding of these issues.

Such a position, however, may be too simplistic. Much ambiguity remains in conceptions of a world "absent" the evaluated element. When we are dealing with a complex social entity—an entity with many ties to other existing entities—a simple absence approach leaves many parts of the picture incomplete. What else about the world changes when we remove the one evaluated element? How broad is the license of an advocate to change reality in order to actuate the absence of that element? In order to address these questions we need to consider an additional concept.

'NEAREST POSSIBLE WORLD'

The notion of "simple absence" is obviously a rough sketch. The general picture of counterfactual absence requires more specificity. The implicit consideration which underlies a consideration of counterfactual absence might be captured in the expression "*ceteris paribus*" or "all other things being equal." If we are, for example, evaluating the influence of a specific event which has happened, we would consider an alternate world which lacks that event, but which is in every other respect identical to our own world. In other words, we would look at the nearest possible world in which the counterfactual is hypothetically true. An explanation of counterfactual claims involving comparison to a "nearest possible world" is generally credited independently to Robert Stalnaker (1968) and David Lewis (1973). Lewis explains:

> 'If kangaroos had no tails, they would topple over' seems to me to mean something like this: in any possible state of affairs in which kangaroos have no tails, and which resembles our actual state of affairs as much as kangaroos having no tails permits it to, the kangaroos topple over. (p. 1)

He continues,

> 'if kangaroos had no tails, they would topple over' is true (or false, as the case may be) at our world, quite without regard to those possible worlds where kangaroos walk around on crutches, and stay upright that way. Those worlds are too far away from ours. What is meant by the counterfactual is that, things being pretty much as they are - the scarcity of crutches for kangaroos being pretty much as it actually is, the kangaroos' inability to use crutches being pretty much as it actually is, and so on - if kangaroos had no tails they would topple over. (p. 8-9)

Entertaining a counterfactual statement, in and of itself, requires a departure from reality. To Lewis, the important point is that this requirement should not be taken as a license to change reality in *unnecessary* ways. To look at the effect of possible legislation on Congressional term limits, we would have to change reality enough to assume its implementation. But we would not have any logically sanctioned ability to assume any other changes in reality, for example a Democrat-dominated Congress. The world we create in order to assess the statement is the world which permits the antecedent (the evaluated condition) to be true, but which permits no additional changes from the actual world.

This solution applied to the advertising resolution would result in conceiving of the nearest possible world in which advertising is absent. Everything but the existence of advertising would be held constant as we examined the hypothetical world without it. At this point, however, ambiguity is still present. Do we look at a world in which literally *everything* else stays the same (i.e., the economy is the same size, people's brand-name recognition is at the same level)? Given the level of media saturation in our society, for example, it may be too difficult or even impossible for us to envision a world absent advertising. The conditions of the nearest possible world are still a picture only partially complete. Here it is helpful to focus on some clarifications that have been made to the concept of a "nearest possible world."

SIMILARITY, UP TO A POINT

In offering a critique of the nearest-possible-world position, G. Lee Bowie (1979) provides an example of a world in which a push of a thoroughly tested and reliable button on the ultimate doomsday machine will cause the universe to explode. Assuming that we are evaluating the counterfactual proposition, "if the button is pushed, then the world will be destroyed," we would be interested in looking at a (counterfactual) world in which the button is pushed and then looking to see if the world is indeed destroyed. Bowie asserts that a nearest possible world position would prefer a world in which the button is pushed but fails to work (because it disintegrates, because a small object momentarily denies the laws of nature to fly under to button and lodge itself, etc.) over a world in which the button is pushed and does actually work, and the universe explodes. Any violation of nature required to stop the button, Bowie argues, would still be a part of a much closer world to ours than a world in which the universe explodes. "Surely a temporary local breakdown in the laws of mechanics would preserve similarity far more than world cataclysm" (p. 485).

Rather than identifying a flaw in the nearest possible world logic, Bowie is actually pointing out that we need only be concerned with the nearness of the possible world up to a specific point. In saying that the compared counterfactual world is the "nearest possible" to the actual world, we are saying that up to a specific point, similarity must be maximized. After that, events take their course. We are absolutely unconcerned about differences which may happen after that point—they are important only in assessing the consequent, not in assessing similarity. Bowie explains,

> Fortunately, there is an easier way to meet the objection. It can be met by making clear that the world we are comparing with ours is not being compared in virtue of its temporal totality. We must require only that its history up to (and perhaps including) the time at which A is true (for counterfactual A []-> B) is most like the history of this world. In the example, we are to imagine standing in the room, finger on the button; the stage is set, and everything so far is as much as possible like things are here. At this point - I have just pushed the button - we stop worrying about how close the worlds are; we just sit back to wait and see what happens. In this case we needn't wait long - the world explodes. (p. 487)

This turning point in history, the point at which we introduce the counterfactual element, is very important to our analysis since it is the point at which we require prior similarity, but disregard posterior similarity. In evaluating the alternate world (a world, for example, absent the national news media's development of a critical press) we need to be concerned about a specific moment in history. Instead of striving for maximal closeness between possible worlds (the world with the media effect and the world without it) we would want to, according to Thomason and Gupta (1981), "maximize closeness only up to some past moment" (p. 305). Thomason and Gupta refer to this as the "condition of past predominance." In the act of evaluating a counterfactual ('if I hadn't bought my car...') we would be concerned about the entire possible history in which that counterfactual would be true. But in the act of selecting the nearest possible world which we will use to evaluate that statement (the world without my car), the condition of past predominance emphasizes that we need only be concerned with an alternate world which is as similar as possible to our actual world only up to the point under evaluation (a world exactly the same as the actual world, up to the point at which I buy my car).

"When time is brought in to the picture," Thomason and Gupta (1981) summarize, "worlds give way to evolving histories... you do not merely want to consider the closest A-world. Rather you want to consider the closest moment-history pair at which A is true" (p. 301). The propositions under consideration then would call for attention to a particular moment in history: a turning point where actual history hypothetically could be seen as changing in the direction of the counterfactual absence of the condition under evaluation. In evaluating the effect of the welfare system on the urban poor, for example, we might look at a historical point at which services for the poor might have taken another path - might have evolved in a way other than the current welfare system.

BRANCHING POINTS

In finding ways in which the real history of the evaluated object or event could have made a transition in the direction of the counterfactual under consideration, attention may turn to historical "branching points" or points at which alternative paths of development seem particularly plausible. Jon Elster (1978) addresses the issue of the historical counterfactual as a matter which is intimately tied to actual history. In assessing the causal relations surrounding a given event, he says "we are free to conduct an imaginary experiment and assume that the event in question never took place, and to ask what would then have been the further course of history " (p. 5). This freedom, however, is not wholly given over to imagination. Elster's central requirement is "that a counterfactual antecedent must be capable of insertion into the real past" (p. 184). Restated, this entails not only that we find a point in history at which we can fiat the counterfactual change, but that such a point is, historically, a "branching point," or "a point in time at which such analytical separations might seem more plausible than at other times" (Engerman, 1980, p. 164).

As a comparative concept, the notion of a branching point creates a basis for assessing the appropriateness of a comparative world. For Elster (1978), the closeness of the branching point bears directly upon the assertability of the counterfactual claim:

If, for example, the antecedent may be inserted into the real world at t_2, whereas we must go back to an earlier time t_1 in order to find a branching point from which a permitted trajectory leads to a state where both the antecedent and the consequent obtain, then the counterfactual is not assertable. Take the statement: 'If it had not been for slavery, the GNP of the US South in 1860 would have been twice as high as it actually was.' This statement would not be assertable if a non-slave South could stem from a branching point no later than, say, 1750, whereas a GNP of the required size would require counterfactual changes going back to 1700. (p. 191)

The notion of a "nearest possible world" then is given meaning in the measurable units of time: a counterfactual is assertable if and only if an antecedent leads to the consequent when inserted into history at the closest possible branching point. "The further back we have to go in order to insert the possible state in the real history," Elster notes, "the greater is the distance to that state" (p. 191). This historical amendment to the general Stalnaker-Lewis requirement for the closeness of the possible world has the potential to play a significant role in combating the ambiguity in counterfactuals containing alternate pasts. As a social historian, Elster's reasoning focuses on utility. It is, at a basic level, most useful to conceive of the absence (or presence) of a given condition by looking at the most recent realistic possibility for that absence (or presence) in our real history. These real historical branching points presumably are more directly applicable to our own experience than would be a contrived purely speculative solution, no matter how 'close.'

While it imparts greater clarity, Elster's requirement of counterfactual insertion into a real past has not escaped criticism. Steven Lukes (1980) calls the requirement "patently excessive" (p. 149) arguing that there are many counterfactuals which would resist insertion into a real past (e.g., If Trotsky held Stalin's post...) but which would be interesting and useful nonetheless. Lukes' point taken, it remains clear that when a counterfactual condition *is capable* of insertion into a real past, then the counterfactual claim which employs that insertion at the closest possible point retains a higher level of assertability then claims which envision insertion at a more distant, less plausible point. In addition, it must be noted that the notion of plausibility is not without problems: it is quite likely that there will be no single point which is unambiguously the only possible point or the most possible point. In an adversary setting though there is no need for an ultimate answer. The branching point becomes a creature of discourse: a construct that is supported to greater or lesser degrees by arguments relating to the plausibility of the alternative.

As a refinement to our answer, the "Branching Points" solution holds promise. We are no longer simply asked to remove the evaluated element and hold all else constant. Nor are we asked to simply chose *a* point in history. Rather, we are directed to answer the question, "what was the most recent point at which the condition under evaluation could have been avoided?" This question cannot be answered with the precision of mathematics, but only within the vagaries of discourse and argument. Nonetheless, it does provide a better foundation for argument on the given proposition type than the other possibilities.

APPLICATION

At this point, we can provide a more precise application of counterfactual analysis to the type of "factual" proposition currently under consideration. The proposition, "Resolved: that the national news media in the United States impair the public's understanding of political issues" could be negated or affirmed with the following argument.

We would start with the acknowledgement that we are comparing the current state of the national news media to its counterfactual absence (in some form). We would reject as irrelevant an analysis which compared the national news media to a new or idealized form of itself. Similarly, we would reject as too simplistic an analysis which simply "removed" the national news media from the current social picture. In comparing two worlds, we want to ensure that the counterfactual world (the world without the present national news media) is the 'nearest possible' world to our own which still permits an evaluation of that antecedent. Knowing that these worlds need logically only be similar up to a specific point, we would want to identify a point in history at which the absence or non-development of this "national" news media could be counterfactually supposed. Knowing that there is a utility in focusing on the most recent plausible transition point at which this absence could be posited, we would consider the question, "what is the most recent historical point at which the development of a national news media could have been plausibly avoided?"

An answer could be found in research on the history of media and politics. Samuel P. Huntington (1975) for example presents the argument that a "national" media seeking to have a critical influence on the public's understanding of political issues emerged at a point in history which is at least roughly identifiable:

> The most notable new source of national power in 1970, compared to 1950, was the national media, meaning here the national TV networks, the national news magazines, and the major newspapers with national reach such as the *Washington Post* and the *New York Times*... 'In the 1960's the network organizations, as one analyst [Michael L. Robinson] put it, became a 'highly creditable, never-tiring political opposition, a maverick third party which never need face the sobering experience of governing.' (pp. 98-9)

Identifying the emergence of the present form of the national news media (as oppositional media) in the 1960's, this analysis facilitates the insertion of the counterfactual non-development of that media at that point in history. While Huntington does not indicate the degree of possibility that can be attached to this *non*-development, it does stand to reason that the non-emergence of something would be more plausible at the point of emergence than at any other time. Elster's (1978) stipulation for a closest branching point could thus be met. The world in the 1960's, according to Huntington, chose a path which led to the development of oppositional media. Absent this choice, the world would have arguably taken the path of continuing its mode of operation as it had functioned in the 1950's (less national and less oppositional news).

This sets up a plausible counterfactual comparison. An advocate would be comparing the world as it presently exists (including the current "national news media") with a world as it counterfactually could have existed absent the emergence of that "national news media" at a given historical point. These two worlds are identical up to the point under consideration (the 1960's), but after that their divergence would be the subject of argument.

For example, an advocate might want to claim that the existence of a critical, oppositional national news media was a causal factor in promoting the development of the Viet Nam anti-war movement. Eyerman writes in 1992,

Like the state and the knowledge industry, the new mass media have helped "create" the new social movements. Coverage in the mass media and the instant attention gained through modern communication technologies have helped build these movements into significant social and political forces and have influenced their internal strategies, organization, and leadership. As Todd Gitlen [of the Students for a Democratic Society] has documented in his brilliant account of the influence of the mass media on the development of the student movement in the United States, the media in many senses became the movement. (p. 52)

At this point, affirmative and negative strategies might diverge. Affirmatives might discuss the geo-political, environmental, and social harms of such movements while negatives might discuss their benefits in, for example, bringing the Viet Nam war to an earlier conclusion and thereby avoiding the use of nuclear weapons.

I do not present this example as a perfect or irrefutable claim. In an adversary setting the appropriateness of this branching point and the conclusions drawn from it could certainly be substantively questioned. It is also certain that many other branching points and many other consequences could be identified. Rather than representing it as a "correct" solution, I use the example to show how counterfactual analysis can be used in a given situation. The function of the example is to demonstrate how the historical specification of the counterfactual turning point can provide a framework for argument. Potential answers to counterfactual questions could be found in the research on any given topic. The solution outlined here does not, of course, answer all potential concerns. Many questions remain to be addressed. An essential starting point for this discussion, however, is that we have a schema: a clear construct of what it means to advance a counterfactual argument.

WORKS CITED

Berube, B. & Pray, K. (1994). Arguing counterfactuals. In D. Berube, *Non-Policy Debating* (pp. 325-339). New York: University Press of America

Bowie, G. L. (1979). The similarity approach to counterfactuals: Some Problems. *Nous, 13*, 477-498.

Broda-Bahm, K. (1994). *Counterfactual ambiguity and problems of infinite regression: A search for a non-arbitrary turning point for the national news media and public understanding.* Paper presented at the meeting of the Speech Communication Association, New Orleans, LA.

Church, R. T. (1995, May). Results of the topic survey. *CEDA-L* [on-line list-server], digest 549.

Creath, R. (1989). Counterfactuals for free. *Philosophical Studies, 57,* 95-101.

Dunning, D. & Parpal, M. (1989). Mental addition versus subtraction in counterfactual reasoning: On assessing the impact of personal actions and life events. *Journal of Personality and Social Psychology, 57,* 5-15.

Elster, J. (1978). *Logic and society: Contradictions and possible worlds.* New York: John Wiley & Sons.

Engerman, S. L. (1980). Counterfactuals and the new economic history. *Inquiry,23,* 157-72.

Eyerman, R. (1992). Modernity and social movements. In H Haferkamp & N. J. Smelser (Eds.). *Social Change and Modernity.* Berkeley: University of California Press.

Graber, D. A. (1984). *Mass media and American politics* (2nd ed.). Washington, DC: Congressional Quarterly Press.

Hilton, D. J. & Slugoski, B. R. (1986). Knowledge-based causal attribution: The abnormal conditions focus model. *Psychological Review, 93,* 75-88.

Hoe, J. (1994). *Counterfactuals in a post-cold war world.* Paper presented at the meeting of the Speech Communication Association, New Orleans, LA.

Huntington, S. P. (1975). The United States. In M. Crozier, S. P. Huntington, & J. Watanuki. *The crisis of democracy: Report on the governability of democracies to the Trilateral Commission.* New York: New York University Press.

Kahneman, D. & Varey, C. A. (1990). Propensities and counterfactuals: The loser that almost won. *Journal of Personality and Social Psychology, 59,* 1101-1110.

Korcok, M. (1994). *The bases of counterfactual comparison.* Paper presented at the meeting of the Speech Communication Association, New Orleans, LA.

Lewis, D. (1973). *Counterfactuals.* Cambridge: Harvard University Press.

Lewis, D. (1979). Counterfactual dependence and time's arrow. *Nous, 13,* 455-475.

Lukes, S. (1980). Elster on counterfactuals. *Inquiry, 23,* 145-55.

Markovitz, H. & Vachon, R. (1989). Reasoning with contrary-to-fact propositions. *Journal of experimental child psychology, 47,* 398-412.

Mill, J. S. (1900). *System of logic*. London: Logmans, Green & Co.

Rescher, N. (1961). Belief contravening suppositions. *Philosophical Review, 70*, 176-196.

Roskoski, M. (1994). *Counterfactual economic history*. Paper presented at the meeting of the Speech Communication Association, New Orleans, LA.

Roskoski, M. (1992). *A defense of counterfactual reasoning in CEDA debate*. Paper presented at the meeting of the Speech Communication Association, Chicago, IL.

Stalnaker, R. C. (1968). A theory of conditionals. In N. Rescher (Ed.), *Studies in logical theory* (pp. 98-112). Oxford: Basil Blackwell.

Thomason, R. H. & Gupta, A. (1981). A theory of conditionals in the context of branching time. In W. L. Harper, R. Stalnaker, & G. Pearce (Eds.), *Ifs: Conditionals, belief, decision, chance, and time* (pp 299-321). Boston: D. Reidel.

Voight, P. & Stanfield, S. (1992). *Shortening Cleopatra's nose: The fallacy of counter factual argumentation*. Paper presented at the meeting of the Speech Communication Association, Chicago, IL.

Wells, G. L., Taylor, B. R., & Turtle, J. W. (1987). The undoing of scenarios. *Journal of Personality and Social Psychology, 53*, 421-430.

Willard, C. A. (1987). Arguing from counterfactuals. In J. W. Wenzel (Ed.), *Argument and critical practices: Proceedings of the fifth SCA/AFA conference on argumentation* (pp. 199-205). Annandale, VA: Speech Communication Association.

Zarefsky, D. (1977). The role of causal argument in policy controversies. *Journal of the American Forensic Association, 13*, 179-191.

NOTES

[1] A counterfactual claim, also known as a "contrary-to-fact conditional" or a "subjunctive conditional," can be defined as an assertion about matters which are not, at present, believed to exist. Counterfactual claims are made whenever speculation centers on what <u>would</u> happen, <u>if</u> something were the case. As Richard Creath (1989) notes, "As a first approximation we might say that a counterfactual is any sentence which says what <u>would</u> happen under specified conditions, even though those conditions do not in fact obtain.... A typical, if somewhat shopworn, example of a counterfactual is: 'If I had struck that match, it would have lit'" (p. 95).

[2] It is important to note that in promoting a *schema* for constructing counterfactual claims, I am not articulating a *test* of their validity as causal statements. There are several well-known tools for evaluating causal statements (e.g., see Mill, 1900, pp. 255-66.). The present essay deals with the question of how to structure, articulate, or set-up the counterfactual claim in the first place. It is a descrip-

tive step: when we make a counterfactual statement, what do we mean?

3 The preceding represents a *necessary* causal relationship (e.g., water causes the plant to grow). In the case of a *sufficient* causal relationship (e.g., temperatures above 95 degrees cause the plant to die) we would also be concerned with uniqueness: absent 'a' *and absent any other sufficient cause* there would be no 'b.' Similarly, in the case of a *contributory* causal relationship (e.g., fertilizer causes the plant to grow) we would be concerned with a unique increment: absent 'a' there would be less 'b.'

4 While it is safe to say that causal statements include a counterfactual element, it is not safe to assume the converse. A counterfactual statement is not necessarily causal (e.g., "If the leaves were turning color then it would be Fall" represents counterfactual reasoning from sign).

5 Some of these "factual" resolutions include:
Resolved: that the national news media in the United States impair the public's understanding of political issues (Fall, 1993).
Resolved: that the Welfare system in the United States has exacerbated the problems of the urban poor (Fall, 1992).
Resolved: that advertising degrades the quality of life in the United States (Spring 1992).
Resolved: that colleges and universities in the United States have inappropriately addressed issues of race or gender (Fall, 1991).
Resolved: that government censorship of public artistic expression in the United States is an undesirable infringement on individual rights (Fall, 1990).

Portions of this paper were included in a presentation at the Annual Convention of the Speech Communication Association, November, 1994, New Orleans, LA.

The author wishes to note the substantial contributions of two excellent anonymous reviewers and to thank Matt Roskoski for raising the issue and for suggesting Jon Elster as a solution. In addition, the SIU Saluki debate squad of Fall 1993 (Mary Bonner, Jason Menzies, Bill Shinn, and Jeremy West) deserves credit for developing and debating the argument which is included in the application section of this essay.

Ken Broda-Bahm (Ph.D., Southern Illinois University) is an Associate Professor in Communication Studies at Towson University, in Towson, Maryland. This essay was originally published in volume 16 (1995) of *Contemporary Argumentation and Debate*, pp. 73-85.

PART FOUR:
FIAT: THE FORCE OF ASSUMED ACTION

The logical limits on the ability of an advocate to specify alternate courses of action have proven to be a vexing concern for debaters and debate theorists over the quarter-century since the appearance of Lichtman and Rohrer's "A General Theory of the Counterplan." The concept of "fiat" or the ability to assume that a given action has taken place, was created of necessity but the challenge has been to construct a rationale and system for fiat which limits the universe of compared worlds to those which reasonably test the resolution. This section provides a sampling of a number of diverse answers to this challenge. **Brian McGee and David Romanelli** in *Policy Debate as Fiction: In Defense of Utopian Fiat* join an earlier debate on the question of whether 'utopian' acts of fiat (e.g., assuming the unproblematic transition to a world government) are educationally justifiable or not. Arguing that the simple policy-making metaphor is too confining, they defend the utopian metaphor for fiat by arguing that debate is best conceived not as a policy-making analog but as a "game played by social critics trying to envision a new order." In *A Counterfactual Theory of Fiat*, **Ken Broda-Bahm** attempts to articulate a broad model which both explains and rationally limits fiat. Instead of seeing fiat as a simple preference for "should" over "would," as a "power" of the advocate, or as a normative wish to include or exclude various arguments, Broda-Bahm urges a concept of fiat as "a servant of relevance" which finds its origins in the counterfactuals that underlie propositions and applies this understanding to difficulties associated with disadvantages, counterplans, and kritiks. **David Berube** in *Fiat and the Circumvention Argument* argues that fiat has been negotiated over time though a series of adjustments which have destabilized the concept. Berube suggests circumvention arguments as a solution to overly expansive views of fiat, arguing that renewed emphasis on this strategy would move the community away from a reliance on warrantless arguments over fiat abuse would would encourage affirmatives to reclaim the issue of inherency. Finally, in *The Decision-Maker*, **Michael Korcok** offers a re-reading of Lichtman and Rohrer's classic article augmented by decision-making theory, in order to produce a comprehensive solution to the fiat problem. Korcok advises that "the appropriate scope of negative fiat is the scope of the authority of the decision-maker choosing whether to adopt the affirmative plan" and argues that this solution avoids the judicial role-playing and normative rule-making which has characterized present piecemeal solutions to fiat. Fiat has long been considered one of the most "magical" elements of policy debate theory, and these essays seek to demystify the idea.

POLICY DEBATE AS FICTION: IN DEFENSE OF UTOPIAN FIAT

Brian McGee
and David Romanelli

The fact of the matter is that in talking about an artificial construct such as debate no language has a prior claim on validity. Indeed, the construct itself is to a very considerable degree actually created by the language. Debate is what we say it is; it is shaped and designated by us out of the terms and syntax of the idiom we are accustomed to apply to it. . . . No single language can exhaust its possibilities.

Douglas Ehninger (29-30)

For decades, intercollegiate debate has been driven by the metaphors used to describe and constrain the discursive and inventional practices of debaters. Despite experiments with social-scientific hypothesis testing (Zarefsky) and public forum (e.g., Weiss) metaphors, the dominant "generating metaphor" (Rowland 191) for understanding intercollegiate policy debate has emphasized the pragmatics of making public policy. Before the authors of this paper were born and to the present day, judges and debaters have been encouraged to treat debate as an exercise in crafting policy, with judges acting like a composite audience of those making deci-

PERSPECTIVES IN CONTROVERSY

sions in the legislative, executive, and judicial branches of the federal and/or state governments. By the 1970s, the development of the idea of "fiat" and counterplan theory (e.g., see Freeley, "Fiat"; Lichtman and Rohrer) led many members of the debate community to increasingly sophisticated analyses of affirmative plans and negative counterplans, with some community members imagining that what they did was a specialized version of the work done in university departments of public policy and management.

Obviously, the metaphors that have been central to the development of academic debate in recent years are not the only possible metaphors that might have influenced such development in the past or might guide such development in the future. If, using the well-known example of George Lakoff and Mark Johnson, one conceived of argument as a kind of interpretive dance, "good" debate might look very different to the intercollegiate debate community, perhaps with the adversarial character of debate relegated to a secondary role or eliminated altogether. There is nothing wrong with metaphor as a guiding force in academic debate or in public discourse. Scholars like Lakoff and Johnson contend that we "live by" such metaphors, since we cannot imagine a theory of the social in which the metaphoric function of language does not shape both language and action. There is no reason to believe that the influence of metaphor can be or should be overcome, and there doubtless are advantages to using familiar metaphors in explaining the esoteric idiosyncrasies of intercollegiate debate to undergraduates.

This essay defends one specific variety of metaphor for interpreting academic debate. To risk turning metaphor into simile, academic debate as currently practiced and as best practiced is usefully described and redescribed as an educational game involving the creation of *utopian literature*, rather than as an exercise in making policy. In other words, debate is a game played by social critics trying to envision the ideal social order. First, the current state of fiat theory in academic debate is examined. Second, the history and function of utopian literature as a social practice is briefly described. Third, the advantages of this metaphor for academic debate, which would legitimize arguments for radical social change in response to proposals for modest, incremental modifications to the policies of the *status quo*, are explained.[1]

A few caveats are necessary before this thesis is developed. Initially, the previous paragraphs already have mixed Alfred C. Snider's ("Fantasy," "Game," "Revisited") metaphoric explanation of debate as a "game" with the utopian literature metaphor for the debate experience. This mixing of metaphors is appropriate because Snider's gaming approach is compatible with a variety of other metaphors, including the policy-making perspective, that explain how the game should be played. For example, one easily could find members of the debate community who accept both the policy-making and gaming metaphors. Recognition of debate's status as an educational game does not render the game unimportant or trivial. Instead, the game is useful precisely because it teaches many important skills that we value as communication scholars. The utopian literature metaphor is designed to supplement, rather than displace, the understanding of debate as an educational game. Further, this essay=s concentration on policy debate is not meant to suggest that non-policy debate is irrelevant or unproductive.

THE PROBLEMS WITH FIAT THEORY

In the history of intercollegiate debate, "fiat" is a relative latecomer. While this essay is not the place to provide a comprehensive account of the development of fiat theory, textbooks in the first half of the twentieth century make no explicit reference to the plans of action that are now the central feature of most intercollegiate policy debates. This early lack of attention to plans of action may be a consequence of the ambiguous relationship between the language used in the resolution and the specific resolutional action advocated by affirmative debaters.

The idea of fiat is simple enough. To avoid uninteresting arguments about whether a policy *would* be adopted by a government that has not yet done so, fiat allows affirmatives (and negatives, when offering counterplans) to assume a counterfactual world in which their new policies exist and the merits of those policies can be evaluated.[2] This minimalist and widely (though not universally) accepted understanding of fiat power increases the educational value of debate without requiring any metaphoric assumption of governmental authority by debaters or judges, since debating *about* policy is not synonymous with *making* policy. However, beginning in the 1960s, the development of fiat theory was driven by the *policy-making metaphor*. Going well beyond the modest dictum that policy debaters deliberate on the best course of action for the government and the nation to take, affirmatives took on the role of acting *as* the government, with the plan typically conceived under the terms of the metaphor as a truncated summary of a Congressional bill, executive order, or Supreme Court decision.

Again, rather than merely debating *about* the merits of public policy, affirmative and negative debaters under the influence of the policy-making metaphor act as if they are *making* policy for purposes of argument development and comparison. By the mid-1970s, David Zarefsky could advocate his own "hypothesis-testing paradigm" (258) by contrasting it with a "policy-comparison paradigm" (260) in which "the judge is regarded as if he [or she] were a decision maker with the power to implement a decision" (257). While much has changed in academic debate since Zarefsky wrote his essay, the policy-making metaphor has remained dominant while other metaphors, including Zarefsky's, have fallen into disuse.

Working out the implications of the policy-making metaphor has not always been easy (e.g., see Solt). Beginning in the 1970s, the advocacy of "utopian" counterplans (e.g., anarchy, decentralized socialism) inspired a sporadic discussion spanning two decades over the appropriate scope of negative fiat (though utopian counterplans have become less fashionable in recent years). Most of the arguments in favor of a limited notion of fiat power and in opposition to utopian fiat were and are grounded in the policy-making metaphor, with opponents of utopian fiat arguing that world government counterplans, for example, demand action beyond that possible by agencies of the U.S. government. Further, Richard H. Dempsey and David J. Hartmann reject the agent-change or "mirror state" counterplan, which usually is not considered utopian, because the simultaneous adoption of a particular policy by all fifty states (at least without federal coercion) is "inconsistent with real world state behavior" (162). Even if states *should* operate in this manner, according to negative debaters, Dempsey and Hartmann contend that fiat power in this case does not extend to negative counterplans because states normally *would* not operate in this fashion.[3]   Dempsey and Hartmann, along with many other members of the debate community, would assent to John P. Katsulas, Dale A. Herbeck, and Edward M. Panetta's contention that "fiat theory should be restricted to assumptions grounded in real world policy making processes" (Katsulas *et al.* 96).

Few scholars would object to the mundane contention that one should compare the merits of competing policy options in policy debate.   This *weak* sense of "making policy" does not require any pretense of government authority or official imprimatur.   In this weak interpretation of "policy" as an adjective modifying "debate," the judge's decision to vote for the affirmative or negative debate team is an act of "intellectual endorsement" (Solt 130) without necessary policy-making consequences.   However, the *strong* version of the policy-making metaphor, which insists that debaters work within the confines of extant policy-making institutions in the United States, is not satisfying.

The prevailing policy-making metaphor, in which debaters play the part of government agents, has three disadvantages. First, this approach would have debaters pretend to argue before a U.S. president, the members of Congress, or some other qualified maker of public policy. This judge role-playing is problematic because very few debate judges thoroughly understand the decision-making processes that elected or appointed federal officials would employ. The inability of judges to meet the requirements of the policy-making metaphor inevitably divorces debate from the "real world" of making public policy that so many defenders of the metaphor prize.   Moreover, judges lack the constraints usually placed on those who craft public policy. A member of Congress is often influenced by her or his hopes for re-election, while the President may support or oppose a certain bill based on its political ramifications. In short, debate judges typically are not capable of meeting the demands of the policy-making metaphor. As Dallas Perkins comments, since "the judge is not in fact a policy *maker*, it is appropriate that resolutions are not typically a tool of policy *making*" ("Counterplans" 148).

Second, while debate facilitates the *discussion* of public policy, debate does not mirror the *making* of public policy. In "real world" policy discussion the number of alternatives would be far greater than those considered in a typical two-hour intercollegiate debate. It would be impossible to discuss all of these options intelligently in a single debate round. Also, as Snider argues, it "seems clear that the best possible policy decision cannot be arrived at after a two-hour discussion" ("Fantasy" 13). Policy options in the "real world" are brought before committees, differences are worked out between House and Senate versions of legislation addressing the same issue, and the U.S. President may put pressure on Congressional leaders to modify legislation or risk a veto.

Third, the policy-making metaphor asks undergraduate debaters to pretend to do something that they probably will never do in the "real world." Most debaters will never hold public office or have a great deal of immediate input in the making of public policy. Their involvement in U.S. politics will be much less direct, though not necessarily unimportant. Insisting that debaters meet the demands of making public policy suggests that the educational goal of debate is to train future generations of bureaucrats and policy wonks. Without accepting the entirety of their analysis, one can sympathize with the contention of Thomas A. Hollihan, Kevin T. Baaske, and Patricia Riley that there "are 'technocrats to spare' in the boardrooms of corporate America, in the defense establishment, and in the rest of the bureaucracy. We need more social critics who are capable of inspiring citizen activism" (186). While the policy-making metaphor undoubtedly encourages a debate *praxis* that teaches students the intricacies of policy analysis, a better metaphor would preserve most of these pedagogical advantages without asking students to take on roles they are not likely to play in the real world. Also, preparing students for life outside formal policy-making circles, where the vast majority of them will find themselves after graduation, is presumptively desirable.

To summarize, the policy-making metaphor, particularly in its strong sense, is unsatisfactory for guiding intercollegiate debate practice. The prevailing metaphor asks too much of debate judges and the debate format, while asking students to reject the "real world" in which most of them will live. The next section provides the context required for understanding an alternative metaphor for the intercollegiate debate experience.

THE PRACTICAL RELEVANCE OF UTOPIAN LITERATURE

To this point, "utopian literature" has been mentioned as an alternative frame of reference for understanding debate. Comprehending this metaphor requires a very brief discussion of the importance of utopian and dystopian literatures in U.S. history. In this discussion, the potential of literature to influence the political process is assumed. (For example, Abraham Lincoln once credited Harriet Beecher Stowe's famous novel, *Uncle Tom's Cabin*, with starting the U.S. Civil War.)

Utopian literature presents an alternative social order as being morally or practically better than the *status quo* in politics, law, economics, and/or interpersonal relations. The transition to this new social order might be sudden and dramatic, but nothing logically prevents a series of small, incremental steps over time from leading to the establishment of utopia. While utopia, the perfectly "good place that is no place" in John Rodden's words (Rodden 1), may not yet exist, American utopians have always struggled to make some counterfactual utopian world a possibility. In the nineteenth century, utopian experiments in agrarian living were numerous in the United States, and familiar names like "Shaker" and "Amana" are the detritus of those experiments. In the twentieth century, utopian novels still appear as commentaries on the problems of American society (see Haschak). Consistently, American utopians have emphasized their desire to demonstrate the practicality of their proposed alternative world and the ease of the transition from the way things are in the current milieu to the way things ought to be (in a sense other than Rush Limbaugh's). Even when criticizing the limits of utopian desire, James Darsey concludes that "utopian desire thwarts complacency by keeping alive dreams that practical politics would consign to the morgue" (Darsey 34).

In contrast with utopian novels, dystopian literatures emphasize the limitations of alternative world views by demonstrating their impracticality or their considerable disadvantages. George Orwell's *1984* and his *Animal Farm* are considered classic examples of dystopian novels, given their harsh criticism of totalitarian government and socialism. If utopian novels demonstrate the advantages of abandoning the current order, their dystopian counterparts warn against the dangers of too quickly abandoning a system that is not wholly dysfunctional. For example, one could argue that Francis Fukuyama's announcement of the "end of history" is simultaneously a proclamation that the capitalist, North Atlantic democracies are utopias and that non-capitalist alternatives have dystopian consequences.

Finally, utopian literature has had an historically important social function. In the nineteenth century, Edward Bellamy's *Looking Backward* inspired the foundation of Bellamy societies and a short-lived political party. In the twentieth century, B. F. Skinner's *Walden Two* has remained in print for several decades and was consulted by some of those who experimented with communal living in the 1950s and 1960s. Today, first- and second-wave feminist utopias, including Charlotte Perkins Gilman's *Herland* (1915), Marge Piercy's *Woman on the Edge of Time* (1976), and Sally Miller Gearhart's *Wanderground* (1979) are embraced by many academic feminists.[4] In short, utopian literature is an important part of the history of American social movement, and there is some reason to conclude that utopian science fictions and other utopian literatures will continue to play a role in future efforts to inspire social change or, in the case of dystopian literatures, to discourage such change.

The next section suggests that envisioning debate as utopian fiction has several practical advantages.

DEBATE AS THE SEARCH FOR UTOPIA

As Alfred C. Snider argued several years ago in defense of his gaming perspective, a suitable paradigm should address "something we can ACTUALLY DO as opposed to something we can MAKE BELIEVE ABOUT" ("Fantasy as Reality" 14). A utopian literature metaphor is beneficial precisely because it is within the power of debaters to perform the desired action suggested by the metaphor, if not always to demonstrate that the desired action is politically feasible.

Instead of debaters playing to an audience of those who make public policy, debaters should understand themselves as budding social critics in search of an optimal practical and cultural politics.

While few of us will ever hold a formal policy-making position, near-ly all of us grow up with the social and political criticism of the news-paper editorial page, the high school civics class, and, at least in homes that do not ban the juxtaposition of food and politics, the live-ly dinner table conversation. We complain about high income taxes, declining state subsidies for public education, and crumbling inter-state highways. We worry about the rising cost of health care and wonder if we will have access to high-quality medical assistance when we need it. Finally, we bemoan the decline of moral consen-sus, rising rates of divorce, drug use among high school students, and disturbing numbers of pregnant teen-agers. From childhood on, we are told that good citizenship demands that we educate ourselves on political matters and vote to protect the *polis*; the success of democracy allegedly demands no less. For those who accept this challenge instead of embracing the political alienation of Generation X and becoming devotees of *Beavis and Butthead*, social criticism is what good citizens do.

Debate differs from other species of social criticism because debate is a game played by students who want to win. However, con-ceiving of debate as a kind of social criticism has considerable merit. Social criticism is not restricted to a technocratic elite or group of elected officials. Moreover, social criticism is not necessarily idle or wholly deconstructive. Instead, such criticism necessarily is a pre-requisite to any effort to create policy change, whether that criticism is articulated by an elected official or by a mother of six whose pri-mary workplace is the home. When one challenges the *status quo*, one normally implies that a better alternative course of action exists. Given that intercollegiate debate frequently involves exchanges over a proposition of policy by student advocates who are relatively unlikely ever to debate before Congress, envisioning intercollegiate debate as a specialized extension of ordinary citizen inquiry and advocacy in the public sphere seems attractive. Thinking of debate as a variety of social criticism gives debate an added dimension of public relevance.

One way to understand the distinction between debate as poli-cy-making and debate as social criticism is to examine Roger W. Cobb and Charles D. Elder's agenda-building theory.[5] Cobb and Elder are well known for their analytic split of the *formal agenda* for policy change, which includes legislation or other action proposed by policy makers with formal power (e.g., government bureaucrats, U.S. Senators), from the *public agenda* for policy change, which is composed of all those who work outside formal policy-making circles to exert influence on the formal agenda. Social movements, lobbyists, political action committees, mass media outlets, and public opinion polls all constitute the public agenda, which, in turn, has an effect on what issues come to the forefront on the formal agenda. From the agenda-building perspective, one cannot understand the making of public policy in the United States without comprehending the confluence of the formal and public agenda.

In intercollegiate debate, the policy-making metaphor has given primacy to formal agenda functions at the expense of the public agenda. Debaters are encouraged to bypass thinking about the public agenda in outlining policy alternatives; appeals for policy change frequently are made by debaters under the strange pretense that they and/or their judges are members of the formal agenda elite. Even arguments about the role of the public in framing public policy are typically issued by debaters as if those debaters were working within the confines of the formal agenda for their own, instrumental advantage. (For example, one thinks of various social movement "backlash" disadvantage arguments, which advocate a temporary policy paralysis in order to stir up public outrage and mobilize social movements, whose leaders will demand the formal adoption of a presumably superior policy alternative.) The policy-making metaphor concentrates on the formal agenda to the near exclusion of the public agenda, as the focus of a Katsulas or a Dempsey on the "real-world" limitations for making policy indicates.

Debate as social criticism does not entail exclusion of formal agenda concerns from intercollegiate debate. The specified agent of action in typical policy resolutions makes ignoring the formal agenda of the United States government an impossibility. However, one need not be able to influence the formal agenda directly in order to discuss what it is that the United States government should do. Undergraduate debaters and their judges usually are far removed—both physically and functionally—from the arena of formal-agenda deliberation. What the disputation of student debaters most closely resembles, to the extent that it resembles any real-world analog, is public-agenda social criticism. What students are doing is something they really CAN do as students and ordinary citizens; they are working in their own modest way to shape the public agenda.

While "social criticism" is the best explanation for what debaters do, this essay goes a step further. The mode of criticism in which debaters operate is the production of utopian literature. Strictly speaking, debaters engage in the creation of fictions and the comparison of fictions to one another. How else does one explain the affirmative advocacy of a plan, a counterfactual world, that, by definition, does not exist? Indeed, traditional inherency burdens demand that such plans be utopian, in the sense that current attitudes or structures make the immediate enactment of such plans unlikely in the "real world" of the formal agenda. Intercollegiate debate is utopian because plan and/or counterplan enactment is improbable. While one can distinguish between incremental and radical policy change proposals, the distinction makes no difference in the utopian practice of intercollegiate debate.

More importantly, intercollegiate debate is utopian in another sense. Policy change is considered because such change, it is hoped, will facilitate the pursuit of the good life. For decades, intercollegiate debaters have used fiat or the authority of the word "should" to propose radical changes in the social order, in addition to advocacy of the incremental policy changes typical of the U.S. formal agenda. This wide range of policy alternatives discussed in contemporary intercollegiate debate is the sign of a healthy public sphere, where thorough consideration of all policy alternatives is a possibility. Utopian fiction, in which the good place that is no place is envisioned, makes possible the instantiation of a rhetorical vision prerequisite to building that good place in our tiny corner of the universe. Even Lewis Mumford, a critic of utopian thought, concedes that we "can never reach the points of the compass; and so no doubt we shall never live in utopia; but without the magnetic needle we should not be able to travel intelligently at all" (Mumford 24-25).

An objection to this guiding metaphor is that it encourages debaters to do precisely that to which Snider would object, which is to "make believe" that utopia is possible. This objection misunderstands the argument. These students *already are* writers of utopian fiction from the moment they construct their first plan or counter-plan text. Debaters who advocate policy change announce their commitment to changing the organization of society in pursuit of the good life, even though they have no formal power to call this coun-terfactual world into being. Any proposed change, no matter how small, is a repudiation of policy paralysis and the maintenance of the *status quo*. As already practiced, debate revolves around utopian pro-posals, at least in the sense that debaters and judges lack the formal authority to enact their proposals. Even those negatives who defend the current social order frequently do so by pointing to the potential dystopic consequences of accepting such proposals for change.

Understanding debate as utopian literature would not elimi-nate references to the vagaries of making public policy, including debates over the advantageousness of plans and counterplans. As noted above, *talking* about public policy is not *making* public poli-cy, and a retreat from the policy-making metaphor would have rel-atively little effect on the contemporary practice of intercollegiate debate.[6] For example, while space constraints prevent a thorough discussion of this point, the utopian literature metaphor would not necessitate the removal of all constraints on fiat, although some utopian proposals will tax the imagination where formal-agenda policy change is concerned.

The utopian literature metaphor does not ineluctably divorce debate from the problems and concerns of ordinary people and everyday life. There will continue to be debates focused on incre-mental policy changes as steps along the path to utopia. What the utopian literature metaphor does is to position debaters, coaches, and judges as the unapologetic social critics that they are and have always been, without the confining influence of a guiding metaphor that limits their ability to search for the good life. Further, this new metaphor does not encourage debaters to carry the utopian litera-ture metaphor to extremes by imagining that they are sitting in a solitary corner and penning the next great American novel. The metaphor is useful because it orients debaters to their role as social critics, without the suggestion that debate is anything other than an educational game played by undergraduate students.

In closing, the best of social criticism and of academic debate always has envisioned possibilities for reconstructing government, the economy, international relations, and interpersonal relationships without bowing to the necessities imposed by the political milieu of the moment. Academic debate would be best served if the debate community embraced this critical, utopian function wholeheartedly, rather than clinging to an overly confining policy-making metaphor. Social critics in the United States have a distinguished history of using utopian literature to popularize and to test alternative ways of organizing society. Advocates of academic debate would do better to embrace this tradition than to maintain their devotion to a central policy-making metaphor that, by itself, does not serve the community well. As Ehninger notes, "debate is what we say it is." To speak of debate as a space for the articulation of utopian thought enriches, rather than impoverishes, debate theory, pedagogy, and practice. Endorsing the utopian literature metaphor will return debate to the real world, rather than further separating debate from that world.

WORKS CITED

Bartanen, Michael, and David Frank. "The Issues-Agenda Paradigm." *The Forensic of Pi Kappa Delta* 69 (1983): 1-9.

Bellamy, Edward. *Looking Backward: 2000-1887.* 1888. New York: Penguin, 1982.

Broda-Bahm, Kenneth. "Counterfactual Possibilities: Constructing Counter-to-fact Causal Claims." *Contemporary Argumentation and Debate* 16 (1995): 73-85.

Cobb, Roger W., and Charles D. Elder. *Participation in American Politics: The Dynamics of Agenda-Building.* 2nd ed. Baltimore: Johns Hopkins, 1983.

Darsey, James. "Utopia and Desire." *Argumentation and Values: Proceedings of the Ninth SCA/AFA Conference on Argumentation.* Ed. Sally Jackson. Annandale, VA: SCA, 1995. 28-35.

Dempsey, Richard H., and David J. Hartmann. "Mirror State Counterplans: Illegitimate, Topical, or Magical?" *Journal of the American Forensic Association* 21 (1985): 161-166.

Edwards, Richard E. "In Defense of Utopia: A Response to Katsulas, Herbeck, and Panetta." *Journal of the American Forensic Association* 24 (1987): 112-118.

Ehninger, Douglas. "Debating as Critical Deliberation." *Southern Speech*

Journal 24 (1958): 22-30.

Fadely, Dean. "Fiat Power and the Mirror State Counterplan." *Speaker and Gavel* 24 (1987): 69-76.

Freeley, Austin J. "Fiat Power: Its Uses and Limitations." *Communication: Journal of the Communication Association of the Pacific* (1977): 79-82.

Fukuyama, Francis. *The End of History and the Last Man*. New York: Free Press, 1992.

Gearhart, Sally Miller. *The Wanderground: Stories of the Hill Women*. Boston: Alyson, 1979.

Gilman, Charlotte Perkins. *Herland and Selected Stories*. Ed. Barbara H. Solomon. New York: Signet-Penguin, 1992.

Haschak, Paul G. *Utopian/Dystopian Literature: A Bibliography of Literary Criticism*. Metuchen, NJ: Scarecrow, 1994.

Hollihan, Thomas A., Kevin T. Baaske, and Patricia Riley. "Debaters as Storytellers: The Narrative Perspective in Academic Debate." *Journal of the American Forensic Association* 23 (1987): 184-193.

Katsulas, John P., Dale A. Herbeck, and Edward M. Panetta. "Fiating Utopia: A Negative View of the Emergence of World Order Counterplans and Futures Gaming in Policy Debate." *Journal of the American Forensic Association* 24 (1987): 95-111.

Lakoff, George, and Mark Johnson. *Metaphors We Live by*. Chicago: U of Chicago P, 1980.

Lichtman, Allan J., and Daniel M. Rohrer. "A General Theory of the Counterplan." *Advanced Debate*. 4th ed. Ed. David A. Thomas and John P. Hart. Lincolnwood, IL: National Textbook, 1992. 365-376.

Mumford, Lewis. *The Story of Utopias*. 1922. New York: Viking, 1962.

Orwell, George. *1984, A Novel*. New York: New American Library, 1961.

—. *Animal Farm*. New York: Harcourt Brace, 1946.

Perkins, Dallas. "Counterplans and Paradigms." *Journal of the American Forensic Association* 25 (1989): 140-149.

Piercy, Marge. *Woman on the Edge of Time*. New York: Fawcett Crest-Ballantine, 1976.

Rodden, John. "State-ly Designs: Toward an Architectonics of the Utopian Imagination." Biennial Wake Forest Argumentation Conference, Winston-Salem, NC, 1991.

Rowland, Robert C. "The Debate Judge as Debate Judge: A Functional Paradigm for Evaluating Debates." *Journal of the American Forensic Association* 20 (1984): 183-193.

Skinner, B. F. *Walden Two*. New York: Macmillan, 1948.

Snider, Alfred C. "Fantasy as Reality: Fiat Power in Academic Debate." Central States Speech Association Convention, Milwaukee, April 1982.

——. "Games without Frontiers: A Design for Communication Scholars and Forensic Educators." *Journal of the American Forensic Association* 20 (1984): 162-170.

——. "Fantasy and Reality Revisited: Gaming, Fiat Power, and Anti-utopianism." *Journal of the American Forensic Association* 24 (1987): 119-129.

Solt, Roger. "Negative Fiat: Resolving the Ambiguities of 'Should'." *Journal of the American Forensic Association* 25 (1989): 121-139.

Stowe, Harriet Beecher. *Uncle Tom's Cabin Or, Life among the Lowly*. New York: Penguin, 1981.

Voight, Phil. "Thinking in Time: The Importance of Temporal Location in Argument." *Contemporary Argumentation and Debate* 16 (1995): 86-97.

Weiss, Robert O. "The Audience Standard." *CEDA Yearbook* 6 (1985): 43-49.

Zarefsky, David. "Argument as Hypothesis Testing." *Advanced Debate*. 4th ed. Ed. David A. Thomas and John P. Hart. Lincolnwood, IL: National Textbook, 1992. 252-262.

NOTES

[1] We are not the first scholars to explore the role of utopian thought in forensic practice. A decade ago, Richard E. Edwards defended "the role of utopianism in stimulating social change" (112) as relevant for debate practice and argued that traditional debate theory was open to the possibility of utopian argument about alternative futures. Unfortunately, the fullest exposition of Edwards's ideas on utopian thought appears in an unpublished 1986 SCA conference paper, to which the authors do not have access.

[2] We recognize that some scholars maintain that debate resolutions are not counterfactuals in some technical, philosophical senses of the term. We use the word here in a minimalist sense to refer only to the fact that plans and counterplans advocate an alternative world that does not yet exist.
For different perspectives on counterfactual analysis, see, for example, the essays of Kenneth Broda-Bahm and Phil Voight.

[3] In a response to Dempsey and Hartmann, Dean Fadely also argued that "Dempsey and Hartmann confuse *should* with *would*" (Fadely 74).

[4] Of course, not all utopias would earn the progressive left-liberal intellectual's seal of approval. As Lewis Mumford observed over seven decades ago, "far too large

a number of classic utopias were based upon conceptions of authoritarian discipline that seemed . . . far from ideal" (4).

5 By citing Cobb and Elder, we are not signaling endorsement of the "issues-agenda" paradigm of Michael Bartanen and David Frank, who base their judging paradigm on Cobb and Elder's agenda-building model.

6 One reader of an earlier draft of this essay asked about the implications of the utopian literature metaphor for the wide range of arguments now called "critiques" in both CEDA and NDT. The differences between the various categories of critique arguments make a succinct answer to this question difficult. Briefly, this metaphor does not constitute a response to critiques that question the epistemological status of argument and/or value claims, since the authors of utopian fictions, no less than members of Congress, make some epistemological assumptions. In contrast, critiques that reject current debate *praxis* as anti-educational might be answered in some instances by reference to the utopian literature metaphor.

Brian R. McGee (Ph.D., Ohio State University) is an Associate Professor of Communication Studies and Chair of the Department of Communication Studies at Spalding University in Louisville, Kentucky. **David Romanelli** (M.A., Miami-OH) is Instructor and Director of Debate in the Department of Communication, Loyola University of Chicago. This essay was originally published in volume 18 (1997) of *Contemporary Argumentation and Debate*, pp. 23-35.

A COUNTERFACTUAL THEORY OF FIAT
Kenneth T. Broda-Bahm

The concept of fiat is not unfamiliar by nature. Certainly "the temporary suspension of concern" (Solt 122) for whether something would be done in order to focus on what should be done is easy enough to conceive and relate to our experience inside and outside a debate setting. The problem is that within the context of academic debate, fiat has been too often approached as a game-rule rather than an issue of argument interpretation or relevance. This essay does not embrace a comprehensive answer to all of the questions of fiat, but instead offers a counterfactual framework for understanding and debating about fiat. After first tracing fiat from its historical roots to its contemporary usage, this essay will build a case for reconceptualizing fiat within the terms of counterfactual theory, and then apply possible counterfactual understandings of fiat to three problematic situations: disadvantage ground, counterplan ground, and critiques of discourse.

FIAT AND THE SEARCH FOR RELEVANCE

As McGee and Romanelli have noted, fiat as a formal concept seems to have emerged only in the past two decades with the increasing particularization of affirmative policy options. Prior to this, the issue of assumed action was relegated to the common sense distinction between "should" and "would." "We may conclude that the word 'should' includes 'could,'" Lambertson wrote in 1942. However, "whether or not Congress or the people 'would' adopt a particular reform at the present time is beside the point" (424). Mills also noted that the word should "implies that action *could* be taken, but not that it will be taken" (80). The distinction was held to be a basic matter of relevance: Summers, Whan, and Rouse argued that questions concerning the likelihood of passage should be dismissed as irrelevant since, "the question is always: *Should* the new policy be accepted" (326). These simple distinctions between "should," "could," and "would" indicate that fiat finds its origin in the need to set aside issues of propensity in the name of relevance. According to this now-classic understanding, an advocate of the benefits of future action intuitively carries a burden to show the possibility and the desirability of their chosen course of action, but not its propensity. Indeed, focusing on propensity in such a case is *non-sequitur* since it answers a question that has not been asked. Answering "we should" with "we wouldn't" simply misses the point.

This conventional distinction appears to have been sufficient until the occurrence of two trends. When affirmative debaters moved beyond simply assuming the enaction of the general policy direction of the resolution by articulating increasingly detailed programs of action, and when negative debaters gained the freedom to choose from a vast array of counterplan options, ranging from the practical to the utopian, fiat became no longer a simple matter of preferring should over would. Something was needed to identify the contexts and the scope of legitimate affirmative and negative arguments. Since fiat was born of an analysis of the word "should" within the context of policy-making, it is no surprise that most theoretical attempts to explain and delimit fiat have generally approached fiat as a "power" which is possessed by debaters, but limited by external normative constraints or game-rules. *The Dictionary of Debate,* for example, defines fiat as "The power of the affirmative or negative to implement the plan or counterplan" and adds the suggested usage, "We have the ability to pass our plan or counterplan into law" (Hanson 67). Freeley also writes of the affirmative's "fiat power" (59) and several writers have advocated various practical limits upon this power (e.g., Dempsey & Hartman; Fadely; Hynes;

Katsulas, Herbeck, & Panetta; Patterson & Zarefsky; Solt). Solt, in particular, has approached fiat theory as a community constraint, suggesting that fiat should be restricted to U.S. domestic policy actors chiefly because the U. S. high school and college policy debate communities have consistently debated topics which have included a U. S. Government agent. He defends his limit of fiat to domestic public actors by essentially saying that alternate "rules" would be worse: "Given some of the current draconian proposals to limit counterplan ground, [limiting fiat to U. S. Government agents] provides a reasonably moderate constraint" (135).

As Solt implies, much of the concern regarding limits to fiat power has centered on the goal of discouraging or promoting specific counterplans. The ubiquity of references to world government, socialism, and anarchy in particular suggests that theoretical attention to fiat has been fueled more by the goal of managing these arguments than by an interest in the argumentative meaning behind the act of fiat. The tendency to treat fiat theory as a means to police undesirable counterplans can be seen most clearly in the debate over utopianism. Katsulas, Herbeck, and Panetta, for example, argue that fiat, "should be restricted to assumptions grounded in real world policy making processes" calling upon debate judges to "enforce" this requirement and to "dismiss" utopian arguments (108). Edwards, on the other hand, champions a less restrictive view based on the argument that fiat should promote a broader view of possibility. Similarly Snider argues that fiat limits should be determined "through a discussion of procedures based on the perceived goals of the game of debate" (125). More recently, McGee and Romanelli use the metaphor of utopian literature to rationalize the act of fiat. Rather than arguing that utopian fiat is relevant to an analysis of claims, they instead justify fiat on the normative value of advocating utopian claims. A broad view of fiat is valued, not for its connection to relevance, but because it "orients debaters to their role as social critics" (33). Neither the critics nor the perceived advocates of utopianism clearly base their case on an analysis of the proposition: utopianism is criticized because it is bad for debate or defended because it is good for debate, in a context removed from the requirements of a particular resolution. What is left unclear is whether a utopian answer is relevant to the question being asked by a given resolution.

If the question governing fiat is, "What issues are best to include?" then utopian and other acts of fiat will be potentially self-justifying. To the advocate of an anarchy counterplan, for example, it is beneficial and even essential for us to envision reality apart from governmental control and hence this instance of fiat must be allowed. The opponent of the counterplan, however, will just as passionately argue that incremental policy-making is our best and most realistic hope for change hence utopian fiat must be avoided. Framed as a normative question, the resolution of this fiat debate is enmeshed in the substantive evaluation of the fiated action itself. If the question of whether we *should* fiat anarchy is addressed by considering the costs and the benefits of anarchy – a consideration which itself requires at least tacit fiat – then we risk begging the question: in order to evaluate this fiat, we must contingently allow it. The question should not be limited to "What is good?" but must also emphasize "What is relevant?"

In broad terms, fiat theory has moved from a basic concern for relevance to a felt need to codify norms as a way of regulating new argument. While the common-sense "should-would" distinction retains the benefit of succinct explanation, it no longer answers questions relating to the scope and form of the myriad of assumed actions in contemporary debate. The resulting case-by-case practice of setting normative limits on fiat has also failed to move beyond *ad hoc* solutions. It is clear that questions of relevance in fiat theory could be better answered by the development of a system for arguing over the propositional relevance of specific acts of fiat.

RECONCEPTUALIZING FIAT IN COUNTERFACTUAL TERMS

One potential framework for reconnecting fiat to argumentative relevance is found in counterfactual theory. When a proposition makes relevant the consideration of something that currently does not exist, that proposition gives rise to a counterfactual statement, or a statement contrary to the factual events as we know them. In evaluating an alternative to the factual world, the central question becomes, what comparisons are most relevant to a particular resolution? This question is potentially answered by considering counterfactuals.

Counterfactuals assert that if an antecedent condition were present, then a specific consequent would obtain: "If it were the case that ___, then it would be the case that ___" (Lewis 2); if I struck that match, it would light; if the Republicans make Congressional gains in the next election, they will pass an income tax reduction; if the federal government were to initiate a carbon tax, greenhouse emissions would decline. "As a first approximation," Creath notes, "we might say that a counterfactual is any sentence which says what *would* happen under specified conditions, even though those conditions do not in fact obtain" (95). Such arguments are obviously commonplace in conventional discussion and in academic debate as well. To say that "A" would be good is to say that in the counterfactual presence of "A," some positive consequent would happen more readily.

In the disciplines of logic, natural language, and philosophy, writers such as Lewis, Stalnaker, Elster, and Rescher have grappled with the issue of how such claims should be understood and evaluated. Within the context of academic debate as well, Berube and Pray, Hoe, Roskoski, Voight and I have discussed the merits and the methods of applying counterfactual analysis to a general understanding of causal claims in argument. Major disagreements have focused on the assumptions that one makes about the world when entertaining a counterfactual proposition, the limits to imagination that should exist when articulating the alternative, and the ways in which the rest of the world can be held constant when a single change is examined. These issues do not merely parallel but actually constitute the concerns of fiat. What is the scope of an advocate's ability to assume an alteration in the world? What other alterations can be made? What else is assumed to remain constant?

The applicability of counterfactual analysis to debate has been called into question (Berube & Pray; Voight; Voight & Stanfield) and defended (Broda-Bahm, "Counterfactual Possibilities"; Broda-Bahm, "Counterfactual Problems"; Roskoski), but it bears noting that most criticism has assumed that counterfactual arguments are solely retrospective arguments, such as "What if Kennedy had survived the assassination attempt?" While much discussion of counterfactuals in logic and philosophy literature does indeed focus on such retrospection, counterfactuals may refer to future conditions as well. In the words of Roese and Olson, the counterfactual is a way of expressing "what might have been and what may yet be" (2). Hoch, for example, discusses counterfactual reasoning as applicable to the prediction of a future outcome (721-22). Johnson and Sherman also write, "Without considering alternatives to reality, we must accept the past as having been inevitable and must believe that the future will be no different from the past. The generation of counterfactuals gives us flexibility in thinking about possible futures and prepares us better for those futures" (510).

All statements about the effects of plans and counterplans are types of counterfactual statements. Even early expressions of the should-would distinction understood proposed policies in counterfactual terms. For instance Musgrave wrote, "The phrase 'should adopt" or its equivalent means that the affirmative must show that the plan, if adopted, would be desirable" (15). "If we passed the Clinton health plan, it would save money" is a counterfactual statement since we have not yet passed the health plan: it envisions a different world than the world that we know. "If we implemented socialized medicine, instead of passing the Clinton health plan, it would save more lives" is a second counterfactual step since it envisions a second hypothetical world to compare to the first. Such counterfactual thinking is impossible to avoid in discussing the implications of any evaluation. As Rescher writes, we necessarily suppose the false to be true in the everyday act of entertaining possibility: "Such suppositions, whose claims we do not for a moment really believe, indeed actually disbelieve, enter essentially into our planning for the future. . . In general, rational deliberation as to the future would be impossible without making false assumptions" (179-80).

In order to be re-conceptualized as a counterfactual construct, fiat should be seen as a natural component of argument, requiring no authority to give it birth, nor to limit its powers, and functioning merely as the servant of relevance. If one argues "I should move to Chicago" and by extension "If I moved to Chicago, it would be good," one *must* hypothesize a world in which one *does* move to Chicago. This assumption is unavoidable if one is to evaluate the claim. The fiat entailed in this assumption promotes relevance by focusing on questions which are important (e.g., the value of a move to Chicago) while dismissing questions which are propositionally unimportant (e.g., the likelihood of a move to Chicago). As a component of argument and a servant of relevance, fiat should find its origin in propositional wording in determining which assumed alterations to reality materially bear upon the question at hand. Rather than being seen as the enabling "power" of a policymaker or as a game rule, fiat should be seen as a logical need to tacitly assume that for the purposes of argument the non-existent actually exists.

The first step in developing a counterfactual theory of fiat is to define fiat in counterfactual terms. Provisionally, we can say that fiat refers to *the hypothetical consideration of any and all counterfactual portions of the claim being supported.* A counterfactual portion of a claim would simply be the antecedent to any conditional claim necessary in evaluating the resolution: If the United States passed health care reform. . . . If Tennessee banned handguns. . . . If all UN nations granted full jurisdiction to the World Court. Any time the claim posits the existence of a condition that does not exist, the claim makes a counterfactual assumption. "Fiat" should be seen most simply as our word for the act of entertaining that counterfactual assumption.

On its face, this redefinition is not a radical move away from conventional interpretations and uses of fiat. Most theorists and debaters would likely agree that fiat is usefully conceived as the act of entertaining a given condition for the purposes of argument. The definition of fiat as a counterfactual concept captures this conventional view, but in some important ways this definition both clarifies and extends the current concept of fiat. Specifically a counterfactual interpretation of fiat can be seen as possessing three advantages: First, it reinforces the propositional origin of fiat; second, it extends the meaning and utility of fiat beyond the policy-making metaphor; and third, it provides a heuristic palette of concepts for arguments over the limits of fiat.

The first advantage of a counterfactual view of fiat is to ground fiat in its propositional origin. Many theorists have not found it problematic to discuss the limits of fiat as a general concept removed from any specific resolution. Freeley, for example, definitively upholds the commonplace belief that, "the affirmative may not fiat attitudes" (59). If fiat is a component of the argument, and not a power of the advocate, however, then the ability to fiat would depend absolutely upon the argument being made. If, as has become generally the case, a proposition focuses on the value of adopting a policy and not on the value of attitudinal endorsement, then the commonplace belief would be correct. We could legitimately assume the policy into being, but there would be no warrant for fiating attitudes surrounding the policy. If, on the other hand, a proposition *does* focus on the value of attitudinal change, then support of that proposition will entail the argument that *"if* such attitude change occurred, *then* it would be good." Hence advocacy would require the provisional assumption – or fiat – that such an attitude change has occurred. Take for example, the resolution on the 1996-1997 CEDA/NDT debate topic ballot, "Resolved: that we should embrace the principles of deep ecology." The advocate of this proposition depends upon the antecedent, "if an embrace of deep ecological principles occurred" and therefore properly fiats that attitudinal endorsement because the question of whether we *would* endorse is irrelevant to whether we *should* endorse. If fiat is seen as the enaction of the counterfactual portion of the proposition, then propositional relevance is the starting point for any claim of fiat and no general rule of what can or cannot be allowed can be sustained.

At a minimum, the counterfactual definition adds clarity to the rationale for fiat. Advocates fiat because they must. Embedded within an evaluative resolution is the conditional judgment, if p were to take place, then a given result q would follow. There is no meaningful way to address that judgment without assuming that p has taken place. Fiat then is not grounded in a game rule, nor in reciprocal power, nor in normative appeals to "good argument," but in a palpable argumentative need to assume the antecedent into being.

The second advantage of a counterfactual view of fiat is that it extends the construct of fiat beyond the narrow frame of policy-making. *Any* counterfactual assumption can be addressed through fiat. To use an extreme example, take a potential resolution of fact from recent news accounts and cinema, "Resolved: that a major asteroid hitting the earth today would end human life." This resolution invokes the conditional antecedent "if a major asteroid strikes the earth today" and hence the evaluation of whether or not such an event would end human life requires that we assume the truth of the antecedent. We must assume for the purpose of argument that "a major asteroid will strike the earth today." In effect, advocates would fiat this occurrence. This act of assumption is literally required by the resolution. The fact that no tracked asteroids are scheduled to approach the earth in the near future may be quite relevant to our own assessment of risk, but that fact is irrelevant to the resolution at hand. Advocates would rightly say, "we are not arguing over whether it *will* hit, we are arguing over what the effect would be *if* it did hit." This argumentative move is parallel to the policy debater's use of fiat, and it makes sense to see it as the same basic construct. Fiat is not simply an analog for the action of a policy-maker, but is a more general way of bringing-into-being the context required for resolutional evaluation. A view of fiat that transcends resolution-type is advantageous, not only because it provides a tool for analyzing all resolutions, but also because it carries more meaning at a time in which many debaters (such as critique advocates) and theorists (e.g., see Mitchell, McGee & Romanelli) are challenging the continued viability of the policy-making metaphor even for resolutions phrased in the most policy-oriented terms.

A final benefit to a counterfactual perspective on fiat is that it supplies a heuristic grounding for debates over fiat. If counterfactual claims are elements of natural language and common-sense thinking, then there should be natural and common-sense limits to fiat linked to the language and meaning of the proposition. The disciplines of philosophy, informal logic, linguistics, and the law all provide numerous explanations of counterfactual problems and solutions. While they have not addressed fiat in particular, several essays within the context of argumentation and debate (Broda-Bahm, "Counterfactual Possibilities"; Borda-Bahm, "Counterfactual Problems"; Hoe; Korcok; Roskoski) and within other contexts (Elster; Lewis, *Counterfactuals*; Rescher; Roese & Olson; Stalnaker) have explored multiple tools for understanding counterfactual claims. The variety of approaches and range of opinion represented within these literatures should supply advocates with multiple avenues of argument. The following sections will illustrate some potential ways that counterfactual terms and concepts can be used to engage the debate over fiat, but they are obviously not intended to exhaust this potential.

COUNTERFACTUAL THEMES FOR ARGUING OVER FIAT

This essay does not seek to provide an answer to the vexing questions of fiat, but instead seeks to develop a set of possible arguments to use in resolving disputes over fiat. This section will turn to counterfactual theory in order to introduce several themes which may be useful for creating such arguments.

In evaluating and consolidating current research on the social psychology of counterfactual claims, Roese and Olson advocate a two-stage model for counterfactual interpretation. The first stage, counterfactual availability, relates to the mere ability to consider some alternate condition, while the second stage, counterfactual content, relates to the actual form of the alternate condition. As it regards fiat, this model might be conceptualized as posing two questions: What allows advocates to consider alternate conditions? What considerations should shape the content of the alternative? Stage one addresses the ability to fiat, while stage two addresses the content of the fiated world. Viewing fiat at both stages as a counterfactual construct suggests several possible arguments.

Fiat Should be Limited by Necessity. Both logically and psychologically, counterfactuals stem from a need to consider a conditional statement with a presently-false antecedent. In writing on the truth-value of counterfactual statements, Stalnaker sets out the requirement that "there are no differences between the actual world and the selected world except those that are required, implicitly or explicitly, by the antecedent" (104). Divorced from this exigence, the generation of counterfactual worlds is argumentatively unwarranted and gratuitous. Rather than being thought of as the intrinsic power of an advocate, the fiating of alternate worlds should be understood as a logical move that is constrained by the condition giving it birth. Limiting fiat to situations in which it is required by a propositionally-relevant antecedent more accurately treats fiat as a feature of an argument, and not as a power of the advocate. For this reason, any act of entertaining a counterfactual through fiat should be justified by referring to the relevant conditional statement that requires counterfactual generation.

Fiat Should Involve the Least Possible Change from the Present

World. Deciding which world offers a relevant comparison is required not just with counterplans, plans, and advantages, but also with even simple statements of causality. When I say that "smoking causes cancer," I assume the counterfactual "if people didn't smoke than they would be less likely to develop cancer." The causal statement entails a comparison between two worlds: our world exactly as we know it, and that same world absent only smoking. In this example, the counterfactual world is that which contains the fewest possible changes from the world as we know it. The counterfactual world changes just enough to allow consideration of the antecedent (less smoking) and no more. To reprise Lewis' famous example, the assertion "If kangaroos had no tails, they would topple over" (1), is an example of a statement that forces us to imagine a given world. While there are myriad possibilities of what that world would look like, including hypothetical worlds in which "kangaroos walk around on crutches" (9), those worlds that involve gratuitous departures from our own world must be rejected in favor of the most circumspect reading of the statement: "What is meant by the counterfactual is that, things being pretty much as they are – the scarcity of crutches for kangaroos being pretty much as it actually is, the kangaroos' inability to use crutches being pretty much as it actually is, and so on – if kangaroos had no tails they would topple over" (9). Given *carte blanche* to characterize the counterfactual world, it would always be possible to either verify or falsify any counterfactual assertion. Lewis' argument that a counterfactual proposition assumes the nearest possible world echoes Stalnaker's advice that assessing the veracity of counterfactual statements requires "that the world selected *differ minimally* from the actual world" (104). He continues, "Further, it means that among the alternative ways of making the required changes, one must choose one that does the least violence to the correct description and explanation of the actual world" (104)

Of course, deciding which world is the closest world can be complicated and interpretations can differ when this idea is applied to debate conventions such as plans, counterplans, and talk about the past. At this point, it should suffice to say that the "closeness" of the counterfactual world offered for comparison is one tool for arguing over its appropriateness.

Fiat Should Include a Plausible Departure from the Present World.
A common sense notion of "should" includes "could," and a counter-factual understanding of "should" does as well. But, it includes a logical and practical refinement on this basic requirement. The advocate of a counterfactual antecedent can be reasonably called upon to account for a likely circumstance by which this antecedent could come to pass. A "branching point" by which the path of the world as we know it transitions to the counterfactual world, is a component of a complete understanding of any counterfactual argument. Instead of creating a fiated world out of whole cloth, the advocate is challenged to explain how the "nearest possible world" they advocate would most likely come into being. Policy advocates, in particular, would interpret the branching point in current politics which would lead to the hypothetical world they defend. Jon Elster's advice "that a counterfactual antecedent must be capable of insertion into the real past" (*Logic* 184) challenges us to investigate the most plausible process for reaching a counterfactual world. The idea of assuming a point in time and a process by which the actual world diverges from the counterfactual can be seen as a refinement to the Stalnaker-Lewis perspective on the nearest possible world.[1] It might appear at first blush that a strict application of the nearest possible world requirement would call forth a world of automatic change – new laws, for example, simply appearing on the books rather than going through legislative processes. Such a world would, however, be much farther from our own than would a world in which change occurred in more or less established ways. The concept of a branching point serves as a reminder that advocating a changed world also entails an understanding that the change has followed an identifiable and conventional process in coming into being. If fiat adheres to conventional ways of thinking about counterfactuals, then policy enaction would entail the assumption not that a policy avoided conventional process, but that the policy survived it.

In keeping with the previous advice that advocates are called upon to only defend the minimum change necessary, it is important to note that the idea of a branching point does not suggest that the proponent of change simply stipulates a preferred branching point. Rather, the most plausible branching point is assumed in the course of normal interpretation. While it may not be possible to prove at the level of truth whether one branching point is "correct" with regard to a potential alternate future, the relative closeness of branching points can be used to mediate the relative assertability of different counterfactual worlds.

APPLICATIONS

A counterfactual view of fiat has the potential to contribute arguments and ways of arguing to several disputes in contemporary academic debate. To demonstrate the utility of viewing fiat from this perspective, three such disputes will be considered.

Fiat and Disadvantage Ground. The availability of fiat to affirmative debaters, in itself, may no longer be seen as controversial, but as it relates to disadvantage opportunities for negative debaters, areas of controversy remain. Conventionally, the affirmative fiat entailed in offering a plan determines negative options and strategically avoids disadvantages. Initially, a counterfactual view of fiat would stress that despite its widespread acceptability, the ability to fiat would still depend on the form of the proposition. If the ability to fiat is limited by necessity, then affirmatives should entertain alternative conditions only when those alternatives form the antecedent of a conditional statement which is demanded by the proposition. Viewed in this way, fiat is not a choice but rather a reading of the resolution. The action that the affirmative fiats is not just their prerogative, it is their interpretation of what the resolution means: it is an argument about how the resolutional antecedent could come into being (or could have come into being).

For example, consider the Spring 1994 CEDA resolution, "Resolved: that the national news media in the United States impair public understanding of political issues." Despite the fact that many affirmatives on this topic advocated a plan to cure the ills of the news media, one could argue that the conditional statement "if the media were improved, then understanding of political issues would improve" is not necessarily entailed by the resolution since saying that the media could be improved is not the same as saying that they have impaired understanding. Based on this argument, the affirmative would not have available fiat to propose future cures because these cures would answer a question which has not been asked.

The question of the legitimacy of affirmative planning has diminished with the increasing policy-oriented consistency of topic selection by CEDA, but the character of the plans themselves has unearthed other fiat issues. For example, in order to avoid a disadvantage relating to Congressional backlash or Presidential popularity, is it germane for the affirmative to specify that their plan is proposed by the President and subsequently passed by Congress, or even passed by a two-thirds majority of Congress in order to override a Presidential veto? If that is viable, then would it also be acceptable to "fiat" that the plan is passed as a bi-partisan joint resolution or to specify that a given Senator votes with the majority? The ability to specify the process in detail seems to inherently impinge on reasonable process related disadvantages. Once affirmative teams are allowed to propose a process, it is not clear in current theory, exactly where that description crosses the line of reasonability.

The argument that the fiated world should involve the least possible change from the present world offers a potential avenue in addressing unrestricted specification by the affirmative team. In order to evaluate the advocated change employing only relevant and not gratuitous fiat, we should compare a world with that change and only that change to the world as we know it. If an affirmative debater defends passage of a regulation of environmental pollutants, then a nearest possible world construct would clarify that this debater defends a world which is as close to the present one as possible, with the addition of the specified new regulations on environmental pollutants.[2] The advocate would be argumentatively required to assume the existence of these regulations – to identify what pollutants would be regulated in what ways – because that is the resolution's antecedent. But if the resolution does not contain any reference to the time the regulation is implemented (e.g., "in two weeks," "after the election," etc.), the form of the regulation's passage (e.g., a congressional override of a Presidential veto), or the form of any compensating budgeting (e.g., an elimination of funding for the Strategic Defense Initiative), then fiat regarding those conditions would be irrelevant to the resolution and would not be argumentatively warranted.[3] Topically, affirmative advocates are required to consider the counterfactual condition of increased regulations, but have no logical reason to entertain counterfactuals addressing other aspects of the policy process: those processes, unlike the "increased regu-lations," already exist and need not be counterfactualized in order to be considered.[4] The affirmative team would fiat the action that the resolution requires, and then the rest of the world would be left to carry on as it otherwise would. Policies would be assumed to be passed based on more or less established procedures regarding time of implementation, method of passage, and strategies in fund-ing.[5] If advantages or disadvantages depended on such details, then evidence of the normal presence (or risk) of those details could be legitimately expected of advocates. By providing for plan imple-mentation in a way which would involve the least amount of collater-al change in the rest of the world, details which are naturally not spelled-out in a 15-second "plan" would be addressed with reference to the conventional political process.

A second opportunity to use conventional process as a way of avoiding gratuitous fiat can be found in the discovery of a plausible branching point for implementation. In advocating an expansion of the North American Free Trade Agreement, for example, we might assume a branching point which begins in the current legislative session. This would provide a basis for affirmative debaters to avoid specification and to assume instead that the plan would take an aver-age amount of time to move through the political process. If a process is already on-going, advocates could simply presume the continuation and favorable conclusion of that process. This would promote a realistic understanding of political process and bring fiat in line with a "natural language" view of advocacy: when I say that "Maryland should control auto emissions," I am not making a state-ment that depends on or assumes the instantaneous enaction of such controls, but neither am I making a statement that is blind to the manner in which such a proposal could come into existence. Instead, I am arguing for a policy change within the context of an existing policy process. A world in which legislators simply wake up one morning to find that a new law is inexplicably on the books is artificial. Conceiving of all the steps of implementation to have taken place "the moment you sign the ballot" similarly divorces the policy change from the policy process. If the creation of a counterfactual world naturally involves a plausible "on-ramp" from the present world as we know it, then it follows that debaters should assume that in advocating a policy change they are advocating the initiation and the favorable conclusion of a *process* of policy change.

The use of a conventional branching point aids in clarifying a natural time-frame for implementation. While in some ways this restricts negative ground (decreasing the relevance of disadvantages which presume instantaneous enaction), it increases opportunities in other ways by providing a basis for transition disadvantages. Legitimate negative consequences stem not only from the operation of a new policy, but also from the inevitable period of time in which a new policy is proposed, debated, and eventually passed.

Fiat and Counterplan Ground. Quite apart from the issue of whether and when the affirmative team can fiat, questions relating to the availability and content of negative fiat also have been very troublesome. Often, negative fiat has been justified on the basis of pragmatic considerations such as reciprocity, a need to defend something other than the status quo, or a preference for considering policy models other than those typically embraced by the resolution. Missing from this analysis is an argumentative grounding for negative fiat: What creates relevance for the negative team's act of proposing an alternative? What conditional statement is negative fiat answering? At least in the case of the conventionally-phrased policy resolution, there are two possible answers to this question, depending on what is meant by the auxiliary verb "should." Perkins has argued that "should" has an incremental sense, meaning that an action would be an improvement on current conditions, and an optimal sense, meaning that an action constitutes the best possible response to a situation (143). Contrasting the incremental "I should go to the movies" with the optimal "I should join the Army," Perkins argues that the statements differ in the comparative base that is suggested. Incrementally justified actions carry an implied comparison to the status quo while optimally justified actions are compared to the universe of other, presumably competitive, options. Perkins concludes that there ought to be no one single, correct use of "should," and that the definition of this term should depend, as other definitions depend, on the choice and the advocacy of the affirmative.

If that is the case, then the choice of a meaning for "should" has clear implications for fiat. If we assume an incremental use of "should," then the argument that we "should expand civil rights protection" is taken to mean that expanding such protection is better than what we are doing now. If counterfactualization springs from necessity, then there is no fiat for the opponent of such a claim. Negative fiat would be superfluous if the incremental "should" only suggests a comparison between the resolution's counterfactual antecedent and the present world as we know it. Viewed another way, the nearest possible world involving *non*-enaction of the affirmative's policy would always be the present world, because the least change is always no change.

If, on the other hand, we follow the more common practice of assuming that "should" is intended optimally, then the clearest argumentative rationale for negative fiat is that it addresses an opportunity cost of affirmation (see Branham). The alternative that we must forgo is relevant in evaluating the alternative that is being proposed. With this rationale, negative advocates can be seen as addressing the relevant conditional statement, "If alternatives which compete with the affirmative team's proposal were pursued instead, then the advantages would be greater." Their argument for legitimate fiat then would be as strong as their argument for considering their alternative as an opportunity cost of affirmation. Since affirmative advocates lack an argumentative warrant for proposing changes not contained or required in the resolution's antecedent, the same standard arguably holds for the negative. Constrained by relevance from alterations not contained or required in the resolution's antecedent, negative advocates should only fiat that which competes with resolutionally required elements of the affirmative's plan. If an affirmative, for example, fiats improved civil rights enforcement but does not fiat time of implementation, relying instead on a current political process then their opponents have no warrant for specifying an alternate process by fiating delayed implementation of the affirmative plan. The reason for this is that the only warrant for considering counterfactual alterations by the negative team is to test the optimal value *of those counterfactual alterations made by the affirmative team.* Negative fiat only gains relevance through competition with that which the affirmative fiats. Thus an affirmative team foreswearing gratuitous fiat regarding implementation details that are not resolutionally required can logically expect the same of the negative.

This limit to affirmative-competitive actions, however may not be seen as complete. A net benefits theory of competition for example would arguably permit all possible agent counterplans once a disadvantage unique to the affirmative agent is discovered. As discussed earlier, several so-called utopian counterplans (such as anarchy or world government) generally meet current standards of competition, but remain controversial nonetheless. One potential interpretation of a "nearest possible world" has the potential to provide an argumentative warrant against such counter-system counterplans. Taking a social-psychological perspective, Roese and Olson make use of norm theory as "the basic mechanism by which counterfactuals are constructed" (8) and as "the dominant theoretical perspective guiding counterfactual research" (16). As a natural limit on counterplan generation, norm theory posits that counterfactuals "recapitulate expectancies" in the sense that people will favor counterfactuals that tend toward what is normal and what is expected (8). In tests of this theory, for example, subjects will frequently be given some scenario and be asked to "undo" the result, or to consider how it could have been avoided. The dominant tendency is to mentally replace exceptional actions with actions tending more toward the norm. For example, "when John learns that he has failed a midterm examination following a particularly pernicious night of drinking, norm theory would predict John's thoughts to be that he would have passed had he drunk in greater moderation" (8). While there are other counterfactuals available to John (if only teachers did not test, if only the 18th Amendment had never been repealed), these actions are more unusual than the action he is evaluating and hence they are less likely to be selected as counterfactuals. This mental undoing of an action in order to evaluate it is parallel to the negative's action in undoing the affirmative, asking, "What if the affirmative proposal were not to be passed, what would the opportunity cost be?" "Counterfactuals are constructed," Roese and Olson conclude, "by converting deviations back into their default expectancies, such that counterfactuals recapitulate expectancies" (43). If we agree with Wittgenstein that meaning can be best conceived as the *use* to which concepts are put in practice among a community of language users, then it seems to follow that the *meaning* of the counterfactual relates to the way it is used by a normal pool of language users. Thus, a reason to prefer counterfactuals that tend toward greater expectancy is that they more accurately capture counterfactual meaning as it is defined in use.

The implication of this is that negative fiat is more legitimate when it alters in the direction of normalcy. This would suggest that negative fiat would be most relevant when it proposes a competitive solution that is *closer* than the affirmative to the norm in a given context. This application provides an alternate rationale for Perkins' solution: "When the affirmative chooses the degree of deviation from the probable by deciding upon a plan, the negative must conform to that choice" (149). Based on this argument, the negative habit of addressing affirmatives by proposing ever more radical alternatives would be suspect because it would not adhere to the conventional use of the counterfactual.[6]

Fiat and Critiques of Discourse. One of the more recent challenges to the meaning of fiat comes from advocates of emergent critiques of discourse, or arguments which seek to problematize some aspect of the language, advocacy, or assumptive framework of one's opponents.[7] Recent critique-oriented arguments have ranged from attacks on militaristic discourse (Dalby), humanism (Spanos), and normativity (Schlag). A central feature of the critique argument often involves a sharp distinction between the actual or extant harms and advantages identified by the critique and the "hypothetical" harms and advantages that exist only in the artificial world of fiat. The familiar expression that "fiat is an illusion" is often used to privilege critique arguments over all arguments grounded in fiat. The view of fiat embedded in many critiques is expressed by Mitchell:

> Advocacy, under this view of fiat, takes place on the plane of *simulation.* The power that backs a debater's command that "we mandate the following. . ." is a mirage, a phantasm allowed to masquerade as genuine for the purpose of allowing the game of political simulation to take place. Debaters have no real authority over the actors they employ to implement their ideas in plans and counterplans, yet the simulation of such authority is recognized as an essential fiction necessary to allow the game of policy debate to unfold (2).

The critique gains its distinction, the argument goes, by transcending this pretense and identifying reasons to accept or reject ideas based only on our status as participants and advocates, not policymakers. Stated in these terms, a critique may not fully account for the "reality" of fiat. While a counterfactual view of fiat should not diminish the importance and utility of critiques, it can promote a more realistic view of fiat as it regards critiques. Specifically, two relevant conclusions can be drawn: fiat is not illusory, and advocates do not bear responsibility for aspects of the world that they are not argumentatively empowered to change.

First, a counterfactual view of fiat provides a rationale for the argument that fiat is not illusory. By examining the argumentative origin of fiat, it becomes clear that the counterfactual world is the antecedent half of a conditional statement. When I muse, "If I stay up to watch the movie, then I will not be able to wake up for work tomorrow morning," I am merely arguing in favor of a relationship between two potential events. In no way am I *pretending* to stay up and watch the movie, and I am not under the *illusion* that I actually have stayed up to watch the movie. In order to entertain the counterfactual, I do *imagine* that I've stayed up to watch the movie, but presuming my mental stability, I am not deceived into actually thinking that I *have* watched the movie, or even that I necessarily will watch the movie. Rather than being a deliberate flight of fancy, counterfactualization is simply a mental test that I or any reasonable person can accomplish without leaving reality. While advocates do truncate claims (e.g., "we will implement . . ." as a shorthand for "we support the implementation of . . .") this does not demonstrably have the psychological effect of causing advocates to begin to believe and act as though their counterfactual suppositions are coming true. The most common sense view of fiat, then, is to regard it as simply a conditional statement, warranted by the resolution that is under discussion, and not as a dangerous lie.

Second, limiting fiat to the least possible change logically would relieve advocates of the responsibility to defend aspects of the world that they are not empowered to change. If advocates defend a world which includes the resolution's antecedent but which makes relevant no additional changes (the nearest possible world), then the affirmative is logically responsible for the addition of the resolution's antecedent (e.g., the plan) but they are not logically responsible for a failure to change the remainder of the world. The argument that by using the current policy process I am "endorsing" its racism, its legal oppression, its sexism, etc., presumes that the act of using current means is a constitutive act. If our perspective is not informed by counterfactual theory, then an affirmative might be seen as doing just that: using fiat to create a fully-formed world, which includes the new plan, but also re-introduces and hence endorses all of the vestiges of the old world which have not been changed. In contrast, based on a counterfactual view, fiat is circumscribed by relevance and thus includes only the resolution's antecedent. The rest of the world remains the same, not because we would like it to remain the same, but because there is no argumentative warrant for its alteration. Elements of the world left unchanged by fiat, then, should not become subject to critique for that reason. Viewed in this context, the advocate who advanced arguments containing hegemonic assumptions would be more open to critique than the advocate who merely endorsed change within a process that is otherwise hegemonic.

The foregoing should not be read as a repudiation of critiques, because critiques do not require the belief that fiat is an illusion nor do they require advocates to defend more than they are responsible for changing. Critiques should matter, not because debaters perpetuate dangerous lies, nor because debaters lack the power to fix all social evils, but because advocacy contains embedded assumptions which should be legitimately open to criticism.

CONCLUSION

Seen as an aspect of argument and not just a feature of debate, fiat stems from a perfectly understandable concern for relevance. Grounding fiat in counterfactual analysis has the advantages of reinforcing the propositional origin of fiat, extending fiat beyond the simple policymaking analogy, and providing a hueristic base for arguments over the appropriate availability and content of fiat. Applying a counterfactual understanding to current controversies in fiat has the potential to clarify the role of political process, to ground and limit negative fiat, and to provide an account of the "reality" of argumentative fiat. While the preceding applications certainly do not answer all of the vexing ambiguities of fiat, hopefully they do suggest a potential argumentative palette for debaters and other theorists. A counterfactual framework reinforces the notion of fiat as a component of argument, not as an external game rule. It also builds a case for natural checks on fiat, encouraging the advocate to investigate the way counterfactual claims are made and understood in conventional discourse. In promoting a reliance on current processes that need not be counterfactualized, this perspective may also act as a substantial inducement for debaters to understand and react to the policy process rather than simply erasing it with the force of assumed action.

WORKS CITED

Berube, David and Kristina Pray. "Arguing Counterfactuals." *Non-Policy Debating.* Ed. David Berube. New York: University Press of America, 1994: 325-339.

Branham, Robert, "Roads Not Taken: Counterplans and Opportunity Costs." *Journal of the American Forensic Association* 25 (1989): 246-55.

Broda-Bahm, Kenneth T. "Counterfactual Possibilities: Constructing Counter-to-Fact Causal Claims." *Contemporary Argumentation and Debate: The Journal of the Cross Examination Debate Association* 16 (1995): 73-85.

—. "Counterfactual Problems: Addressing Difficulties in the Advocacy of Counter-to-Fact Causal Claims." *Contemporary Argumentation and Debate: The Journal of the Cross Examination Debate Association* 17 (1996): 19-31.

Broda-Bahm, Kenneth T. and Thomas L. Murphy. "A Defense of Critique Arguments: Beyond the Resolutional Question." *CEDA Yearbook* 15 (1994): 20-32.

Dalby, Simon. *Creating the Second Cold War: The Discourse of Politics.* New York: Guilford, 1990.

Dempsey, Richard. H. and David J. Hartman. "Mirror State Counterplans: Illegitimate, Topical or Magical? *Journal of the American Forensic Association* 21 (1985): 161-166.

Edwards, Richard E. "In Defense of Utopia: A Response to Katsulas, Herbeck, and Panetta. *Journal of the American Forensic Association* 24 (1987): 112-118.

Elster, Jon. *Logic and Society: Contradictions and Possible Worlds.* New York: John Wiley & Sons, 1978.

—. Reply to Comments. *Inquiry* 23:2 (1980): 213-32.

Fadely, Dean. "What Makes a Fiat Run?" *Debate Issues* (November 1985): 7-9.

Flaningham, Carl D. "Concomitant vs. omparative Advantages: Sufficient vs. Necessary Conditions." *Journal of the American Forensic Association* 18 (1981): 1-8.

Freeley, Austin. *Argumentation and Debate: Critical Thinking for Reasoned Decision Making* 9th ed. New York: Wadsworth, 1996.

Hanson, Jim. *NTC's Dictionary of Debate.* Lincolnwood, IL: National Textbook Company, 1990.

Hoe, Josh. "Counterfactuals in a Post-Cold War World." Paper presented at the meeting of the Speech Communication Association, New Orleans, LA, 1994.

Hoch, Stephen J. "Counterfactual Reasoning and Accuracy in Predicting Personal Events." *Journal of Experimental Psychology: Learning, Memory, and Cognition* 11:4 (1985): 719-731.

Hynes, Timothy J. *Debating Counterplans: Modern Theory and Practice.* San Francisco: Griffin Research, 1987.

Johnson, Marcia K. and Steven J. Sherman. "Constructing and Reconstructing the Past and the Future in the Present." *Handbook of Motivation and Cognition: Foundations of Social Behavior* Vol. 2. Eds. E. Tory Higgins and Richard M. Sorrentino. New York: Guilford, 1990: 482-526.

Katsulas, John P., Dale A. Herbeck, and Edward M. Panetta. "Fiating Utopia: A Negative View of the Emergence of World Order Counterplans and Futures Gaming in Policy Debate." *Journal of the American Forensic Association* 24 (1987): 95-111.

Korcok, Michael. "The Bases of Counterfactual Comparison." Paper presented at the meeting of the Speech Communication Association, New Orleans, LA, 1994.

Lambertson, F. W. "The Meaning of the Word 'Should' in a Question of Policy." *Quarterly Journal of Speech* 28 (1942): 421-424.

Lewis, David K. *Counterfactuals.* Cambridge: Harvard University Press, 1973.

McGee, Brian R. and David Romanelli. "Policy Debate as Fiction: In Defense of Utopian Fiat." *Contemporary Argumentation and*

Debate: The Journal of the Cross Examination Debate Association 18 (1997): 23-35.

Mills, Glen E. *Reason in Controversy: On General Argumentation* 2nd ed. Boston: Allyn & Bacon, 1968.

Mitchell, Gordon. "Reflexive Fiat: Incorporating the Outward Activist Turn Into Contest Strategy." Paper presented at the meeting of the Speech Communication Association, San Antonio, TX, 1995.

Musgrave, George McCoy. *Competitive Debate: Rules and Techniques* 3rd ed. New York: H.W. Wilson, 1957.

Patterson J. W. and David Zarefsky. *Contemporary Debate.* Boston: Houghton Mifflin, 1983.

Perkins, Dallas. "Counterplans and Paradigms." *Journal of the American Forensic Association* 25 (1989): 140-149.

Rescher, Nicholas. "Belief Contravening Suppositions." *Philosophical Review* 70 (1961): 176-196.

Roese, Neal J. and James M. Olson. "Counterfactual Thinking: A Critical Overview." *What Might Have Been: The Social Psychology of Counterfactual Thinking.* Eds. Neal J. Roese and James M. Olson. Mahwah, NJ: Erlbaum, 1995: 1-55.

Roskoski, Matt. A Defense of Counterfactual Reasoning in CEDA Debate. Paper presented at the meeting of the Speech Communication Association, Chicago, IL., 1992

Schlag, Pierre. "Normativity and the Politics of Form." *University of Pennsylvania Law Review* 139 (April, 1991).

Snider, Alfred C. "Fantasy and Reality Revisited: Gaming, Fiat Power, and Anti-Utopianism." *Journal of the American Forensic Association* 24 (1987): 119-129.

Solt, Roger. "Negative Fiat: Resolving the Ambiguities of 'Should.'" *Journal of the American Forensic Association* 25 (1989): 121-139.

Spanos, William V. *Heidegger and Criticism: Retrieving the Cultural Politics of Destruction.* Minneapolis: University of Minnesota Press, 1992.

Summers, Harrison Boyd, Forest Livings Whan, and Thomas Andrew Rouse. *How to Debate: A Textbook for Beginners.* New York: H.W. Wilson, 1950.

Stalnaker, Robert C. "A Theory of Conditionals." *Studies in Logical Theory.* Ed. Nicholas Rescher. Oxford: Basil Blackwell, 1968:

98-112.

Voight, Phillip T. "Thinking in Time: The Importance of Temporal Location in Argument." *Contemporary Argumentation and Debate: The Journal of the Cross Examination Debate Association* 16 (1995): 86-97.

Voight, Phillip T. and Susan Stanfield. "Shortening Cleopatra's Nose: The Fallacy of Counter Factual Argumentation." Paper presented at the meeting of the Speech Communication Association, Chicago, IL, 1992.

Wittgenstein, Ludwig. *Philosophical Investigations*. Trans. G. E. M. Anscombe. 3rd ed. Oxford: Basil Blackwell. 1968.

NOTES

[1] While Elster states that his goal is "to demolish the Lewis-Stalnaker theory of truth conditions in terms of possible worlds" (*Logic* 182), by criticizing the idea that fully-formed possible worlds can be rank-ordered in measurable units of "closeness," he also makes clear that he accepts the general idea that a compared world needs to be as close as possible to the actual world. In discussing Hitler as a cause of World War II, for example, he notes, "What we want to say is that the Second World War would not have occurred if we assume the early death of Hitler and *a minimum of other changes*" (*Logic* 186). On the subject of requiring the minimum of alterations, Elster says, "any account of counterfactuals that ignores this requirement is a non-starter" (*Reply* 220).

[2] It might be charged that a nearest possible world approach would encourage the smallest conceivable affirmative plan: an environmental regulation permitting the emission of just one fewer carbon dioxide molecule, for example. This would be an inaccurate application of the theory. The construct calls not for the "nearest possible antecedent" but rather for the antecedent, however specified, to be true in the nearest possible world. How the resolution's antecedent is characterized is a matter of how the advocate chooses to define and operationalize the terms of the resolution.

[3] This solution is similar to one advocated by Carl Flaningham. Referring to the results of actions not directly necessitated by the resolution as "concomitant advantages," Flaningham argues that these advantages stemming from the *manner* of affirmation detract from a comparative focus on the resolution and its alternatives.

[4] It is conceivable that a resolution could propose a change for which there is no "normal" process of implementation. The proposal of such a change, *would* seem to argumentatively necessitate some specification of process, but a process closest to *status quo* implementation procedures otherwise in force would still be preferred.

5 This is not to suggest that current policies and procedures ("normal means") are best, or even that they are good. Avoiding an alteration of these procedures through fiat merely follows from a recognition that there is no resolutional warrant for counterfactually altering these procedures.

6 This is not to suggest that radical counter-system proposals are unrealistic or harmful to the debate process (as has been suggested by others, e.g., Katsulas, Herbeck, & Panetta), but to instead suggest one way of arguing that such solutions are less relevant to the evaluation of incremental policy alternatives.

7 Such arguments are frequently referred to as "Kritiks" as a way of highlighting their affinity for continental schools of thought in philosophy.

Ken Broda-Bahm (Ph.D., Southern Illinois University) is an Associate Professor in Communication Studies at Towson University, in Towson, Maryland. This essay was originally published in volume 20 (1999) of *Contemporary Argumentation and Debate*, pp. 1-23.

FIAT AND THE
CIRCUMVENTION ARGUMENT
David M. Berube

In the mid-nineties, hardly a high school or college student has been able to avoid customizable card games such as Wizards of the Coast, Inc. 'Magic: The Gathering™' and its clones. Competent game designers understand the importance of moves and countermoves. For every move, there must be a plausible countermove otherwise the game would be won by whomever could afford the most catastrophic, most rare, and most expensive card. Moreover, card designers must avoid cascading, whereby an action forecloses or makes redundant other actions, nullifying incidentally implicated strategies and tactics. For example, computer programmers and debuggers know from experience that changing a single line of text can have fatal consequences throughout a program.

My thesis is that like inexperienced game designers and computer programmers, we have attempted to resolve paradoxical problems in academic debate by moves and countermoves, but the gestalt of these adjustments has not made debate such a great game to play.[1] Two occurrences will be examined below. First, we surrendered the stock issues model for the systems analysis model without shucking all the stock issues baggage. Then, we changed the meaning of inherency from "why non-topical actions have not and could not get the affirmative advantages or solve the affirmative harms" (Schunk, "Affirmative Fiat" 87) to "uniqueness of actions taken, rather than uniqueness of benefits claimed" (Flaningham, "Inherency" 233).[2] These two events have profoundly affected our understanding of fiat and the legitimacy of solvency arguments such as circumvention. The essential purpose of this essay is to defend the circumvention argument as a viable counterbalance to the expansive interpretation of fiat.

Consider the following illustrations. A negative policy debater argues that the plan, say the extension of Title VII protection to cases involving same-sex harassment, will never be enforced: the Equal Employment Opportunity Commission (EEOC) will disfavor cases involving gays, and poverty and public interest lawyers will not take up the cases. She argues the EEOC are political creatures who reflect the biases in society at large. The affirmative responds: "Fiat!" The negative claims: "This is fiat abuse!" In another round, a negative policy debater argues that adoption of this plan will need some shifting of constituencies or blocs in Congress to accommodate the changes in thinking needed to implement the plan mandates. Those shifts might preclude consideration of important policies, which would compete with the political capital of the plan. The affirmative policy debater responds: "We fiat through that problem – the plan is implemented and any argument occurring before that point is 'should-would' and not germane." The negative responds: "This is fiat abuse!"

While the abuse claimed by the negative in both illustrations might be difficult to sustain, our understanding of fiat is so unclear that we have no basis for arbitrating fiat abuse claims when dealing with implementation based arguments. The following will try to clarify some of these issues.

DEFINING "SHOULD"

Before we can have any handle on determining what fiat abuse means, we need to understand how the term "should" is used in policy resolutions. Since fiat is assumed to trump policy arguments which exist outside the scope of should, the term's meaning is elementary to understanding fiat's purpose in debating.

"If should means 'ought to be' but not necessarily 'will be,' then

. . . affirmative teams are not required to consider political obstacles to adopting their policy suggestions" (Lichtman and Rohrer 241). Arguments which are grounded in such obstacles have been dubbed "should-would" arguments. There seems to be good reason for distinguishing between arguments grounded in "should" and those grounded in "would," since the latter are questionably productive. Schunk and others argue against predicting the behavior of policy makers for two primary reasons: it would encourage research about bureaucratic behavior which may not be pedagogically defensible for contest debaters, and determining the rationale for voting behavior is highly suspect since self-reporting is often aspirational rather than realistic, and interpretive assessment might be impossible given the remoteness of the actors.

While "should" might not mean "would," it surely means "could." One of the earliest debate references to the "could" or "can" duty associated with "should" and "ought" statements was made by Lambertson more than five decades ago. "The word 'should' includes the word 'could'. . . . The word 'could' connotes that the remedy is within the realm of possibility" (424, 423). Fitzgerald offers a simple standard to delineate between "could" and "would" considerations:

> The "could" dimension pertains essentially to the mechanics of the plan: to issues of workability and the ability of the proposal to reconcile the inherency problems of the present system. The "would" dimension, on the other hand, will encompass the motivational forces that speak to the practical concerns of getting a proposal implemented: practicality or issues of enactment and enforcement (102).

For Fitzgerald, we "ought" not do what we "cannot" do; the affirmative plan must solve for the shortcomings of the present system that impede the plan. Once resolved, however, it is fair to assume that opposition to the plan will be resolved as well and sufficient resources to bolster the plan will be forthcoming. So, once the shortcomings are solved, motivations associated with and potentially disruptive to the plan will be solved. Unfortunately, it is not that simple.

Before considering the range of options, it is prudent to learn more about "should" as "could." The first reason "ought" means "could" is steeped in pragmatics. Even when we ought to do a thing, obligations are relaxed, if not voided, when we cannot do that thing. Indeed, "we may excuse a man [sic] on the ground that he [sic] could not do what he [sic] ought to have done; circumstances prevented him [sic] from acting appropriately" (Margolis 37). The principle is straightforward: "If a person has no control over what he [sic] can or cannot do, over what he [sic] could or could not have done, in short, over his [sic] life, there might well be no wrong or blameworthy action" (Stocker 316). Consider Radin's discussion of the Rule of Law:

> To regulate conduct, and thereby achieve the social coopera-
> tion necessary for justice, rules must have certain characteris-
> tics associated with the Rule of Law: "Ought implies can." The
> addressees must have the ability to conform, and the authori-
> ties must act in good faith. Impossibility of conformance, there-
> fore, must be recognized as a defense (788).

This doctrine has been applied frequently. "That an agent could not have done the act that he [sic] allegedly ought to have done (or could not have omitted what he allegedly ought not to have done) is also sometimes offered as a defense against the charge of wrongdoing. This appeals to the principle that 'ought' implies 'can'" (McConnell 437).

Another reason is grounded is essentialism. "The 'ought implies can' principle requires that normative advice in epistemological matters not be designed to ideal knowers, but to real-world knowers. . ." (Leiter 815). Lipkin provided a classic illustration: "For men to be obligated not to have abortions, they must be capable of having abortions, which means they must be capable of having children. Since men are incapable of having abortion, it is physically impossible for the state to impose the same burden on them as on women" (1080).

A third reason treats "could" in reference to free choice. "Whatever else the principle that 'ought implies can' means, it seems to be telling us that there is an important connection between 'ought' statements and freedom. . . . The idea is that actions that a person cannot avoid doing are not ones that he ought to do. Nor, of course are they ones that he ought to avoid doing" (McConnell 440). Tranoy sets a much more definitive standard:

> It is no more than common sense that it is not legitimate (or not permissible, unjustifiable, unreasonable) to ask the impossible, to demand more than (you know) you can get from a person.... "Ought implies can" can be read as a general restriction placed on the right of any person b to act as a norm giver (norm authority) for a norm subject (norm-receiver) a. ... If an action p is (known to be) impossible to perform for a person a, then no other person b is permitted (is justified, is entitled, has the right) to order a to do p or to place a under an obligation to do p (120).

While this precept is framed in terms of individual action, debate resolutions generally are not written with individual agents in mind. Unless you can assume institutions are individuals, this point of view on the "couldness" of "should" might be problematic. However, we know that institutions have emergent characteristics that exceed the totality of the individuals so incorporated, hence they are individuating. As such, the "ought implies can" principle has been applied to institutions. "Because ought implies can, governments cannot be held responsible for failure to produce systems they cannot realistically create" (Balkin 1969).

It would be academically irresponsible to lead the reader to conclude that "ought" always means "could." There are many exceptions, but they can be grouped into two categories. The first deals with statements expressing ideals. "In what might be called an ideal-expressing or axiological mode – it would be good [or better or best] if – 'ought' clearly does not imply 'can.' A moral "ought" can also be taken in a deontological way, given by such obligation notions as 'obligatory,' 'duty,' 'wrong not to do'" (Stocker 304).

"Ideal-expressing 'oughts' – such as in the statement, 'there ought to be no war' – do not imply 'can'" (McConnell 438). In fact, many people are faced with the duty to do the impossible. "The alcoholic may be placed under a prohibition not to touch liquor by well-meaning and ignorant moralists. A soldier may be ordered to do that which it is impossible for him to do. . ." (Tranoy 118, 122).

Tranoy and others perceive a few problems with these ideal

expressing statements, one of which Tranoy calls the "bridge principle:"

> In any moral system there must, then, be at least one moral ele-
> ment, which cannot be the logical consequence of any other
> moral or non-moral element (or combination of elements) in the
> system. Yet it must be possible to argue and to give reasons in
> support of such a primitive moral element. If these two conditions
> are not fulfilled, a normative ethics is again made impossible:
> either it would founder on a violation of Hume's thesis or on the
> threat of an infinite regress, or it would have to be the product of
> unprincipled arbitrariness. . . . Moreover, it takes but little
> reflection to see that a primitive norm (the bridge principle) must
> not be conceived to be tautologous, or analytic, or self-evident and
> "intuitively certain," or again the outcome of arbitrary stipulation.
> . . . Furthermore, we know that systematically and deliberately
> asking, requiring, ordering, pressing people to do the impossible,
> and to abstain from the necessary/indispensable, leads to their
> undoing. This is elementary. But I think I am trying to say more
> than that. Acceptance of the meta-norm (the bridge principle) is
> prior to all moral agreement and disagreement; it is a necessary
> condition for the possibility of a moral point of view. It is in this
> sense that it is constitutive of any and all forms of life (124,
> 128-129).

Also, if the impossible can be demanded of a norm-receiver, Tranoy
foresees an incredible normative paradox:

> A generally, universally valid norm permitting norm-givers to
> order norm subjects to do the impossible might, indeed, serve to
> make any form of human life impossible if it were to be practiced
> on an extended scale. It would legitimate the existence of inhu-
> man worlds. It might thus be held to be a normatively self-defeat-
> ing norm (123).

The second major category of exceptions are linguistic in nature.
There is the definitional issue. There are many "oughts": the ought of
prediction (she's never late for a round, she ought to get here soon);
the ought of duty (she promised to complete her assignment, it ought

to be on your desk); the ought of urging (she can speak clearer and ought to try); the ought of wishing (there really ought to be free on-line text retrieval for everyone); the ought of advising (you ought to debate at a better university) (Smith 362-363); and the ought of the superogatory (one ought to accept the loss and turn the other cheek) (Dahl 487). For me, what happens in debate may be closer to advising or the superogatory, since people involved in the debate are not empowered to resolve the action contemplated within the resolutional statement. As such, definitional quibbling does not seem the fracture the "ought-could" conjunction.

An exception to a strict interpretation also has been grounded in the speech act itself. "Part of any adequate theory of conversation is to treat instances critically and not to take them at face value" (Martinich 327). Martinich's reservations have been voiced elsewhere, but J. L. Austin gave the finest criticism.

> If, for example, the speaker is not in a position to perform an act of that kind, or if the object with respect to which he [sic] purports to perform is not suitable for the purpose, then he [sic] doesn't manage, simply by issuing his [sic] utterance, to carry out the purported act. . . . Now people have, I know, the impression that where a statement, a constative utterance, is in question, the case is quite different; anybody at all can say anything at all. What if he's [sic] ill-informed? Well then, one can be mistaken, that's all. It's a free country, isn't it? To state what isn't true is one of the Rights of Man [sic]. However, this impression can lead us into error. In reality nothing is more common than to find that one can state absolutely nothing on some subject, because one is simply not in a position to state whatever it may be – and this may come about, too, for more than one reason. . . (14, 19-20).

Hence, the distinction between the speech act in a debate, for example, and the constative of a promise or command is arbitrary. Consequently, speech act associated exceptions to the ought implies can principle are suspect.

This examination has led me to conclude that arguments favoring a strict "could" obligation associated with a "should" statement are important to improve the play of the game of debating. It has produced two important conclusions: "should" does not imply a "will" or "would" obligation, yet does imply a "can" or "could" obligation. Enter fiat as the wild card.

THE GENESIS OF FIAT

Fiat is one of the most powerful, if not pernicious, conventions established in debating. In the days of stock issues, students were taught about stases. Two stases, blame and cure, were incorporated into policy debate as the stock issues inherency and solvency. Evidently, it was perceived that inherency and solvency might be difficult to prove without contradicting oneself. In response, the debate community decided that arguments associated with the conflict between these two stock issues would be short-circuited: we would call them "should-would" and we would exclude them from the decision calculus of the critic.

It is likely that fiat was introduced into policy debate to avoid the should-would conundrum. In essence, fiat is "the authority of the word should" (McGee 16). It allows an advocate to assume policy adoption, so system implications, desirable and undesirable, can be compared. In describing how fiat works, a metaphor was used: It is like an act of God. In time, the metaphor grew legs and became a power in itself.

Unfortunately, as our way of thinking about the game of debating changed, the fiat rule remained unchanged. Along with Lichtman and Rohrer and, more recently, Madsen, a competing paradigm, systems analysis or policy-making, surfaced and was extended. This paradigm transformed debaters and the critic(s) into policy makers (legislative or judicial), and they approached the debate as their real world counterparts might approach making law.

Systems analysts, a.k.a. policy makers, changed debate profoundly. Their first effect was on inherency. For the policy systems analyst, at least, inherency assumed a probability function, an essentially new role.

> Inherency, in short, answers the question, why is one system more likely than another to maximize the desired goal? What makes one system more efficacious than another. . . ? The essence of the problem is that the present system chooses not to pursue absolute goals. It chooses not to commit its energies and resources in the pursuit of a particular value in a vacuum. In policy arena after pol-

icy arena, this is the only reasonable explanation as to why presumably good people tolerate evil (Pfau, "Part One" 82).

In order to remove the debate from some of the real world considerations of politics, fiat was embraced again. To remove constituency sating, porkbarreling, partisan or party line voting, and vote trading, etc., from the purview of the debate and the judge, the would part of the debate was again short-circuited with fiat.

The affirmative, in a better position to demonstrate probable efficacy for their proposal because of affirmative single-mindedness, chose to move from inherency as a barrier to inherency as a description of the status quo. In other words, the plan does not exist, hence it is inherent; fiat makes it exist, hence it resolves the inherency in the system. Indeed, the highly misleading term "existential inherency" has been used to describe the status quo. In systems analysis speak, the plan was secured via fiat to reprioritize policy decisions to favor the affirmative plan.

Other developments followed. In time, systems analysis allowed the introduction of the comparative advantage case. As cost-benefit analysis became part of budget planning during the Kennedy administration, it pervaded policy discourse. The cost-benefit calculus seemed to favor even fine improvements over the status quo by undervaluing any innate merit to inaction. Therefore, affirmatives argued that any improvements over a working status quo were grounds for adoption as long as the benefits of the plan exceeded disadvantages to it.

One result was the further weakening of inherency. By its nature, "in the so-called comparative advantages case. . . , strictly speaking, the affirmative does not indict the status quo, the inherent need flows from the fixed point which might be phrased as follows: If there is a better way to solve a problem (all things being equal), then that solution should be adopted" (Mader 20). "The affirmative does not necessarily have to demonstrate specific inherent problems in the status quo. Rather, they may choose to focus on the necessary (one might even say inherent) possibility that harms will accrue from minor defects in the machinery of existing policy. This possibility is cause by the very existence of the status quo" (Cronen 247).

Though the emphasis may have shifted, Zarefsky argues the obligations had not changed and that any dichotomy is false. "What is required for a determination of inherency is to decide what is the essence of the present system, and whether that essence must be changed to achieve the goals of the proposal. . . . In addition, the advantages alleged by the affirmative must, logically, inhere in the proposal adopted" ("The Traditional Case" 13, 14). Nonetheless, plans were driven by descriptive (or existential) inherency, and affirmatives rejected essentializing their advantages to the plan, thereby avoiding "intrinsicness" considerations.

Systems analyst innovator Kunkler disagreed with Zarefsky, arguing that inherency in policy making is field dependent and that its discovery lies in the comparison of two systems. Essentializing the *per se* advantages would not be necessary:

> The affirmative demonstrated inherency when it showed that the new system has characteristics different from the old and that they are not only responsible for the gained positive effects, but that they also flow from the proposition. So the substantial nature of inherency, which varies from topic to topic, is discovered more from a comparison of two systems rather than from a causal analysis of present circumstances (cited in Brock et al. 157).

Negative strategies against the comparative advantages case have become problematic. Traditionally, the negative would have "show[n] that the advantages can be obtained from the status quo itself, or from minor repairs of the status quo. . ." (Thomas and Anderson 156). They continued: "The second line of argument against the causal connection between the plan and the advantages is to show how the advantages can be obtained without adopting the plan, that is, to prove that the plan is not a necessary cause for the alleged effects. ... If the alleged advantages can be gained by means other than the affirmative plan, the affirmative team has the burden to prove that its plan is superior to those other means" (157). The minor repair briefly became the hypothetical counterplan, before becoming an unconditional one. Testing for necessity started as justification, became the intrinsicness argument, and was rejected as infinitely regressive.

Next, systems analysis popularized attitudinal inherency. In an attempt to mirror more exactly the issues confronting policy makers, motives crept back into the discussion of inherency. This time it was about attitudes. Attitudinal inherency refers to the affirmative argument that the reason the present system is not considering the policy at issue is an irrational (read as not persuadable by rational affirmative claims) predisposition against it:

> Generally the attitudinal inherency case is developed by arguing that the present system's inability to achieve a given goal is a function of that system's control by a group of men [sic] who are attitudinally opposed to that goal, or who find other conflicting goals more desirable. Thus, it is the attitudinal bias of powerful men [sic], rather than an inherent structural flaw, which prevents the system from optimal performance vis-a-vis a given goal (Ling and Seltzer 278).

Cherwitz and Hikins not only argued that ". . . all inherency arguments are attitudinal since all institutions are rooted in motives," but also demanded that the inherency burden not stop at fingerpointing (89). Attitudinal inherency can be mitigated by the plan mandates.

> What makes a problem truly inherent is the point at which attitude, structure, implementation, and means merge. In short, it is only the bringing together of final, formal, efficient, and material cause that attests to the status quo's inherent capacity to rectify a problem. For that reason, all affirmative cases are reflecting of the properties of attitudinal inherency; but, no matter what one calls them, they must not be confined to a delineation of attitude alone (89-90).

Therefore, either the plan should deny power to the presently controlling group or the plan should be enacted through a second group unaffected by the attitudinal bias. An example of the first would involve removing the EEOC from its gatekeeping role if the EEOC was insensitive to the civil rights of a proscribed group. An example of the second can be drawn from history. The federal government secured civil rights for African-Americans in the 1950s when it became clear the states were not rising to the challenge.

This view did not abandon the notion of "structural flaw" which pervaded the old inherency. The new inherency viewed a structure that allowed perverse attitudes to affect it as "a flawed structure," but rather than repair it they argued to replace it with one which was not flawed.

In essence, fiat was perverted when affirmatives decided to avoid their inherency by fiating it away. "If as the affirmative case argues, policy makers do not currently want the affirmative policy, then they will find ways to see that the affirmative plan is not put into effect. Affirmative debaters, wanting to have their cake and eat it too, have responded with the magical power of fiat, mandating policy action to override these currently opposing attitudes" (Schunk, "Affirmative Fiat" 84). At times, the affirmative, as if seduced, blindly uses fiat as a way to cancel the inherency claim rather than using the plan to avoid the inherency construct; as such, they fiat solvency with the plan. Some critics have found this practice self-defeating.

> It is the affirmative who has introduced a "would" dimension into the debate. However, having introduced it, the affirmative is unwilling to be bound by this "would" dimension in the consideration of the affirmative proposal. . . . When they "will" their plan into existence or depend upon an act of God, they are saying, in effect, that they cannot change the attitudes of men [sic]. They are saying that ultimately men [sic] cannot be convinced by reason to change their way of thinking . . . If such a premise is accepted, it then follows that debate is a meaningless activity because decision making is outside the realm of rational processes (Ling and Seltzer 280).

Nonetheless, attitudinal inherency is pervasive, but plans that actually resolve the bases or mechanisms of the attitudinal inherency are not.

Finally, systems analysis introduced the concept of "normal means." Systems analysis and fiat compressed the process of adoption: inception, composition, construction, discussion, amendment, compromise, veto, override, and judicial interpretation were undertaken by "normal means." Arguments such as "Congress will repeal the affirmative plan after its adoption," "Congress will refuse to fund the plan," "an executive agency will refuse to enforce the plan," "the Supreme Court will strike down the plan," etc. might be labeled should-would and considered not germane to implementation, but arguments associated with the effects of implementation on the political culture were retained. Witness the prevalence of political process disadvantages.

Some may think that the notion of should – and affirmative fiat –

obviates the need to consider all political variables associated with the implementation of policy. This assumption seems erroneous. For example, post-fiat, the impacts of the plan on political capital and resources are rich grounds for disadvantages of all sorts.

> The political tension, generated both by the adoption of a particular policy and by the use of affirmative fiat, will result in costs which manifest themselves in terms of thwarting of present system alternatives – both present and future . . . [and] affirmative plans, which mandate action in pursuit of one objective, will reduce the total pool of inputs . . . which makes them less available for some future agenda. (Pfau, "Part Two" 149).

Nevertheless, "acts of fiat" disadvantages remain particularly absurd. Occasionally, we find the word "fiat" used in discourse about government and politics. Nearly without exception, such fiat is derided. Some debaters have tried taking the "fiat" referred to in political discourse, comparing it to "fiat" associated with "should-would" arguments in debate, cross-applying the discursive commentary, and claiming affirmative fiat should be rejected. On one level, the "fiats" are incomparable and the reference requires equivocation. One another level, there are no costs associated with the act of fiat because fiat is not real: actually, it is never used. It is paradoxical in that it never happens, it only happened. It has no spatial location, hence, it has no effect in real time and space. It predicates nothing. Fiat was designed merely to suspend the examination of some political variables in order to foster a more complete comparison of effects. It does not absolve the affirmative from the political consequences of "normal means."

The issue before us is: What, if any, political issues pre- and compressed-fiat remain outside the realm of "should-would" arguments. Prior to and during fiat (within the compressed time), all political capital which is expended, but left uncompensated by the plan, is relevant and not suspended by the should-would label or the fiat magic wand. Fiat does not empower the affirmative to cancel their inherency. They remain obligated to design a plan that either eliminates the motive for the attitude(s) or the mechanisms through which the attitude(s) find expression.

All these policy-making developments have confounded the status of fiat in contemporary debating practice. We have reached the point whereby affirmatives may fiat de facto advantages by ignoring the inherency of the problem, merely wishing it away. The negative has tried to respond. If the debate community was not willing to rewrite the fiat rule, negatives would find strategies and tactics to circumnavigate it. And, the cascading of the game began.

THE NEGATIVE RESPONDS TO FIAT

Fiat abuse fired up the negative to fight for disadvantage links. For example, Cheshier warned that fiat removes from consideration important implementation details, which need to be recaptured as ground for the negative.

> The politics of enactment are very much part of the policy landscape, but too often these arguments are dismissed as inappropriate to policy debate (they are "should-would" arguments; "fiat lets us assume Congress will support the plan"; "political capital consequences that would result in weakening of the plan's mandates can be ignored – we can fiat over that," and so on). Although we permit, by kind of mutual agreement, some political capital arguments (thus the popularity of the Clinton disadvantage, movement arguments, etc.), others are almost arbitrarily excluded (n. pag.).

As the negative began to see its ground recede, ground from which to draw link stories, we began to see the end of the disadvantage as an argument form. Though not the only cause of its demise, ground loss has contributed to its near extinction. The death of the disadvantage has become painfully evident with the popularity of a mere handful of dubious ones.

For example, consider a popular political disadvantage, currently code named "Clinton." This argument assumes the plan will be perceived by constituents, either the electorate or legislative colleagues, as evidence of strength/weakness that, in turn, increases/decreases the likelihood of some action upon which the fate of the world revolves. Beyond the obvious (Clinton can positively/negatively distance himself from any policy, his leadership characteristics are hardly tagged to the policy instant, his sexual peccadilloes have made his administration appear ludicrous, etc.), the disadvantage is nothing more than a race for updated link and internal link stories from on-line full-text retrieval services. In many instances, the team with the fastest and best connection, and who can afford to travel with a card-cutting assistant, wins the disadvantage.

Disadvantages became highly problematic when the affirmative was given the power to suspend the discussion of problems linked to the plan at various stages of implementation. When conceived, a policy direction can cause groups to coalesce and mobilize because they are excluded from the payoff; an unwise or impractical agenda might be adopted and people might be seriously harmed. When adopted, vested interests and political actors might employ anticipative and responsive strategies that are counterproductive on many different levels, e.g., a group might amend legislation to secure interests risked by the adoption of the plan. While this normally occurs within the confines of the bureaucracy, it is fractured by fiat. When implemented, actors might espy shifts in actual or perceived self-interest and they mitigate the execution of the plan by implementing compromising legislation. They might overreact and gut the provisions of the plan altogether.

While we can categorize some of these arguments as "would" issues, it is important to realize that they become issues because the affirmative has grown unwilling to do what needs to be done to avoid their inherency. Why? Avoiding the inherency is costly and breeds disadvantage link stories. A clear example of this is the absolute unwillingness by affirmative teams to spend money at any level. Under the guise of normal means, they discount all spending arguments by claiming fiat on one level of another. In general, the affirmatives have been allowed to discount the execution costs of the plan.

> Fiat . . . "turbo-charges" arguments elevating their propensity for occurrence to the status of inevitability, when the actual likelihood of adoption is slight or non-existent. . . . [O]ne can always imagine ways to change the world (through fiat) so as to make competing proposals irrelevant or undesirable. . . (Cheshier n. pag.).

And negatives did just that, simply counterplanning their disadvantages into the debate. "Consider the difference between a federalism disadvantage and a state counterplan with a federalism net benefit. The only difference is that the former requires debate over likelihood of occurrence – can anyone really defend the view that disadvantage debates are worse than counterplan debates?" (Cheshier n. pag.). In response, the negative had no choice but to convert their disadvantages into counterplan mandates. Claiming comparable fiat, they mandated the link story.

This practice has been assisted by current interpretations of counterplan competitiveness. We decide whether a counterplan mutually excludes a plan by examining the net benefits of the permutation(s). Branham suggested that we view counterplan competitiveness as opportunity-cost directed choices. "Succinctly, one disadvantage of the affirmative plan may be that its adoption significantly reduces the chance of implementing the superior counterplan" (62). Therefore, Branham considered the counterplan as a disadvantage. "If the aim of the negative is believed to be the establishment of the counterplan as a disadvantage, it makes sense to think of competitiveness as a link, a relationship of varying probability between plan adoption and the ability to implement and gain the benefits of the counterplan" (62).

Another negative move designed to counter expanding affirmative fiat has been to replace the traditional policy disadvantage with the kritik. While surely not the sole reason for the kritik, fiat abuse was a powerful one. For Shanahan, one of the assumptions in debate worthy of examination was the reality of fiat. He wrote that a "necessary precondition for any kritik is uncovering assumptions critical for the arguments and evidence being debated" (A-7). Shrader paraphrased the fiat basis for kritiks: "Fiat is an illusion; nothing happens when you vote affirmative. The change in thinking patterns or patterns in discourse are the biggest impacts of all, since they're the product of this [sic]" (n. pag.). He continued; we may "imprint one another with our perverse habits of thinking" and "if our preparations have included actions that are destructive of the environment and detrimental to the fortunes of future generations, then a real impact has occurred" (n. pag.). Shrader concluded: "The events of the debate which are external to the thought-experiment (are) actually more important than the odd cyberworld of fiat-constructed reality" (n. pag.). Hence, kritiks have become pre-fiat considerations that are neither unique nor need a threshold, and they cannot be outweighed by the anticipated advantages of the plan.

Recently, Gehrke tried extending kritiks to post-fiat arguments. While his view of kritik as policy criteria needing normative retuning is interesting, he does not explain how systems analysis employs this method in pragmatic decision making. There may be moments in history that call for such retooling, e.g., pre-Depression America, post-Tito Yugoslavia, etc., but these instances are rare events. Furthermore, his view of kritiks within interpretive analysis casts them as internal link stories to a traditional disadvantage, e.g. "advocacy may alter belief systems, provide new paradigms..." (31). For Gehrke, the disposition of these kritiks is not unlike disadvantages with issues such as threshold, uniqueness, etc. His idealism seems misplaced, conveniently ignoring that thinking people forego challenging decision making calculi not because they are unenlightened, but rather because utility demands that some challenges wait for another day. Nonetheless, he hints at the obvious: disadvantages masquerade as kritiks.

Fiat has been especially at issue in terms of disadvantages framed as radical counterplan strategies. While fiat may be an issue with any counterplan, it is inextricably associated with two: utopian counterplans and advocacy counterplans.

Utopian counterplans are premised on repopulating the world with utopians. "Debaters who advocate (utopian) counterplans populate the globe with perfect individuals; they fiat structures which allow only the goodness of humanity to flourish. In other words, debaters magically create a perfect world community" (Herbeck and Katsulas 108).

The debate over utopian counterplans has occurred elsewhere.[3] However, the three strongest arguments against utopian counterplans each implicate fiat. Allowing the negative to move from a non-utopian setting into full-fledged and operating utopia is a classic illustration of the problem with fiat in negative counterplanning. First, the agent of the utopian counterplan is not prone to considering the policy in question (Katsulas, Herbeck and Panetta "Negative view" 106-107). Second, the utopian counterplan ignores solvency burdens by fiating past the transition from reality to utopia (Herbeck and Katsulas 109; Katsulas, Herbeck and Panetta "Negative view" 130). Third, fiat is skewed toward the negative, for the counterplan can be run against any and every case (Perkins 144).

A second counterplan is more radical still. The advocacy counterplan was designed to circumnavigate plans premised on weak or non-existent inherency claims. As such, they are well tailored to reveal some of the fiat related problems discussed earlier. The negative argues that the descriptive or existential inherency justifies action by the negative team as advocates. While hardly popular, it is worth exploring below.

Zarefsky discussed why good people tolerate evil. Their motives range from altruistic acts of selflessness to symbolic statements to reassure a constituency. Unearthing core motives might involve determining patterns of consistency between word and deed. To clarify, he offered a list of seven core motives: self-interest, roles, role conflicts, self-esteem, conflicting values, jurisdictional concerns, and perversity ("Causal Argument" 185). To this I would add oversight. In other words, sometimes evil occurs merely because people simple lack foresight. For example, legislation in California requiring riders in the bed of a pickup truck to be restrained was introduced after a bizarre accident in which a young child was thrown into the windshield of the car following a truck. The California legislature reacted immediately, passing legislation to preclude such a disaster from recurring. Hence, the reason a problem may exist is that no one seemed to notice it was a problem. The warrants for descriptive or existential inherency might easily be simple oversight.

As such, debaters have advocated counterplans to resolve these oversight problems. Mitchell references an example "involving the coaching staff of a given university undertaking a study of the panoptic dimensions of the criminal justice system . . . and another involving the appointment of debaters as energy czar. . . . Against an affirmative plan which called for a reversal or a particular court decision, the negative might have presented an action plan which directed debaters to organize an amicus brief initiative designed to influence an appeals court to issue a judgment. . ." (12). The negative might opt to flash mail the affirmative plan to members of Congress for immediate consideration.

While the first two illustrations might be bizarre and extravagant, the remaining two are quite more realistic. In these instances, the construct of fiat is engaged "within the spatio-temporal boundaries of the contest round" – a concept Mitchell tags as "reflexive fiat" (11). Reflexive fiat "collapses the gulf separating advocate from agent of action. . . , makes fiat a tangible mandate for concrete action. . . , explodes the spatio-temporal limitation of the contest round itself. . . , and pragmatically grounds [fiat] in the physical presence of advocates" (11-12). Mitchell concluded: "Unlike the temporally ephemeral political commitment entailed in the defense of simulated plans, the commitment to future action makes the reflexive fiat carry with it an outward activist imperative" (11-12). The negative is the activist. Mitchell argues that such counterplans compete rhetorically, and any affirmative permutation would tarnish the persuasiveness of the counterplan advocates as rhetors entering the public sphere. To advocate both plan and counterplan "would involve assuming a hypocritical or inconsistent rhetorical stance in the public sphere, something which would limit their political efficacy and jeopardize solvency of the action plan" (12).

The advocacy counterplan is most effective when used by the negative in response to descriptive or existential inherency. The counterplan demonstrates that the affirmative fails to establish an inherency requirement for the plan. The counterplan, whether visiting Washington in person, writing letters, or flashmailing a transcript, demonstrates the plan is not a unique solution to whatever ills or advantages the affirmative offers for consideration.

Unless we want pre-emptory advocacy counterplans run to flush out inherency that then serves as a solvency challenge, unless we want to allow affirmatives to run plans which are costly yet cost nothing because fiat cancels the link story to the potential disadvantage, and unless we want rounds riddled with mini-kritiks, often hidden within other arguments, such that every debate seems to frame the judge as the arbiter of all truth and understanding in the cosmos, then we might want to restrain fiat by encouraging negatives to argue plan circumvention. This argument would compel affirmative debaters to rewrite the fiat rule themselves.

THE CIRCUMVENTION ARGUMENT

The fiat exclusion of "should-would" arguments does not amnest the affirmative from political reality

> Negative teams can, of course, argue that even if instituted, an affirmative proposal could not be effectively implemented and enforced. . . . [N]egative teams can contend that the government will act to undermine its intent . . . or the government either will not or cannot enforce the proposal. . . . By raising enforcement and circumvention arguments, advocates attempt to diminish the proba-

bility that the plan will achieve desirable outcomes even when adoption of the proposal is not an issue (Lichtman and Rohrer 242).

Of course, for any of these potential arguments to be effective, a bright-line of sorts needs to be drawn that fences in fiat. Circumvention arguments are viable only when the affirmative does not choose to expend capital (political, monetary, etc.) to evade the inherency issues, selecting to complete adoption by canceling the inherency and situating themselves among their solvency claims.

While Lichtman and Rohrer hedged that the negative is "prohibited from alleging that decision-makers will repeal the affirmative plan" (242), their conclusion seems to be groundless. In instances when the affirmative merely fiats away the motives and mechanisms which tolerated the absence of the plan, arguments such as repeal seem to be a viable test of the affirmative plan and clarifies the abuse of fiat. On the other hand, if the affirmative "buys off" or "buys out" the inherency, repeal arguments using the affirmative inherency arguments as a warrant are groundless simply because the post-fiat world is not the pre-fiat world; the motives and mechanisms which might lead to appeal are different. The affirmative inherency argument no longer identifies a viable motive or mechanism for circumvention, including repeal.

Repeal is, of course, an extreme form of the circumvention argument. There are many other types. Circumvention arguments can address issues associated with insufficient personnel, expertise, or budgets, misguided interests, concerns, or values, etc. The circumvention argument has three formal elements: (a) a discussion of motive(s) that have been illegitimately discounted by fiat; (b) an examination of mechanisms available to agents who have motivation to scuttle the plan; and (c) some evaluation of the relative impact of the motive and mechanism upon the solvency of the plan mandates. The circumvention argument would function post-fiat, and would punish arbitrary discounting through affirmative fiat.

It has been argued that the search for inherency and its incorporation into contest debates might make them less "magical" and more grounded in the machinations of policymaking. The same might be said of the circumvention argument.

In the search for inherency, we discover a multitude of configurations, which are the substance of the resolutional field. The laws, or overarching structure, are related in unique harmony/disharmony with the particular expression of administrative order. An understanding of the relationship between laws and the embodiment of those laws will produce an understanding of reality for each topic which provides the ability to link general to specific, predicate to object, and even cause to effect. Additionally, such an understanding may reveal how systems of knowledge and acts may conjoin in constructing the real (Goodnight et al. 239).

Consider the use of "side payments" and package deals as acceptable strategies in constructing the "real." Zarefsky suggested: "It may be possible to propose action which will 'buy-off' objectors by outweighing their current motives with positive incentives for compliance . . . including 'side payments' – additional benefits to persons other than those for whom a program is designed. . . ("The Role of Causal" 188). Wilson wrote, "When change does come, it tends to come in packages. . . . To have a new policy. . . , it is usually necessary to make side payments, giving other people as a condition of acquiescence something that they want. The total package becomes much bigger, and a single change tends to be imbedded in a cluster of simultaneous changes" (21-22). The affirmative plan's true costs become clarified as the affirmative promulgates reasonable solutions to multivariate problems. "Given a society as diverse as ours and given the kind of decentralization of formal authority that exists, perhaps the cheapest way to keep the system moving with a minimum of organizational strain may be to engage in economically efficient 'package deals'" (Wilson 22). The circumvention argument demands that actors and agency be resolved by plan mechanics. The plan mandates would need to compensate the forces, attitudinal and/or structural, that preclude the realization of the affirmative advantage. If the status quo routinely ignored the plight of a class of citizens, then those involved would be replaced or their jurisdiction restrained. If the status quo refused to assist a class of citizens for a single or confluence of externalities, then those externalities would need to be resolved as well.

Consider this broad illustration. The Equal Employment Opportunity Commission has not functioned efficiently, and civil rights goals associated with employment remain unfulfilled. Why? Because the EEOC is perverse? (If so, the negative could argue that the plan would be equally problematic.) The EEOC has insufficient resources? (If so, unless the plan hires more civil servants and provides them with an adequate budget, the negative could argue that the post-plan EEOC will also fall short, or that it will merely expose another class of litigants to discrimination as a trade-off.) The EEOC does not realize the problem because it has not received appropriate complaints? (If so, unless the plan publicizes its mandates and provides increased resources for poverty and public interest lawyers, the negative could argue that the EEOC will remain ineffective.) Hence, the circumvention argument uncovers the motives for the descriptive inherency and uses the motives to construct a link story.

Next, the circumvention argument evaluates plan mechanics to determine which means remain available through which the motives are expressed and these are used to construct an internal link story. Finally, the consequences of the interplay of motives and mechanisms are evaluated against the claimed advantages. While it may be difficult to argue that circumvention would nullify the solvency of the plan, when wedded to other arguments in the debate (presumption, solvency presses and take-outs, disadvantages, etc.), it might tip the balance away from the descriptive inherency and expansive fiat.

CONCLUSIONS AND COMPLAINTS

To counterbalance expansive fiat, critics have had to listen to the following arguments: (1) tit-for-tat – whereby the negative claims comparable fiat privileges, adopting wildly bizarre counterplans; (2) crime and punishment – whereby the negative claims some procedural violation by the affirmative should be punished with an *a priori* disposition against them, somewhat like the traditional topicality argument; and (3) whining and counterwhining – whereby both teams make charges and countercharges, often without warrants, opening the discussion to intervention by the critic. While most judges find these "arguments" tiresome, debaters have added little or nothing to their argumentative arsenal that might avoid such questionable rejoinders.

Since the policy debate community seems unable to locate fiat, or even resolve why it exists at all, some controls on its escalation seem sensible. The circumvention argument might compel affirmatives to resolve inherency rather than making it dissolve into the ether like a cheap parlor card trick. By rewriting the fiat rule for debating as it is practiced presently, we might improve the game play for debating. Minimally, it deserves its day, at least until something better or cleaner rises in its place.

WORKS CITED

Austin, J. "Performative-Constative." *The Philosophy of Language*. Ed. John R. Searle. Oxford: Oxford UP, 1917. 13-22.

Balkin, J. M. "Populism and Progressivism as Constitutional Categories." *Yale Law Journal* 104 (May 1995): 1935-1990.

Branham, Robert. "Roads Not Taken: Counterplans and Opportunity Costs." *Journal of the American Forensic Association* 25 (Spring 1989): 246-255.

Brock, Bernard L., James W. Chesebro, John Cragan, and James F. Klumpp. *Public Policy Decision-Making: Systems Analysis and Comparative Advantages Debate*. NY: Harper & Row, Pub. 1973.

Cherwitz, Richard A. and James Hikins. "Inherency as a Multidimensional Construct: A Rhetorical Approach to the Proof of Causation." *Journal of the American Forensic Association* 14 (Fall, 1977): 82-90.

Cheshier, David. "Debate Without Fiat: A Thought Experiment." Outline presented at the Speech Communication Association Convention. San Diego. November, 1996. N. pag.

Cronen, Vernon E. "Comparative Advantage: A Classification." *The Central States Speech Journal* 19:4 (Winter 1968): 243-249.

Dahl, Norman O. "'Ought' Implies 'Can' and Deontic Logic." *Philosophia* 4 (October 1974): 485-511.

Edwards, Richard E. "In Defense of Utopia: A Response to Katsulas, Herbeck, and Panetta." *Journal of the American Forensic Association* 24 (Fall 1987): 112-118.

Fitzgerald, John. "The 'Should-Would' Dichotomy: A Philosophical Position." *Proceedings of the National Conference on Argumentation*. Ed. James Luck. Ft. Worth, TX: Texas Christian UP, 1973. 100-112.

Flaningham, Carl D. "Concomitant vs. Comparative Advantages: Sufficient vs. Necessary Conditions." *Journal of the American Forensic Association* 18 (Summer 1981): 1-8.

—. "Inherency and Incremental Change: A Response to Morello." *Journal of the American Forensic Association* 20 (Spring 1984): 231-236.

Goodnight, Tom, Bill Balthrop, and Donn W. Parson. "The Problem of Inherency: Strategy and Substance." *Journal of the American Forensic Association* 10 (Spring 1974): 229-240.

Gehrke, Patrick. "Critique Arguments as Policy Analysis: Policy Debate Beyond the Rationalist Perspective." *Contemporary Argumentation and Debate* 19 (1998): 19-40.

Herbeck, Dale A. and John P. Katsulas. "Point of Theory: Utopian Counterplans." *The Forensic Quarterly* 59/3 (Fall 1985):108-110.

Katsulas, John P., Dale A. Herbeck, and Edward M. Panetta. "Fiating Utopia: A Negative View of the Emergence of World Order Counterplans and Futures Gaming in Policy Debate." *Journal of the American Forensic Association* 24 (Fall 1987): 95-111.

—. "Fiating Utopia, Part Two: A Rejoinder to Edwards and Snider." *Journal of the American Forensic Association* 24 (Fall 1987): 130-136.

Kruger, Arthur N. "The Underlying Assumptions of Policy Questions III. Inherent Evil." *Speaker and Gavel* 2 (March 1965): 79-82.

—. "The Inherent Need: Further Clarification." *Journal of the American Forensic Association* 20 (September 1965): 109-119.

Lambertson, F. W. "Plan and Counter-Plan in a Question of Policy." *The Quarterly Journal of Speech* 29 (1943-1944). 48-52.

Leiter, Brian. "The Epistemology of Admissibility: Why Even Good Philosophy of Science Would Not Make for Good Philosophy of Evidence." *Brigham Young University Law Review* 1997 (1997): 803-819.

Lichtman, Allan J. and Daniel M. Rohrer. "The Logic of Policy Dispute." *Journal of the American Forensic Association* 16 (Spring 1980): 236-247.

Ling, David A. and Robert V. Seltzer. "The Role of Attitudinal Inherency in Contemporary Debate." *Journal of the American Forensic Association* 5 (Winter 1972): 278-283.

Lipkin, Robert Justin. "The Quest for the Common Good: Neutrality and Deliberative Democracy in Sunstein's Conception of American Constitutionalism." *Connecticut Law Review* 26 (Spring 1994): 1039-1092.

Mader, Thomas F. "The Inherent Need to Analyze Stasis." *Journal of the American Forensic Association* 4 (Winter 1967): 13-20.

Madsen, Arnie. "General Systems Theory and Counterplan Competition." *Argumentation and Advocacy* 26 (Fall 1989): 71-82.

Margolis, Joseph. "One Last Time: 'Ought' Implies 'Can.'" *The Personalist* 48 (Winter 1967): 33-41.

Marsh, Patrick O. "Terminological Tangle: A Reply to Professor Kruger." *Speaker and Gavel* 2:2 (January 1965): 54-59.

Martinich, A. P. "Obligation, Ability and Prima Faciae Promising." *Philosophia* 17:3 (October 1987): 323-330.

McConnell, Terrance R. "'Ought Implies Can" and the Scope of Moral Requirements." *Philosophia* 19:4.(December 1989): 437-454.

McGee, Brian and David Romanelli. "Policy Debate as Fiction: In Defense of Utopian Fiat." Paper presented at the Speech Communication Association Convention. San Diego, November 1996.

Mitchell, Gordon R. "Reflexive Fiat: Incorporating the Outward Activist Turn into Contest Strategy." *The Rostrum* 72 (January 1998):11-20.

Perkins, Dallas G. "Counterplans and Paradigms." *Journal of the American Forensic Association* 25 (Winter 1989): 140-149.

Pfau, Michael. "The Present System Revisited Part One: Incremental Change." *Journal of the American Forensic Association* 17 (Fall 1980): 80-84.

—. "The Present System Revisited Part Two: Policy Interrelationships." *Journal of the American Forensic Association* 17 (Winter 1981):146-154.

Radin, Margaret Jane. "Reconsidering the Rule of Law." *Boston University Law Review* 69 (July 1989): 781-819.

Schunk, John F. "A Farewell to 'Structural Change': The Cure for Pseudo-Inherency." *Journal of the American Forensic Association* 14 (Winter 1978): 141-149.

—. "Affirmative Fiat, Plan Circumvention, and the 'Process' Disadvantage: The Further Ramifications of Pseudo-Inherency." *Speaker and Gavel.* 18:3 (Spring 1981). 83-87.

Shanahan, William. "Kritik of Thinking." *Health Care Policy: Debating Coverage Cures.* Winston-Salem, NC: Wake Forest University, Debater's Research Guide, 1993. A-3 - A-8.

Shrader, Doyle. "Critiques Answering Lovechild." [discussion]. CEDA Discussion List. [Online]. CEDA-L/EDEBATE@UVM.EDU (1 February 1994).

Smith, James Ward. "Impossibility and Morals." *Mind* 70 (1961): 363-375.

Snider, A. C. "Fantasy and Reality Revisited: Gaming, Fiat Power, and Anti-Utopianism." *Journal of the American Forensic Association* 24 (Fall 1987.):119-130.

—. "Stalking the Big Game: An Introduction to Gaming as a Paradigm for Academic Debate." Department of Theatre, University of Vermont. Unpublished. April, 1988.

Stocker, Michael. "'Ought' and 'Can.'" *Australasian Journal of Philosophy* 49:3 (December 1971): 303-316.

Thomas, David A. and Jerry M. Anderson. "Negative Approaches to the Comparative Advantages Case." *Speaker and Gavel* 5:4 (May 1968): 153-157.

Tranoy, K. E. "'Ought' Implies 'Can': A Bridge from Fact to Norm." *Ratio* 14:2 (December 1972): 116-130.

Wilson, James Q. "An Overview of Theories of Planned Change." *Centrally Planned Change*. Ed. Robert Morris. NY: National Association of Social Workers, 1964. 12-29.

Zarefsky, David. "The 'Traditional Case - Comparative Advantage Case' Dichotomy: Another Look." *Journal of the American Forensic Association* 6 (Winter 1969):12-20.

—. "The Role of Causal Argument in Policy Controversies." *Journal of the American Forensic Association* 13 (Spring 1977): 179-191.

NOTES

[1] A. C. Snider, who popularized gaming as a metaphor for debate, felt that "academic debate already possesses the characteristics of a game." Gaming is unlike evaluative paradigms such as policy making and hypothesis testing, he wrote, in that they are "prescriptive-external" and "require debate to be modeled after some outside phenomenon." Gaming, on the other hand, is "descriptive-internal because it uses the characteristics internal to academic debate to describe it" (Snider, "Stalking" 5-6). For Snider, his metaphor was extrapolated into a paradigm. Here, gaming is used merely as a metaphor.

[2] For a detailed analysis of the history of inherency, see: Marsh; Kruger; Cronen; Goodnight; Cherwitz and Hikins; Zarefsky; Schunk; Lichtman and Rohrer; and Flaningham.

[3] See Herbeck and Katsulas; Katsulas, Herbeck and Panetta; Edwards; and Snider "Fantasy."

David Berube (Ph.D., New York University) is an Associate Professor of Speech Communication and Director of Carolina Debate at the University of South Carolina in Columbia, South Carolina. This essay was originally published in volume 20 (1999) of *Contemporary Argumentation and Debate*, pp. 24-46.

THE DECISION-MAKER
Michael M. Korcok

Who decides?" matters. One manner in which the outcome of a decision depends upon the decision-maker is that decision-makers differ in their motives, interests, and values. A second manner in which decisions depend on the decision-maker is the quality of decision-making styles and processes. But "Who decides?" matters in another way: the outcome of a decision depends on the decision-maker's scope of authority over competing alternative courses of action. Understanding this last manner in which "Who decides?" matters dissolves the now long-standing problem in academic debate about the appropriate scope of negative fiat. This essay argues that the appropriate scope of negative fiat is the scope of the authority of the decision-maker choosing whether to adopt the affirmative plan.

Let us suppose that we are evaluating whether the debate team of Smart and Feisty should participate in the Academy tournament next month. Let us initially posit that the debaters are making the decision about whether to participate. This decision ought to be made by weighing the value of participating in the tournament against the best competitive alternative course of action that could be chosen by Smart and Feisty. Let us assume that the best alternative is attendance at a campus social function. Smart and Feisty might well decide that participating at a debate tournament would offer more value than yet another beer-fest. Our deliberation whether to endorse the debaters' choice could bring to bear a rather different set of values, interests, and concerns. The intellectual evaluation of others' choices is, furthermore, not a simple, passive, nor inconsequential exercise. For this example, however, let us suppose that we neither disagree with the decision-makers' valuations of their options nor that we problematize our role as evaluators and intellectual endorsers. After examining their decision, let us endorse the choice to participate at the Academy tournament.

Now, however, let us posit that Wise, the Director of Forensics, is making the decision about whether Smart and Feisty should participate in the Academy tournament. Director Wise ought to make this decision by comparing the value of the debaters' participation against the best competitive alternative course of action that could be chosen by Wise. Let us assume that best alternative available to Director Wise is entering the debaters in the Collegium tournament instead. In this situation, Wise might well decide that the debaters should not participate at the Academy because she prefers the Collegium tournament. In auditing this choice, let us suppose that we neither disagree with Director Wise's valuation of her options nor that we problematize our role as evaluators: let us endorse the choice not to participate at the Academy tournament.

Whether Smart and Feisty should participate in the Academy tournament next month hinges upon who faces that decision even though there may be no difference between the decision-makers in respect to motives, interests, values, or decision-making styles and processes. Furthermore, the outcome of our evaluation of whether the debaters should attend the Academy tournament hinges upon "Who decides?" without involving any differences in our role as evaluators. The different outcomes are simply the result of decision-makers' differing scopes of authority to choose alternatives.

Finally, before leaving this introductory example, let us ask whether Smart and Feisty should participate in the Academy tournament without specifying a decision-maker faced with making this choice. We might, perhaps, attempt to take the perspective of an ideal, rational decision-maker. There is no satisfying way to proceed. If we are committed to endorsing participation if and only if the value of participation is greater than the value of the best competitive alternative to participation, then we are left with a simple quandary:

Which of the universe of possible alternatives are legitimate reasons to reject participation? If University funding were to be quadrupled by the Regents next week, a decision we would surely applaud, then Smart and Feisty could be sent to a colloquium in Paris instead. If the Dean were to select Feisty as the scholar of the year, then the debaters ought to stay home for the presentation ceremony. If the Academy decided to offer another tournament later in the year, attending the subsequent tournament instead could be a reason not to participate next month. And of course we could add to this list of possible competing alternative courses of action *ad infinitum.* Our quandary is that there is no scope of authority over alternative courses of action that adheres to ideal rational decision-makers: they can imagine a horde of possible competitive alternatives and they have authority over none of them. This quandary is exactly the problem of the appropriate scope of negative fiat in contemporary debate.

Initially, this essay reviews the modern history of the problem of the appropriate scope of negative fiat, then proffers a solution within an "opportunity cost" grounding of counterplans, and finally, examines the role of the debate critic as an evaluator of decisions.

FOOTNOTE THIRTEEN

Allan Lichtman and Daniel Rohrer, in their 1975 classic "A General Theory of the Counterplan," observed in footnote thirteen, their only consideration of negative fiat, that:

> It is assumed, of course, that decisionmakers being addressed have the power to put a counterplan into effect. An individual or governmental unit can reasonably be asked to reject a particular policy if an alternative promises greater net benefits. If, however, a counterplan must be adopted by another individual or unit of government, the initial decision-maker must consider the probability that the counterplan will be accepted. Debate propositions often affirm that a particular policy should be adopted by the federal government. Even if adoption of this policy by the individual state governments would be more beneficial, a reasonable critic would still affirm the resolution if state adoption were highly unlikely. The federal government should refrain

from acting only when the net benefits of state and local action, discounted by the probability that such action will occur, are greater than the net benefits of federal action (74).

The general solution to the problem of the appropriate scope of negative fiat hinted at but not elaborated upon by Lichtman and Rohrer, it is fair to say, has been ignored by academic debate during the intervening two and a half decades. Lichtman and Rohrer limit the scope of negative fiat to all and only those actions that the "decision-makers being addressed" can put into effect. Negative fiat does not extend to competitive alternatives outside of the scope of authority of the appropriate decision-maker: these alternatives are subjected to calculations of propensity and probability of adoption; they are mere consequences of action rather than alternatives which could be chosen, and they are no different in kind than disadvantages. There are at least three very different ways to read this footnote. The first involves a conflation of debate critics and decision-makers, the second was incorporated into Walter Ulrich's resolution of negative fiat, and the third is substantially the position taken in this essay.

CONFLATING CRITICS AND DECISION-MAKERS

According to one reading of the footnote, the "decisionmakers being addressed" in an academic debate are debate critics: they are, after all, deciding whether the affirmative plan should be adopted. This reading is problematic for at least two related reasons: the first is that debate judges typically have no authority to put either the affirmative plan or any interesting counterplan into effect, and the second is that conflating debate judges and decision-makers creates the problem of an appropriate scope of negative fiat. The first difficulty is that typical debate critics have neither the authority nor the power to put either plans or counterplans into effect; that authority typically resides in legislatures, executives, corporations, movements, and other loci of power and does not reside in graduate students and academics. We could, for the purposes of debate, pretend that debate critics do have the authority to put the plan into effect and we could also extend our imaginations to give debate critics the authority to enact counterplans. A second difficulty would immediately arise: Which counterplans should we pretend that debate critics have the authority to enact? This is the problem of the appropriate scope of negative fiat, and our inability to answer this quandary in a satisfying manner argues against a reading that conflates decision-makers and debate critics.

This initial reading of footnote thirteen is also tortured. Lichtman and Rohrer clearly and appropriately assume that the "decisionmakers being addressed" are "individual and governmental units" with the "power to put a counterplan into effect" (74). That does not describe debate judges. They furthermore argue that negative fiat cannot legitimately extend to counterplans which must be adopted by "another individual or unit of government" (74). That characterization makes no sense if debate critics and decision-makers are equivocated. Lichtman and Rohrer clearly do not conflate decision-makers and debate critics.

It may seem curious that this misreading has persisted at all. It is clearly a tortured reading of the Lichtman and Rohrer view and it immediately gives rise to the problem of the appropriate scope of negative fiat. Traditional debate theory equivocated debate critics and decision-makers without difficulty. Deciding whether the affirmative plan is better than the *status quo* does not give rise to problems of negative fiat precisely because there is only one alternative to the affirmative plan, the expected course of action if the affirmative plan is rejected. From the traditional debate theory perspective, neither debate critics nor decision-makers need to decide which of the universe of possible competing alternatives to the affirmative plan are legitimate. Since the debate critic and the policy-maker faced exactly the same decision in traditional debate theory, it was a simple matter to understand the debate judge as a policy-maker. The traditional conflation of debate critics and decision-makers has persisted despite its obvious incompatibility with Lichtman and Rohrer's reformulation of counterplan theory and has, in no small measure, served to prevent solution of the problem of the appropriate scope of negative fiat.

THE ULRICH READING.

Walter Ulrich, one of the few to mention Lichtman and Rohrer in the context of discussions regarding negative fiat, read Lichtman and Rohrer faithfully, arguing that negative fiat should extend to all and only actions of the resolutional agent. In his 1979 essay "The Agent in Argument," Ulrich read Lichtman and Rohrer thus:

> I would argue that the judge should adopt the role of the agent specified in the resolution. The debaters should argue as they would if they were arguing before the agent in the resolution. Thus, if the resolution calls for Congressional action, the policymaker should be viewed as Congress. If the topic calls for international action, the policymaker should be one controlling an international organization. The resolution thus serves the function of designating the agent that is being addressed (11).

Ulrich's reading of footnote thirteen was too narrow: Although Lichtman and Rohrer assumed that the appropriate decision-maker was the resolutional agent, the more important insight of footnote thirteen was that negative fiat legitimately extends only to actions within the authority of the appropriate decision-maker. Ulrich justifies some limitation of negative fiat and makes a plea for the educational value of teaching debaters personal limitation and responsibility, but assumes that the affirmative plan actor is the resolutional agent. There was no reasoning connecting fiat limitation, the affirmative actor, and the resolutional agent. No serious consideration of other potential decision-makers, such as the resolutional agent, the affirmative plan actor, or even an ideal rational citizen was present. Ulrich simply did not reach the central insight of footnote thirteen.

In his 1981 essay "The Judge as an Agent of Action: Limitations on Fiat Power," Ulrich developed his solution to the problem of the appropriate scope of negative fiat. Ulrich's solution had two components: the debate critic should role-play as the appropriate decision-maker and the appropriate decision-maker is the resolutional agent. Ulrich argued on behalf of this "role-playing the resolutional agent" solution:

> One possible solution to the problem of fiat power is to alter the current view of the role of the judge in a debate. Rather than having the judge adopt the plan/negative policy through the

use of fiat power, the judge should play the role of the agent specified in the resolution. As a result of this perspective, the judge would not fiat any policy into existence, but would rather decide whether or not, based on the arguments in the round, the agent in the resolution would take the action recommended by the affirmative team. Thus, if the resolution called for the federal government to take some action, the judge would evaluate the arguments in the round based on the way that a federal policy maker would respond to the arguments. This view of the role of the judge would have several desirable implications that would help resolve many of the problems that are created by the use of fiat (2).

The first component of Ulrich's solution, that for the purposes of the debate the critic role-plays as the appropriate decision-maker, may appear curious at first glance. Debate judges are not, after all, ASEAN or the United States Federal Government, or Congress – they are themselves. Ulrich took this position with a view to reforming previous practice. As mentioned above, the conflation of debate critics with decision-makers is an artifact of traditional problem-solution debate theory. Prior to the modern theory of counterplans, it was sufficient to view the debate critic as the policy-maker deciding whether to enact the affirmative plan: the debate critic was thought to exercise "fiat power," an ability to bring the affirmative plan into being. This view is problematic because the debate critic typically has no actual authority to enact either the affirmative plan or any interesting negative counterplans. More importantly, the lack of a defined scope of authority over possible alternative courses of action creates the problem of the appropriate scope of negative fiat. By recasting debate critics as role-playing appropriate decision-makers, Ulrich attached to debate critics a scope of authority over possible alternatives and disposed of the fiction that debate judges actually bring policies into existence by "exercising fiat power."

The second component of Ulrich's solution, that the appropriate decision-maker is the resolutional agent, was suggested in Lichtman and Rohrer's classic reformulation of counterplan theory. The appropriate scope of negative fiat becomes a non-issue for this view precisely because the judge is given a specific scope of authority over possible alternative courses of action. The appropriate scope of negative fiat is the scope of the resolutional agent's authority over competitive alternatives. Stated differently, considerations of propensity are irrelevant for all and only those actions that the resolutional agent can undertake. He illustrated how his view of judge role-playing as resolutional agent solved the problem of negative fiat:

> The first implication of viewing the judge as the agent specified in the resolution is that the options available to both teams would be limited. If the judge is a federal policymaker, for example, the only options open to him/her are options to enact potential federal programs. This would mean that a negative team arguing for a state counterplan would have to prove that the counterplan will be adopted, since the action that is being advocated falls outside the jurisdiction of the judge. Inherency arguments would be limited to those programs that the federal government COULD adopt, or those programs that other levels of government ARE adopting ("Judge" 2).

Both components of Ulrich's solution are problematic. That debate judges pretend to be something that they are not and could not be is an artifice, one that must strike even the casual observer as an *ad hoc* gimmick. This artifice has been persistently troubling to debate theorists who have argued on behalf of more parsimonious views of the role of the debate critic. Dallas Perkins, in his 1989 essay, "Counterplans and Paradigms" argued on behalf of an "intellectual endorsement" or "policy evaluation" view:

> Thus the outline of a possible "debate paradigm" begins to emerge: the judge is to act as if she were called upon to witness an argument and endorse the position of one side or the other, but not to take any further action. Several things about this new paradigm make it attractive. First, it is what resolutions are all about. These are not designed to promote policy making, but rather policy evaluation. They are more often than not, as in our case, adopted by private groups, though they may deal with matters of public policy. The adoption of a resolution constitutes an endorsement, not implementation. Since the

judge is not in fact a policy maker, it is appropriate that resolutions are not typically a tool of policy making (148).

The rejection of role-playing as an artifice in favor of an intellectual endorsement or policy evaluation view substantially undermined the Ulrich solution. If the debate critic is just the debate critic, then why should they be limited to considering only policies from the perspective of the decision-maker they are role-playing? The objection to judicial role-playing in general was furthermore related to concerns about the particular agents which debate judges might be asked to role-play. This concern is simply stated: "Why should the debate critic be limited to taking only the perspective of the resolutional agent or any other particular decision-maker?" Roger Solt connected the general objection to role-playing with a rejection of limitations upon negative fiat which would constrict discourse to "official" policy in his 1989 essay, "Resolving the Ambiguities of Should:"

> I believe that the judge should not assume any particular role, be it member of Congress or social scientist, in evaluating the debate. Rather, the judge should reflect the perspective of an ideally impartial, informed, and eclectic viewpoint. Most consistent with this view of the judge seems to be a view of fiat simply as an act of intellectual endorsement. If intellectual endorsement is all that occurs at the end of the debate, there is no real reason why the judge should be precluded from endorsing options outside the political mainstream – if they are competitive with the affirmative (130).

Because Ulrich had interwoven the two components of his solution to the problem of the appropriate scope of negative fiat, these compelling objections to the artifice of judicial role-playing served as well to undermine the argument that the appropriate decision-maker is the resolutional agent. This may seem curious at first, but if the debate critic is just the debate critic rather than the resolutional agent or any other particular decision-maker, it seems only natural to ask: "Why should the debate critic label some competitive alternative courses of action as illegitimate, as inappropriate to the decision to lend or withhold an intellectual endorsement of the affirmative plan?" And to this question, Ulrich had no compelling answer.

The second component of Ulrich's solution, that the appropriate decision-maker is the resolutional agent, is also problematic. Simply put, there appears no connective logic in Ulrich's essay which argues that the appropriate decision-maker ought to be the resolutional agent rather than some other governmental decision-maker, the affirmative plan's actor, a non-governmental organization, or even an ideal impartial evaluator. Solt explained this sort of objection:

> Ulrich's standard, however, posits a very narrow policy-making view of the debate process. It assumes that the judge actually adopts the role of a federal decision maker, or whatever the topical agent may be. I have already indicted the idea that the judge should assume such a critical perspective. Many who consider questions of public policy are not actual decision makers, and for such non-decision makers, a question such as the comparative desirability of state versus federal action (which Ulrich's approach would exclude) might well arise (132).

This objection had force primarily because Ulrich offered no reasons for the resolutional agent as decision-maker; he presented arguments for limiting negative fiat and then demonstrated that his solution did so elegantly. Ulrich's strategy left his solution largely defenseless against objections which simply asked "But why the resolutional agent?"

This second component of Walter Ulrich's solution, that the appropriate decision-maker is the resolutional agent, is a special case of the solution presented in this essay. Ulrich's arguments, however, do not justify the special case. The argument presented by Ulrich that went furthest in warranting the limitation of negative fiat by way of specifying a particular decision-maker merely entailed that the affirmative and negative ought to be limited to the same decision-maker:

> Humans are choice making animals, who are forced to accept their limitations and to act upon those limitations. Consider the types of arguments and decisions our students face. In decid-

ing what graduate school to go to, the issue is not, in the best of all possible worlds, where should the student go. This approach would enable students to argue that Harvard or Yale should accept them. Instead, the student is forced to accept the actions of others as a given, and he/she is forced to decide among those options open to him/her and only those options open to him/her. While there are examples of people who sit back and try to decide who is the ideal agent to perform a task, at the point that any action is converted into reality, only one agent is involved. To allow discussion of what other agents should do would allow an individual to live in a fantasy world, ignoring his/her own obligation to act in the hopes that another person beyond their control will act. While both types of argument exist in the real world, the most relevant type of argument is the argument that takes place when an individual recognizes the limits of being human and attempts to decide, not what would be the best of all possible worlds, but what option available to him/her is the most productive option ("Judge" 5).

Taken together, the objections to Ulrich's solution were compelling: judicial role-playing is an inelegant artifice; constraining debate to mainstream political discourse is unwarranted; and tying judicial perspective to a particular viewpoint appears to be logically arbitrary. Entwining the two components of Ulrich's solution, judicial role-playing and resolutional agent as appropriate decision-maker, was a fatal mistake as theorists developed a compelling case against judicial role-playing. Most importantly, Ulrich's exposition, by focussing on the advantages and disadvantages of judicial role-playing of the resolutional agent, failed to reach what this author takes to be the important insight which dissolves the problem of the appropriate scope of negative fiat: the scope of negative fiat is constituted by the scope of authority of the decision-maker.

Unfortunately, the success of these objections has led to the rise of a theoretical perspective which can fairly be described as "fiat *ala carte*." The contemporary view seems to be that fiat ought to be granted to or withheld from those counterplans which meet or fail to meet a standard or standards selected from a theoretical smorgasbord. Rarely are the selected standards connected to the logic of counterplans or grounded in a theory of counterplans. A decade after Solt commented upon the unresolved problem of the appropriate scope of negative fiat, his words still ring true:

> There is clearly, however, no such consensus where negative fiat is concerned. With the rise to prominence of the counterplan as a negative strategy, it is negative rather than affirmative fiat which is increasingly contentious. While affirmative fiat is a necessary consequence of the resolution's wording, negative fiat is definitely more problematic. If affirmative fiat involves imagining that the affirmative plan were adopted, negative fiat is the act of imagining alternatives to the affirmative. While the resolution usually places some constraints relating to realism on the affirmative, the non-resolution places no such constraints on the negative. Consequently, the potential (and actual) abuses of negative fiat could fill a forensic wax museum (122).

The basic problem with the contemporary approach to the appropriate scope of negative fiat is that it fails to understand the fundamental insight pointed to by Lichtman and Rohrer in footnote thirteen: "It is assumed, of course, that decisionmakers being addressed have the power to put a counterplan into effect" (74).

RE-READING FOOTNOTE THIRTEEN

The preferred reading of footnote thirteen is substantially the position defended in this essay: negative fiat legitimately extends to all and only those competitive alternatives within the scope of authority of the appropriate decision-maker. Our introductory example illustrated the logic underlying this reading: decisions should be made by comparing the value of the choice under consideration against the worth of the best competing alternative choice, different decision-makers possess different scopes of authority over alternative choices, and evaluating a decision without specifying the decision-maker is incoherent. The example presented in footnote thirteen illustrates how this view operates to dissolve the problem of negative fiat in academic debate. If the appropriate decision-maker faced with choosing whether to adopt the affirmative plan is taken to be the federal government, then alternative courses of action, such as state and local initiatives which the federal government does not have the authority to enact, are subject to calculations of propensity. All and only those actions which the federal government has the authority to enact are immune to calculations of propensity – they are promoted from being mere consequences and elevated to the rank of possible counterplans. Even though "A General Theory of the Counterplan" is widely credited with initiating the contemporary theory of counterplans, the fundamental insight contained in footnote thirteen was generally ignored and the problem of the appropriate scope of negative fiat has been intractable.

The solution to the problem of negative fiat is not that the judge ought to role-play the resolutional agent, but rather that *the appropriate scope of negative fiat is the scope of the authority of the decision-maker choosing whether to adopt the affirmative plan.* This section proceeds by first addressing the most important pragmatic implication of this solution, after that, offering an extended example of how this solution functions, and finally, grounding the solution in decision-making processes.

DETERMINING THE DECISION-MAKER.

This solution is incomplete in the sense that it does not particularize the scope of negative fiat for all debates: it does not imply that the scope of negative fiat is constituted by the scope of authority of the federal government, the affirmative plan's actor, the resolutional agent, nor any other particular decision-maker. The logical force of the arguments presented below extends only to this solution and does not go so far as to particularize the appropriate decision-maker. Likewise, adequate grounding in considerations of decision-making processes extends this far and no farther.

The incompleteness of the solution presented here is a feature, not a bug. If we come to understand that the appropriate scope of negative fiat is constituted by the scope of the authority of the decision-maker choosing whether to adopt the affirmative plan, then the problem of the appropriate scope of negative fiat is dissolved. What is left is a question: "In any given debate, who or what is the appropriate decision-maker?" This question can be addressed in at least three ways: by arguing over the appropriate decision-maker in the debate itself; by creating a community consensus that the resolutional agent is the appropriate decision-maker; or by selecting the decision-maker contemporaneously with the resolution. The first option leaves to debaters the task of explaining how any given counterplan fits within the authority of the decision-maker choosing to adopt the affirmative plan. Debate about who ought to be the appropriate decision-maker for the particular affirmative plan at issue might well ensue, since that determination would fix the scope of legitimately fiated counterplans. Many of the extant arguments for limiting negative fiat to domestic public actors, expanding negative fiat to include international bodies, checking negative fiat through the relevant resolutional literature, or attempting to locate the site of controversy could be marshaled in defense of one or another particular decision-maker.

The second option extends the role of the resolutional agent. The agent in the resolution currently serves as a parameter which delimits the affirmative's choice of plan actor. A second role the resolutional agent can play is as the decision-maker choosing whether to adopt the affirmative plan. This option ought to function because, in most instances, governance is hierarchical. If the federal government is the resolutional agent, for example, then actors within the federal government (potential affirmative plan actors) are also within the scope of its authority (as are other potential counterplan actors). This option is not logically implicated by the solution presented in this essay and requires an agreement by at least the affirmative and negative debaters that the resolutional agent ought to serve as the decision-maker. Absent a community consensus that the resolutional agent ought to serve as the appropriate decision-maker, this option reduces to the first: the debaters themselves would be faced with the task of justifying their particular choice of decision-maker.

The third option, selecting the appropriate decision-maker contemporaneously with the resolution, may seem radical at first glance. How compelling this option is ultimately depends upon how pessimistic one might be with regard to the quality of arguments debaters might muster about the appropriateness of given decision-makers. It is a reformulation of an idea first proposed by Solt when he suggested that a satisfying resolution of the problem of the appropriate scope of negative fiat may never be found and that the community might need to select the range of acceptable counterplans along with the resolution:

> A second approach would be to write a kind of negative resolution. The resolution could contain two sentences, one indicating the scope of affirmative choices, the other the scope of negative choices. Such a negative resolution might state that policy alternatives germane to this resolution are those which operate within present government structures and which could be adopted by domestic public actors (138-139).

Solt proposed the artful delimitation of the list of acceptable counterplans. In this form, his solution is unacceptable for at least two reasons: it unduly intrudes upon substantive issues more appropriately resolved by the debaters themselves and it offers no connecting logic between the delimitation of acceptable counterplans and the evaluation of the affirmative plan. The natural question to ask is: "Why these counterplans and not others?" So long as there was no satisfying solution to the problem of the appropriate scope of negative fiat, the only answer available was: "Because we have to limit negative fiat somehow. Do you have a better idea?" The solution proffered in this essay allows us to reformulate Solt's proposal. Because the appropriate scope of negative fiat is the scope of the authority of the decision-maker choosing whether to adopt the affirmative plan, we need only select an appropriate decision-maker. The problem of the appropriate scope of negative fiat is unresolvable without specifying a decision-maker and, conversely, specifying a decision-maker resolves the ambiguities of fiat. The natural question to ask becomes: "Why this decision-maker?" The answer to this question is: "Because we cannot decide whether any affirmative plans should be chosen unless we specify the decision-maker faced with making that decision." We do not wish to intrude on substantive questions about the desirability of the affirmative plan, nor can we anticipate potential alternatives to affirmative plans, but those questions are incoherent without a decision-maker. Lastly, we believe that arguing about the identity of the appropriate decision-maker is not as valuable as the other issues which will face debaters on this resolution."

AN EXTENDED EXAMPLE.

An extended example serves to illustrate the application of this essay's solution to the problem of the appropriate scope of negative fiat. Let us posit the following:

Resolution: the U. S. Department of Defense should increase its security assistance to Southeast Asia.

Affirmative plan: the U. S. Army gives Laos forty-seven Blackhawk helicopters.

Now, let us begin by considering several potential decision-makers that might have authority to decide whether to adopt the affirmative plan:

Decision-maker 1: The United States Federal Government.

Decision-maker 2: The United States Department of Defense (the resolutional agent).

Decision-maker 3: The U.S. Army (the affirmative actor).

Initially, the decision whether to adopt the affirmative plan may well hinge upon the identity of the decision-maker. In particular, each of the three candidate decision-makers has a different scope of authority over possible competitive alternative actions. There are options available to the Department of Defense, for example, which are unavailable to the Army. Furthermore, if we fail to select a particular decision-maker faced with the decision to adopt the affirmative plan, we will be unable to proceed: the affirmative plan should be adopted if and only if it is preferable to the best competitive alternative, and the nature of that alternative is necessarily dependent on the decision-maker. Finally, by way of introduction, the appropriate scope of negative fiat is unresolvable unless we specify the decision-maker. How nice it would be if those who threaten Laos decided to surrender, if ASEAN funded assistance to Laos themselves, or if global harmony ruled the day. These possibilities, however, are satisfyingly rejected as unreasonable if and only if we are able to select a decision-maker that would not have these alternatives as choices.

Now, let us examine several possible counterplans and assess whether fiat legitimately extends to them under the assumption that the appropriate scope of negative fiat is all and only those actions for which the appropriate decision-maker has authority.

Counterplan 1: Missouri sends state troopers to Laos. This counterplan is illegitimate even if it competes with the plan because none of the candidate decision-makers would have the authority to choose it. Now, it might be the case that there are reasons to believe that Missouri has some non-zero propensity to send their troopers to Laos absent the plan that would decrease if the plan were enacted. In this case, we might have a disadvantage, but not a counterplan: fiat would be neither necessary nor appropriate.

Counterplan 2: France sends Mirages to Laos. This counterplan, even if it competes with the affirmative plan, is illegitimate because none of the candidate decision-makers has the authority to choose French actions. Whether the Army should send Blackhawks to Laos would and should include considerations of the consequences of that act with respect to French reaction: but that is a matter of assessing advantages and disadvantages and not an appropriate object of fiat. Similarly, that US pressure might convince France to send Mirages to Laos is a far cry from an extension of fiat that waives considerations of the likely success of such pressure.

Counterplan 3: The CIA sends operatives after enemies of Laos. This counterplan's legitimacy is a more complex issue. Presumably, if the United States Federal Government were successfully defended as the appropriate decision-maker, then this counterplan would be legitimate. If, however, the appropriate decision-maker is the Department of Defense or the U. S. Army, neither of which has authority over the actions of the CIA, then this counterplan would not be legitimate. A negative team advancing this counterplan would be faced with justifying the federal government as the appropriate decision-maker rather than the Department of Defense (the resolutional agent) or the US Army (the affirmative plan's actor).

GROUNDING NEGATIVE FIAT.

The problem of the appropriate scope of negative fiat has been notoriously resistant to solution. In part, the problem's intractability has been a consequence of the method used to address it: previous theorists have either sought after a standard or standards that limited negative fiat fairly or they looked to attack or advocate particular types of counterplans. This approach to debate theory is problematic because it fails to examine the logical underpinnings of negative fiat. It is not enough to present a solution, offer a few motivating comments, and illustrate its applications. The solution presented in this essay is entailed by an adequate grounding of the concept of negative fiat in decision-making. Given the perspectives and arguments presented thus far, we are now ready to ground negative fiat.

The problem of negative fiat has two aspects that are in tension. On the one hand, it appears that all competitive counterplans are reasons to reject the affirmative plan, thus it may be asked: "Why and how does one decide that some of those reasons should be disallowed?" On the other hand, it appears that any use of negative fiat circumvents calculations of the propensity of counterplan action absent implementation of the plan, and it may be asked: "Why and how does one decide that negative fiat should extend to any counterplan actions?" One way to address both of the above concerns is to ask: "Under what circumstances is it appropriate to eliminate considerations of the propensity of actions which trade-off with the affirmative plan?"

The suggested solution addresses both aspects of the problem of the appropriate scope of negative fiat and is contiguous with our intuitions about legitimate negative fiat. I first introduce the concept of opportunity cost, then examine why fiat does not extend to some competitive counterplans, and finally, explain why it is legitimate to ignore considerations of propensity for some counterplans.

BEGINNING WITH OPPORTUNITY COST.

Human beings and human agencies confront every decision in a context of constraint. One choice necessarily forecloses other choices, either because of the mutual exclusivity or the mutual undesirability of some paths. Few choices, thankfully, foreclose all other options, but no decisions, because they are decisions, can be made without selecting one choice at the expense of others.

The problem of valuation begins as a simple question: "How much is a given choice worth?" A presumably simple and commonplace answer is available: the value of a given choice is the anticipated difference between its benefits, the good which is expected to ensue, and its costs, the bad which is expected to ensue. This answer to the problem of valuation is insufficient for decision-making, however. That a particular choice has positive value or, absurdly, seven hundred and three utils, tells us very little about whether it should be selected: there are always other, sometimes competing, choices we could make. If choices were like multiple-choice tests, a delimited menu of alternatives, one and only one of which could be selected, then there might yet be a way to proceed: we would select the highest-valued alternative. But only rarely are decisions so simple. We must typically decide whether to take a given course of action, knowing that many alternative choices with complex possibilities for combination and permutation are barely specified but possible.

For decision-making purposes, a seemingly simple but ultimately subtle answer to the problem of valuation is available: the value of a choice is the difference between its worth and the worth of the best alternative that must be foregone. The worth of the best alternative that must be foregone is called a choice's *opportunity cost.* James Buchanan, the 1986 Nobel Prize recipient in economics, defined the concept of "opportunity cost" in his *The New Palgrave* exposition:

> Choice implies rejected as well as selected alternatives. Opportunity cost is the evaluation placed on the most highly valued of the rejected alternatives or opportunities. Opportunity cost, the value placed on the rejected option by the chooser, is the obstacle to choice; it is that which must be considered, evaluated, and ultimately rejected before the preferred option is chosen (720).

Once the concept of opportunity cost is in hand, the above solution to the problem of valuation leads to a simple decision-rule: affirm a choice if and only if it is better than its opportunity cost.

In academic debate, the concept of opportunity cost is instantiated in competitive counterplans. The negative team presents counterplans as opportunities that would be sacrificed if the affirmative plan were to be adopted. Counterplan competition with the affirmative plan is just the idea that adoption of the plan would foreclose the opportunity of enacting the counterplan. The decision-rule applied is that the affirmative plan should be adopted if and only if it is better than the competitive counterplan.

Fiat does not extend to competitive counterplans that are not opportunity costs. The first aspect of the problem of the legitimate scope of negative fiat can be summarized in the question: "Why and how does one decide that some competitive counterplans should be disallowed?" If the affirmative plan is undertaken, then competitive counterplan action cannot or should not be taken: we must choose between the plan and the counterplan. It appears that all competitive counterplans are thus opportunity costs of plan action. From this perspective, any and all competitive counterplans can be legitimately fiated. A counterplan theory grounded in decision-making, however, does not sanction all competitive counterplans: only some competitive counterplans represent legitimate opportunity costs of plan action.

A counterplan represents a potential opportunity cost of taking plan action only if the counterplan competes with the plan and the decision-maker choosing whether to undertake plan action has the ability to do so. Opportunity costs are necessarily situated within choice-making contexts. It is not any alternative action which must be foregone if a posited action is undertaken which could be an opportunity cost, only those actions foregone which are open to choice in a given decision-making context are potential opportunity costs. Actions that you cannot undertake, for example, can never present opportunity costs for you: they are not alternatives open to choice. Similarly, the independent actions of others cannot present opportunity costs for you: you cannot choose these alternatives, only others can.

Thus, not all competitive counterplans represent relevant objections to an affirmative plan. Only those competitive counterplans that the decision-maker deciding whether to undertake plan action has the authority to choose are relevant objections to plan action.

Fiat extends to competitive counterplans that are opportunity costs. The second aspect of the problem of the legitimate scope of negative fiat can be summarized in the question: "Why and how does one decide that fiat legitimately extends to any counterplans?" Counterplans have no propensity: the action specified by a counterplan will not occur. Evidence is not presented for the likelihood of counterplan action in the absence of plan action and the probability that such action would be undertaken in the absence of plan action is not an issue for counterplans. A counterplan operates to reject affirmative plan action because taking plan action would prevent counterplan action that wouldn't occur anyway. It appears that counterplans are not really costs of plan action after all. On this view, the negative properly gets no fiat. Why should the propensity of actions which plan action would sacrifice ever be ignored?

The correct answer to this question is: "Because opportunity costs are not subject to calculations of likelihood or propensity – they are coequal alternatives for a decision-maker choosing whether to take plan action." The worth of any choice is its value in comparison to its opportunity cost: the value of the best choice that must be foregone but could be chosen otherwise. Opportunity costs are necessarily situated within choice-making contexts. A decision-maker's own calculation of the likelihood, propensity or probability of choosing one or another alternative is literally nonsensical. Decision-makers would be in the bizarre position of attempting to predict what they would do if they chose differently. Opportunity costs nullify calculations of propensity and likelihood.

Thus, at least some competitive counterplans represent relevant objections to an affirmative plan. Those competitive counterplans that the decision-maker choosing whether to undertake plan action has the authority to choose are relevant objections to plan action without calculation of propensity.

THE JUDGE

In academic debate, the intractability of the problem of the appropriate scope of negative fiat is, in part, the result of conflating debate critics with decision-makers. The solution to the problem of the appropriate scope of negative fiat offered in this essay neither equivocates between debate critics and decision-makers nor asks debate critics to role-play decision-makers. For decision-makers, the appropriate scope of negative fiat is the scope of their own authority over alternative choices. For debate critics, the appropriate scope of negative fiat has nothing to do with the critic's own authority but, rather, remains the scope of authority of the decision-maker. An immediate entailment of this view is that debate judges can and should remain themselves: critics, evaluators, pundits, and endorsers rather than decision-makers.

The problem of the appropriate scope of negative fiat is no different in debate than in other contexts. Advisors, consultants, pundits, evaluators, endorsers, and critics must understand the set of competing alternatives available to the relevant decision-maker because an action ought to be taken if and only if it is the best of the competing alternatives available to the appropriate decision-maker. This view separates critics from decision-makers in an appropriate manner. Unlike solutions which conflate critics with decision-makers or that ask critics to role-play decision-makers, there is no suggestion in this perspective that critics ought to accept *uncritically* the motives, interests, and values of the decision-maker whose choices they audit. Understanding that negative fiat is constituted by the authority of the decision-maker does not imply that critics ought to endorse the decision-maker, the decision-maker's decision processes, or the decision-maker's valuation of the choices facing them.

This view does not relegate critics to a simple, passive, or inconsequential role: rather, a discursive space for critical arguments is framed by the separation of critic and decision-maker. The act of endorsement is distinct from the act of policy decision-making. A debate critic is asked by the debaters to lend or withhold intellectual endorsement for the affirmative plan. It is, of course, assumed that a critic's intellectual endorsement ought to depend, in some manner, upon whether the affirmative plan ought to be chosen by the decision-maker. Intellectual endorsement is a distinct choice faced by critics, however, which potentially involves additional considerations that do not speak to a decision-maker's deliberations.

It is now a commonplace for debaters to present critical arguments that directly address the debate judge's act of endorsement. These arguments often include the observation that "fiat is illusory," that is, no real policy change will occur as a result of the debate. This observation, while true, misses the mark. The debate critic's act of endorsement does not bring a policy into being any more than does endorsement by any other critic, advisor, or auditor. This does not argue, by itself, that endorsement ought not to depend upon the desirability of the affirmative plan. Nor does it somehow disable the reasons for an endorsement of the affirmative plan. This argument is meant to create the space for arguments that directly address the act of endorsement. By reminding critics that they are critics only, reasons to withhold an endorsement that do not speak to the decision-maker's options are enabled.

There is also an emerging trend in academic debate to "permute" critical arguments, even though critical arguments are not typically offered as competitive alternatives to the affirmative plan. This argumentative move is intuitively appealing. The act of intellectual endorsement is, in one important sense, no different from any other human action. It ought to be undertaken if and only if it is better than the best competitive alternative. Critical arguments, if they are to be relevant, must also function as reasons for the judge to take some action that competes with an endorsement of the affirmative plan. A "permutation" of the criticism is little more than a test of whether the criticism offers a reason not to endorse the affirmative plan.

In the context of critical arguments that directly address the debate critic's act of intellectual endorsement, the question of fiat is not especially complex. In this context, the debate judge is a decision-maker rather than a pundit, advisor, and endorser of others' choices. As for any decision-maker, the critic's own scope of authority over competitive alternatives constitutes the legitimate scope of negative fiat. After all, the critic faces directly the decision of whether to endorse the affirmative plan and they should do so if and only if endorsement of the affirmative plan is the best of the competing alternatives available to the judge.

WORKS CITED

Buchanan, James. "Opportunity Cost." *The New Palgrave: A Dictionary of Economics.* Eatwell, John, Murray Milgate, and Peter K. Newman. eds. Vol. 3. 1987: 718-721.

Lichtman, Alan and Daniel Rohrer. "A General Theory of the Counterplan." *Journal of the American Forensics Association* 12 (1975): 70-79.

Perkins, Dallas. "Counterplans and Paradigms." *Journal of the American Forensics Association* 25 (1989): 140-149.

Solt, Roger. "Resolving the Ambiguities of Should." *Journal of the*

American Forensics Association 25 (1989): 121-139.

Ulrich, Walter. "The Agent in Argument: Toward a Theory of Fiat." Paper presented at the meeting of the Speech Communication Association. San Antonio. November 1979. Education Resource Information Center ED170800 (1980): microfiche.

—. "The Judge as an Agent of Action: Limitations on Fiat Power." Paper presented at the meeting of the Speech Communication Association. Anaheim. November 1981. Education Resource Information Center ED210739 (1982): microfiche.

Michael Korcok (M.A. Kansas State University) is a Doctoral student in Communications Theory at Florida State University in Tallahassee, Florida. This essay was originally published in volume 20 (1999) of *Contemporary Argumentation and Debate*, pp. 49-68.

The author wishes to express thanks to Jessica Wojtysiak for her invaluable assistance in working through some of the ideas contained in this essay.

PART FIVE:
CRITIQUES – EXPANDING THE
ARGUMENTATIVE DOMAIN

This section addresses critiques (or "Kritiks"), an argument type whose resistance to neat categorization is indeed one of its defining elements. While it is best left to the included authors to provide their own definition of this argument type, a common element is that critiques are at least commonly seen as standing outside of the conventional weighing of advantages and disadvantages that most often characterizes policy debate. For that reason, critiques are seen as opening up academic debate's frame of analysis and including issues that may otherwise be overlooked. The essays included in this section provide diverse perspectives on this argument trend. **Ken Broda-Bahm and Thomas Murphy** in *Defense of Critique Arguments: Beyond the Resolutional Question* provide an example of an early attempt to define, defend, and categorize the argument form. Defining critiques narrowly as arguments which attempt to supercede the resolutional question, the essay seeks to describe and support normative critiques tied to specific arguments or argumentative contexts as well as resolutional critiques which reject the legitimacy of the resolution's framework. They conclude that critiques are potentially viable arguments which question "whether the resolution is a worthy and capable subject for debate, and whether some event or argument has real effects which are important enough to demand preeminent evaluation." **David Berube** in his essay *Contexts, Texts and Retexts: Textual Analysis Re-Examined, Criticizing Kritiks*, offers a critical perspective on critiques. Berube views kritiks within the framework of textual analysis to argue that the kritik is "mostly worthless and has little, if any, truth value in academic debate." By failing the basic criteria of good argument, kritiks imperil dialogue and substitute power for reasoning. Finally in *Critique Arguments as Policy Analysis: Policy Debate Beyond the Rationalist Perspective*, **Pat Gehrke** argues that both sides of the controversy over critiques "marginalize critique arguments by positioning them outside of policy deliberation." By exploring the policy studies literature, Gehrke argues that policy analysis inevitably involves the construction of value systems and moral premises and can incorporate interpretive theories as well. Gehrke concludes that repositioning critiques as policy analysis offers an opportunity to overturn some common assumptions that have contributed to the general mystification that has surrounded the argument form.

A DEFENSE OF CRITIQUE ARGUMENTS: BEYOND THE RESOLUTIONAL QUESTION

Kenneth Broda-Bahm and Thomas L. Murphy

The definitional issues of the resolutional question are <u>non sequitur</u> to what we're discussing which is the framework and the procedure that you established for us as thinkers in this room and the judge and the panel and for what we're supposed to debate. We are arguing that the framework that you present is objectionable (Brey *Transcript* 22-23).

The final round at the 1989 CEDA National Tournament featured a negative team advancing the argument that an objection to the affirmative's legal framework of interpretation mattered more than an answer to the resolutional question. Since this time, arguments labeled "critiques" have become increasingly prevalent and have extended debate beyond the issues of resolutional truth and falsity. Such arguments have recently included First Amendment objections to the use of "public understanding" as a standard for performance of the national news media on the Fall 1993 CEDA topic,[1] and language-based criticism of the use of geopolitical security discourse in the Spring 1994 CEDA topic.[2] In each of these arguments, the negative had taken no position on the veracity of the affirmative case, and instead had argued that the framework for the debate was inherently flawed. Is such a strategy legitimate? On what basis could it be a voting issue against the affirmative?

Regardless of what we would think about their substantive merits, it is clear that arguments such as these would violate many of the debate community's common presumptions about the role of the resolution. Scholars of debate generally have assumed that, because the proposition is the starting point of debate (Brey *Use and Misuse* 203, Murphy & Murphy 6) relevant arguments are limited to the issue of resolutional truth. This essay seeks to expand the conception of relevance beyond that assumption. Specifically we will argue that while debate generally takes as its focus the task of answering a resolutional question, at times it may be justified to instead focus on the legitimacy of the resolutional question, the ability to answer the resolutional question, or the normative effects of arguments or practices within the framework of the debate. This essay will advance a definition of critique, develop a general defense of critiques, forward a taxonomy of critiques, and offer a more specific defenses of several forms of critique.

THE MEANING OF "CRITIQUE"

Current usage of the term "critique" is vague enough that it may cover a wide array of arguments. This essay should not be considered a defense of all such positions. In an attempt to clarify our focus, we define a critique as any argument which does not provide an answer to the resolutional question[3] but which does provide a reason for superseding the resolutional question in importance. The essence of the critique is a justification for some non-resolutional argument to be considered in lieu of the resolutional question. This essay focuses on critiques which obtain their link at the level of advocacy rather than in the resolutional terms which are the subject of evaluation (in fact/value resolutions) or the action called for (in policy/quasi-policy resolutions).

To say that critiques do not answer the resolutional question is not to say that critiques have nothing to do with the resolution. In some cases, the critique will focus on the practical possibility or normative value of answering the question. In other cases, the critique will focus on the climate in which debate on the resolution is occurring. In all cases, however, the critique as we view it will offer a reason why another specific concern must come before our need to answer the text of the resolution.

Critiques may additionally be characterized based on what they are not. Rosen, for example, has noted that on the Spring 1993 CEDA topic[4] some negatives obtained an unwarranted strategic advantage by labeling their argument that "The Universal Declaration on Human Rights entrenches Western culture" a "critique." Based on our definition, this argument would supply a reason for negating rather than superseding the resolution (we should not implement the declaration because it entrenches Western culture) and as such it would be a disadvantage rather than a critique. Only if the argument provided a reason to avoid debate on the resolution (for example, if it claimed that we in the West should not put ourselves in the position of discussing what is best for the world) could it be seen as a critique. Aside from separating them from disadvantages, critiques may also be distinguished from topicality and justification which seek to reinterpret, rather than reject, the framework for the debate.

One further defining characteristic of critiques is that they, like topicality and justification, claim *a priori* status as voting issues. If a critique succeeds in justifying the claim that the resolution either cannot or should not be used as the basis of decision, then the critique itself becomes the decisive issue. While this may be seen as violating "argument equality"[5] it seems more appropriately viewed as a consequence of the sequential nature of argument: some claims must necessarily be resolved before other claims. Most judges consider procedural arguments, such as topicality, to require evaluation prior to the affirmative's case. Disadvantages are also sequential in nature since a judge must consider the links prior to the impacts and if the links are not valid, then the evaluation of the disadvantage goes no further. Similarly, the critique argument is sequentially a voting issue. If the framework for the debate is flawed, then it makes little sense to enter that framework in order to evaluate arguments. You must know whether a question is worth answering before you answer it. For a large number of critiques, it would be senseless to engage in a simple weighing of the consequences of affirmative and negative arguments. On the Spring 1994 topic, for example, a judge would not be able to weigh the advantages of an air strike in Bosnia against the disadvantages of militaristic discourse or sexist language. The critique would be evaluated first, and only if the critique were rejected would the judge be able to consider the value of the air strike.

While many of the examples so far have focused on the critique as a tactic of the negative, they are not exclusively the negative's ground. Affirmatives have an equal ability to develop a critique against a framework for the debate imposed by the negative. Critiques are more commonly seen as a tool of the negative only because current practice tends to afford the affirmative a broader interpretive ability.

As a final characteristic, critiques are best seen as comprehensive strategies. In this sense they are more likely to be broad encompassing positions than isolated acts of rejoinder. There is a natural tension between arguing that a flawed framework justifies superseding the resolutional question and making other arguments which seek to answer that question and in the process presume the value of answering it. The concept of the "waiver" which Murphy articulated in the context of topicality argumentation seems to apply here. If a negative offers a critique suggesting that advocacy over the resolutional question, in general, is harmful and then proceeds to generate substantive arguments against the affirmative, they are equally susceptible to the critique. At that point, the negative could be judged to have waived their critique position.

A PRELIMINARY DEFENSE OF CRITIQUES

All propositions can be seen as containing two levels of meaning. The first, and most familiar level, is propositional truth: is the proposition true or false? Addressing the level of propositional truth presupposes that we have decided that the proposition is worth addressing. The second level, the level of propositional legitimacy, is the realm of the critique. Critique focuses on the worth or the consequences, not of the proposition, but of the discussion itself. Should we be having *this* debate over *this* proposition? All that is required in order to accept the concept of critique is to accept the possibility that at times a question of propositional legitimacy might override a question of propositional truth.

The ability to potentially focus on the worth of the debate can be justified. Communication educators acknowledge the benefits of introducing students to critical issues regarding language and advocacy. The development of an awareness of the social construction of experience through language, the relationships between language and power, and the connections between speech and action are seen as integral to a collegiate education on communication. The development of critique argumentation in debates would provide an educational laboratory for the consideration of these questions. As believers in the benefits of the debate process we feel that these issues should not be addressed simply by coaches, but should be explored by placing them in the dialectic of the round which, despite its limitations, remains the central laboratory of our educational activity.

Many contemporary communication theorists recognize a multitude of factors relevant to the communication process that extend well beyond the simple question of the truth or falsity of a proposition. Eloise Buker notes that an emphasis on language is becoming increasingly important:

> Contemporary social analysis has turned to linguistic analysis as a way to understand the basic structure of social/political action. With this linguistic turn, citizens have become more aware of how language shapes their daily lives and how language and speech empower certain actors and inhibit others (70).

Likewise, many theorists can be marshalled to demonstrate the importance of a broad conception of the variety of communication influences at work in a given argumentative setting. Edwin Black, for example, notes the effect of language in creating a persona in auditors which should be subject to evaluation. "In all rhetorical discourse," he notes, "we can find enticements not simply to believe something, but to *be* something. We are solicited by the discourse to fulfill its blandishments with our very selves" (119). Simon Dalby argues that U.S. miliary discourse, a field for many debate impacts, has effects of its own. "It is precisely these discourses of security," Dalby notes "that define and delimit the bounds of political discussion, acting to reproduce the militarization of culture and politics" (181). Focusing on law, another frequent arena for debate arguments, Lance Selva and Robert Bohm exhort us to consider not just the truth-value but the effects of legal discourse. The imperative is to "challenge the discourse that mediates the perception of the way people feel and think about social reality" (255).

In the context of a widespread academic recognition of the important effects contributed by discourse style, a debate forum requiring an exclusive focus on the simple truth-content of the resolutional question seems to preclude many important avenues for analysis. Following G. Thomas Goodnight and David Hingstman, we feel that debate should bear a closer relationship to communication theory. Providing the forum of the debate round with a fair way to consider issues related to discourse and advocacy would allow debaters to confront the critical issues of communication philosophy. This highlights another practical benefit to allowing critiques: their inclusion would align the debate community with a more contextualized and contemporary view of communication. This is an important benefit, since academic debate as an institution often is perceived as being at odds with the communication departments that sponsor it.

Independent of the pragmatics of a focus on communication in the debate forum, the value of such a focus must also stem from the realization that advocacy has consequences. Many rationalize debate practices with the statement, "nothing happens at the end of the round." Such a position, however, fails to account for the effects of advocacy on both advocate and auditor. Whether in a laboratory setting, such as competitive intercollegiate debate, or in a real-world context, the act of advocating is a real act with consequences. Indeed, as the only non-hypothetical element in a debate round, advocacy could be seen as being the area of effects most worth talking about.

Most importantly, if we believe that our advocacy is real and has consequences, and if we believe that the debate format can be a vehicle for addressing the conditions and consequences of real advocacy, then we should admit the possibility of raising legitimate critique arguments in the debate forum.

A TAXONOMIC DEFENSE OF CRITIQUES

As arguments that do not answer the resolutional question but instead provide a reason for superseding the resolutional question, critiques can be differentiated based on their reason for superseding the resolutional question. We see two general reasons which could be important enough to overcome the need to answer the resolution: the rejection of a given occurrence in a debate round, and the rejection of the resolution as a flawed framework. The first form, which we will term *normative critique*, regulates the norms for acceptable action within the debate context. The second form, which we will term *resolutional critique,* challenges the worth of operating within a resolutional framework. This distinction is not meant to be all-inclusive, but is instead intended to differentiate between two major reasons an argument could focus debate away from answering the resolution. We will explain and subsequently defend each of these critique forms.

NORMATIVE CRITIQUES

The Normative critique is based on the assumption that in order to be productive and humane, a debate should function within certain norms. At a minimum, a debate should take place in an environment which is at least relatively free of behaviors which would oppress or silence the dialogue of participants. A major premise is that while coaches, judges, and the larger community all have a role to play in maintaining, or revising, these norms, the debate round itself should be a potential forum for invoking or challenging the acceptable conditions of dialogue.

FORMS OF NORMATIVE CRITIQUES

The creation of a normative framework for the debate can focus on factors related to context as well as to specific arguments.

Context critiques. Critiques of context advance the position that some element of the argumentative situation is important enough to require attention in a manner more basic than the resolutional question. A common context critique is that the use of sexist-language by a team should constitute a voting issue (West). Other conceivable context critiques would include racist-speech or dehumanizing delivery. One context critique which is widely accepted, if rarely used, relates to evidence challenges. The charge of evidence fabrication or taking evidence out of context has status as a voting issue in the minds of many judges. If a team committed such an offense, but still managed to prove or disprove the resolution with unchallenged evidence, few judges would vote for them. The reason for voting against a team that fabricated evidence is based, not on a failure of the team to live up to their obligation with respect to the resolution, but on their failure to live up to their obligation with respect to the process.[6] Most members of our community seem to feel that a charge of evidentiary dishonesty is a legitimate critique, provided it can be substantiated, and an argument which would supersede the resolutional question in importance. The charge of evidentiary dishonesty can thus be viewed as a normative critique of context by highlighting the principle that the violation of trust matters more than any answer to the resolution. A context critique related to sexist-language use would similarly posit that the violation of egalitarian interaction matters more than any answer to the resolution. The impact of the argument differs, but not its fundamental form.

The effect of these arguments, if successful, is to generate discursively mediated "rules of the game." A team against which a successful challenge is made loses the debate, regardless of the truth or falsity of the resolution. This *a priori* status stems from the impossibility of evaluating normative critiques in comparison to other arguments in the context of the debate. How, for example, could a judge weigh a sexist-language critique against the claimed risk of nuclear war solved by affirmative's hypothetical policy? Necessity requires that the arguments be evaluated separately and the sequential nature of the critique requires that the context be evaluated first. Only if the context is judged to be fair for debate, should evaluation proceed to the resolutional question.

Argument critiques. Critiques against particular arguments advanced in the debate also have the potential to challenge or establish norms for acceptable practice. Argument critiques advance the position that the rejection of a particular argument is important enough to supersede the resolutional question. Examples of argument critiques might include an affirmative position which suggests that a negative position on "Islamic Fundamentalism" plays to racist stereotypes (Ahmed 229), a position which argues that the use of John Birch Society sources and conspiracy theories fosters anti-semitism, or a position stating that arguments based on racial differences encourage genocide. In each of these cases, whether such an argument is a critique must be assessed by reference to its function. If the purpose of the argument is simply to defeat the affirmative argument, then it is refutation rather than critique. If, on the other hand, the function of the argument is to establish itself as an issue more fundamental than the resolutional question, it would be a critique.

While there tend to be strong norms in the debate community which typically prevent the introduction of highly offensive claims, exceptions remain. The benefits of patriarchy, the truth of biological determinism, and the advantages of AIDS have all, to a greater or lesser degree, been advocated by debaters in recent memory. The 1991-1992 NDT topic for example allowed for some clearly offensive cases such as overruling a Supreme Court decision which permitted interracial marriage.[7] The argument critique is based on the premise that some arguments degrade the forum enough that more than simple refutation is warranted.

A DEFENSE OF NORMATIVE CRITIQUES

Normative critiques are not hypothetical arguments. They are based on the possibility of real and immediate harm resulting from allowing a specific action to continue. Sexist language, for example, would be grounds for a critique, not based on just the abstract claims of authors, but based upon its effect in creating a hostile environment in which the value of continued debate over the truth of the resolution would be negated. This level would not necessarily be met by the use of a generic "he" in a quote. The persistent use of demeaning language by a debater in a round, however, could create an environment in which the value of further debate on the resolution would be outweighed by harm to the participants. More directly, persistent hostile language could result in a situation in which productive debate on the resolutional question would be impossible.

Real and immediate harm can also be measured based on damage to the debate forum and on the impossibility of reasoned choice when the forum becomes the vehicle for racist, sexist, or demagogic arguments. In our view the normative critique plays a valuable role in empowering debaters to create, advocate, and enforce self-regulating norms for humane argument and behavior in a debate context.

This is not to say, however, that we believe that all attacks on a team's behavior or arguments would constitute potential critiques. Clearly, preventing infinite regression is a major concern in advocating normative critique. What would keep a team from arguing that their opponents should lose a debate because of their failure to use recycled paper, which contributes to the destruction of the environment? Or that a team should lose because they were wearing watches made in China, thus supporting human-rights violations? What gives a critique such as the use of sexist-language greater importance that these examples?

The distinguishing feature of normative critiques is their norm-generating function. In essence, they create "rules of the game." Normative critiques would only become infinitely regressive if the debate community permits them to. This is unlikely. The success of the sexist-language critique seems to represent a collective judgement by the debate community that genderized language is a problem which is serious enough to warrant correction.

Normative critiques should also be distinguished from simple *ad hominems*. The advocate of a normative critique must show not only that a bad effect results from a given argument or practice, but that a climate is created (such as a sexually harassing climate) or that a harm is created in the debate round (such as the conscious use of racist stereotypes) which would negate the benefits of further consideration of the resolutional question. A challenge to the opposition's practices (their choice of paper or watches) can be true without being a critique. The essential ingredient is a justified reason why the challenge would come before the resolutional question in importance.

In advocating the potential critique of specific practices and arguments, we want to clarify that we are not advocating censorship or a "politically correct" silence on certain issues. We are advocating that objectionable speech should be met with more speech. Actions or claims that are oppressive should be openly challenged with reasoned discourse.

RESOLUTIONAL CRITIQUES

Critiques which are more germane to the resolutional question, but which still supersede rather than answer that question can be termed *resolutional critiques*. Resolutional critiques are fundamentally challenges to the possibility or the worth of debate on the resolutional question. They are based on the assumption that the resolution, as a framework for the debate, must be both worth discussing and capable of being discussed. A resolution which could not foster valuable debate would be rejected *a priori*.

FORMS OF RESOLUTIONAL CRITIQUES

The resolution can be rejected as a inappropriate framework either because a flaw in the resolution renders it incapable of proof, or because a legitimacy question renders the resolution unworthy of proof.

Resolutional-flaw critiques. Critiques based on a resolutional-flaw contend that the resolution is incapable of proof. They advance the argument that the existence or absence of a given state of affairs renders proof impossible. A hypothetical example of a resolutional-flaw critique might be generated with the resolution, "Resolved: that red ducks fly." If the negative is able to prove that no red ducks exist, the resolution cannot be proven true.[8] More realistic examples of potential resolutional-flaw critiques stem from the Spring 1994 CEDA topic. Some negative teams attempted to critique this proposition by arguing that the Cold War had not yet ended, or that democracies cannot be fostered.

Due to their absolute nature, a skepticism regarding the status of the resolutional-flaw as a voting issue may seem justified. We could make the assumption that because a topic has been chosen for debate, it is necessarily capable of proof. Or we could posit that some parts of the proposition can be *assumed* to be true as in "assuming we are in a post-Cold War world, is military intervention justified?" The pragmatic desirability of this position is often captured in the adage that if the resolutional-flaw was true, "all teams would have a .500 record."

On the other hand, this skepticism fails to resolve the difficulty in handling a topic that has been proven to be unprovable. If there are no red ducks, what ducks do we debate? And how can we assume ducks are red for the purpose of debate if no red ducks exist?

This form of critique obviously carries a very high standard of proof. It is one thing to say that a resolution is problematically phrased and quite another to say that it cannot be proven true or false under any interpretation. At a conceptual level at least, however, the argumentative possibility of a true resolutional-flaw remains.

If a resolutional-flaw, such as the non-existence of red ducks, was demonstrated in such a way as to prove the resolution false then it would constitute a refutation rather then a critique. If however, the resolutional-flaw renders the resolution as ambiguously neither true nor false (based on, for example, a strict avoidance of the fallacy of argument from ignorance) then a critique based on the resolutional-flaw would seem warranted. Assuming that it can be proven, the resolutional-flaw critique is justified as an *a priori* issue based on the claim that the affirmative carries a unique burden to prove the resolution, including all of its constituent elements. If the resolution cannot be proven true then affirmation is impossible and negation becomes the default option.

Resolutional-legitimacy critiques. Critiques based on resolutional-legitimacy suggest that the resolution is not worthy of discussion based on the claim that debate using the resolution as a framework would result in some specified harm. These critiques are at times language-based, for example focusing on "race or gender" as inappropriate categorizations in the proposition. These legitimacy critiques argue that the meaning created by terms in the resolution engenders negative effects or sets a harmful precedent (Bahm). Often, legitimacy critiques are institution-based, for example focusing on the harms of an exclusive focus on governmental solutions to environmental problems. These legitimacy critiques argue that debating within the institutional framework specified by the proposition carries a negative value.

The basic philosophy of the resolutional-legitimacy critique is illustrated by the resolution, "Resolved: That a chick should be

President."[9] In a technical sense, it would be possible to "prove" this resolution by arguing that "chick" is slang for "a woman" and that a woman should be President. A more intuitive response to this proposition, however, would be to argue that its oppressive language destroys the legitimacy of the claim, and the critique of legitimacy is more important and more valuable than any argument relating to the truth of the proposition. While this proposition is clearly debatable, one should question whether it is worthy of debate, given its pejorative labeling, and one should also be concerned about the precedent which would be set by engaging in debate on such a question.

While few would dispute lack of legitimacy in this proposition, recent topics debated by CEDA and NDT pose similar, yet more subtle, questions. Past CEDA topics, for example, have included evaluative terms such as *foreign* (Spring 1991), *censorship* (Fall 1990, Spring 1984), and *terrorist* (Fall 1985). While these terms come out of specific fields and carry complex meanings, it remains possible to argue that the terms, in context, carry meanings and effects which are unnecessarily pejorative. The term "terrorist" for example is easily characterized as a label which is selectively applied to criminal acts and frequently based on one's opinion of the political persuasion of the criminal.

Aside from the specific terminology, it is also possible to argue that the larger field of discourse, for example militarism (Dalby, Enloe), in which a proposition is embedded taints the value of debate on that proposition. In addition, the institutional-framework in which a resolution is debated can be subject to a legitimacy critique. All policy topics, whether NDT or CEDA, seem to work within existing political institutions and frameworks and to see them as the solution to societal ills. While counterplans such as socialism and anarchy could be seen as denying the value of the affirmative's agent, it is also conceivable that such arguments could be forwarded as resolutional-legitimacy critiques if, for example, debate on the resolution precluded the discussion of these alternate solutions. In describing Rich Edwards' position on such utopian counterplans, John Katsulas, Dale Herbeck, and Ed Panetta note:

> He perceives debaters who today are advocating anarchy, socialism, world government, authoritarianism, and technocracy to be engaged in a type of *criticism* which is analogous to the

> utopian literary criticism offered by Thomas More in the *Utopia* (97, emphasis added).

The expansive notion of fiat advocated by Edwards in response to his critics seems to encompass the possibility that, at least in policy debate, utopian counterplans operate outside the boundaries of the resolution. This represents a shift away from the view that "fiat limits affirmative and negative teams to advocating only incremental shifts away from existing policy" (114).

Resolutional-legitimacy critiques focus on the negative consequences which might arise from advocacy within a resolutional framework. A successful critique in this case would function as an *a priori* voting issue based on the premise that a challenge to the resolution as a framework would require adjudication separate from, and prior to, adjudication of arguments within that framework.

A DEFENSE OF RESOLUTIONAL CRITIQUES

Resolutional critiques permit a more complete focus on the argumentative task involved in justifying a proposition. Questions regarding the possibility and desirability of resolutional debate are not arbitrarily excluded or decided by other authorities, they are entrusted to the debate round. At this level, resolutional critiques should appeal to those who believe that both sides in a debate have an obligation to equip themselves with a contextual understanding of the resolution. A close analysis of many resolutional critique arguments shows that they impose and enforce just such a burden on affirmative and negative teams by encouraging them to gain a complete knowledge of the resolution prior to debate. In this manner, resolutional critiques serve a valuable function in improving the quality of debate.

While we recognize problems regarding resolutional-flaw critiques, and consider true resolutional flaws to be rare, we are unwilling to reject arguments over what may be important components of a resolution. While debatability may be preserved by holding resolutional-flaw critiques to a comparatively high standard of proof[10], we believe that a solution may additionally lie in more appropriately considering some critiques labeled *resolutional-flaw critiques* as actually resolutional-legitimacy critiques. The argument on the Spring 1994 CEDA topic positing that the resolution is incapable of proof because the Cold War was not over, or because there never was a Cold War, might be more accurately viewed as resolutional legitimacy critiques. The reason many foreign policy analysts reject the *Cold War* label seems to have less to do their *descriptive* view of the world than with their *evaluative* assessment of the effects of the *Cold War* label on policy decisions. The critique may be seen as saying, in effect, not that the Cold War doesn't exist, but that it is harmful to debate within a Cold War mindset.[11] Relabeling this critique, and all others which depend on an evaluative rather than descriptive assessment of the resolutional framework, would have the effect of improving the ground for the affirmative by permitting them to contest the evaluation.

A common criticism against both resolutional-flaw and resolutional-legitimacy critiques is that they penalize affirmatives for something that is essentially beyond their control: the framing of the resolutional question. On its face this seems to be a persuasive criticism. As previously noted, however, the tendency for resolutional critiques to be argued most frequently against the affirmative stems from the affirmative's presumptive power to interpret the resolution. Many resolutional critiques, thus, occur with affirmative complicity: the affirmative's use of their power to interpret brought about the critique, or could have been used to avoid the critique. An additional response to this criticism is that it is not unique to critique positions: affirmative is also bound to issues of resolutional truth in a way which is beyond their control. Why should the affirmative be responsible for proving the resolution, but not responsible for whether the resolution can be proven true or is worth proving true? An obligation to defend against the critique can be seen as part of the affirmative's ground: a natural consequence of their participation in advocacy of the resolution.

CONCLUSION

Critique arguments appear to be an emerging strategy in intercollegiate debate. The purpose of this essay has not been to defend any critique argument in particular. Individual critiques are often controversial at a substantive level since they frequently seek to question conventional practices. This essay has sought to advance a theoretic taxonomy and rationale for critiques, so that their substantive merits might be more clearly discussed in debate rounds. While we have long assumed that the only issue in a debate is resolutional or exemplar truth, critique arguments demonstrate that there may be other relevant issues in a debate. Those issues include whether the resolution is a worthy and capable subject for debate, and whether some event or argument has real effects which are important enough to demand preeminent evaluation. With appropriate development, critique arguments have the potential to serve valuable argumentative and normative functions.

WORKS CITED

Ahmed, Adbar S. *Postmodernism and Islam: Predicament and Promise.* New York: Rutledge, 1992.

Bahm, Kenneth T. "Meaning as Language Use: The Case of the Language-Linked Value Objection." *CEDA Yearbook* 12 (1991): 67-78.

Black, Edwin. "The Second Persona." *Quarterly Journal of Speech* 56 (1970): 109- 19.

Brey, James. "The Use and Misuse of Criteria in CEDA Debate Rounds." *CEDA 1991: 20th Anniversary Assessment Conference Proceedings.* Ed. David A. Thomas and Stephen C. Woods. Dubuque, IA: Kendall/Hunt, 1993. 199-220.

—. Ed. "1989 National CEDA Tournament Final Round." *Transcript.*

Buker, Eloise. "'Lady' Justice: Power and Image in Feminist Jurisprudence." *Vermont Law Review* 15 (1990): 69-87.

Dalby, Simon. *Creating the Second Cold War: The Discourse of Politics.* New York: Guilford, 1990.

Edwards, Rich E. "In Defense of Utopia: A Response to Katsulas, Herbeck, and Panetta." *Journal of the American Forensic Association* 24 (1987): 112-18.

Enloe, Cynthia. "The Masculine Mystique." *The Progressive* 58.1 (1994): 24-26.

Goodnight, G. Thomas. "The Reunion of Argumentation and Debate Theory. *Dimensions of Argument: Proceedings of the Second Summer Conference on Argumentation.* Ed. George Ziegelmueller and Jack Rhodes. Annandale, VA: Speech Communication Association, 1981. 415-32.

Hingstman, David B. "Lessons Learned: The Philosophy of Ordinary Language and the Theory of Debate." *Argument in Transition: Proceedings of the Third Summer Conference on Argumentation.* Ed. David Zarefsky, Malcolm Sillars, and Jack Rhodes. Annandale, VA: Speech Communication Association, 1983. 772-91.

Katsulas, John P., Dale A. Herbeck, and Edward M. Panetta. "Fiating Utopia: A Negative View of the Emergence of World Order Counterplans and Futures Gaming in Policy Debate." *Journal of the American Forensic Association* 24 (1987): 95:111.

Murphy, Thomas L. "Assessing the Jurisdictional Model of Topicality." *Journal of the American Forensic Association* 26 (1990): 145-50.

Murphy, Thomas L. and Melinda L. Murphy. "Resolutional Relevance: A Primary Standard for Evaluating Criteria in Non-Policy Debate." *CEDA Yearbook* 11 (1990): 1-8.

Rosen, Jeremy. "Re: Critique Arguments." *CEDA-L Digest* 42 (12 Dec. 1993).

Sandoval v. Martinez 109 N.M. 5, 780 P.2d 1152 (Ct. App.), *cert. denied* (July 27, 1989).

Selva, Lance H. and Robert M. Bohm. "Law and Liberation: Toward an Oppositional Legal Discourse. *Legal Studies Forum* 11 (1987): 243-66.

Toffler, Alvin and Heidi Toffler. *War and Anti-War: Survival at the Dawn of the 21st Century.* Waltham, MA: Little, Brown, and Company, 1993.

West, Mark. "Let's Let Everyone Play." *West Coast Debate: The Negative Handbook.* Ed. Jim Hanson and Matt Taylor. Spanaway, WA: West Coast. 8-10.

NOTES

[1] "Resolved: that the national news media in the United States impair public understanding of political issues."

[2] "Resolved: that United States Military intervention to foster democratic government is appropriate in a post-Cold War world."

[3] We use the term "resolutional question" with the understanding that it has become accepted practice to affirm the resolution with reference only to an affirmative's parametric case. Given this, the resolutional question would most often manifest itself as the truth or falsity of the affirmative's case.

[4] "Resolved: that United Nations implementation of its Universal Declaration on Human Rights would be beneficial."

[5] This criticism was suggested by Jeremy Rosen of Cornell University through the CEDA Listserv.

6 In *Sandoval v. Martinez*, for example, the New Mexico Court of Appeals held that a district court may dismiss a plaintiff's lawsuit as a response to the plaintiff lying in interrogatories. Their justification for the decision had nothing to do with the merits of the case; they held that the rationale for dismissal was the plaintiff's disruption of the discovery process.

7 The topic was "Resolved: that one or more United States Supreme Court decisions recognizing a constitutional right of privacy should be overruled." Some judges, in fact, recused themselves from judging on this topic for reasons that argument critiques may address.

8 Philosophers might refer to such a statement as "trivially true." Due to the non-existent nature of the subject (and the resultant non-falsifiability) it would be technically valid to say that "red ducks fly," but equally valid to say that "red ducks cannot fly."

9 We use this term with the understanding that its conventional use is insulting; we use it to demonstrate that some propositions clearly are more deserving of legitimacy critique than refutation.

10 Most debate arguments are probably evaluated according to a *preponderance of evidence* standard (Which position is most likely true?). Perhaps a stricter standard, such as *clear and convincing proof*, could be applied to resolutional-flaw critiques. Higher standards of proof are already recognized in other contexts (such as the argument that the affirmative must be proved "100% non-topical" in order to lose on that issue).

11 This seems to be a central thesis in Toffler and Toffler's *War and Anti-War*. They seem to argue that thinking in *post-Cold War* terms entrenches a Second Wave mindset, rendering us unable to develop Third Wave peace strategies.

We wish to achknowledge the contributions of several individuals whose conversations on this subject, via the CEDA Listserve, were instrumental in shaping the content of this article. These individuals include Doyle Srader, Jamey Dumas, Jeremy Rosen, and others. We would additionally like to thank the *CEDA Yearbook* editor and the anonymous reviewers who made direct and substantive contributions to the style and the content of this work.

Ken Broda-Bahm (Ph.D., Southern Illinois University) is an Associate Professor in Communication Studies at Towson University, in Towson, Maryland. **Thomas Murphy** is an attorney with the Public Defender's office, 5th Judicial District, in Hobbs, New Mexico. This essay was originally published in volume 15 (1994) of *CEDA Yearbook* (now known as *Contemporary Argumentation and Debate*), pp. 20-32.

CONTEXTS, TEXTS AND RETEXTS: TEXTUAL ANALYSIS RE-EXAMINED CRITICIZING KRITIKS

David M. Berube

I. INTRODUCTION

Textual analysis is and seemingly will remain an analytical quagmire. To illustrate some of the weaknesses of textual studies, I have chosen to examine kritiks as argumentative strategies in interscholastic and intercollegiate debate. I conclude they not only yield little, if any useful understanding, but also they confound and obscure meaning as well.

"A kritik is an argument that has a special disposition. Presumably, a kritik is resolved prior to any substantive issues in a debate (*a priori*)" (Berube, 1996, 13). In other words, they are pre-fiat arguments. In practice, kritiks can be experienced on three, sometimes overlapping levels.

A language kritik blames the advocate for misuse of language. Whether an ethnic slur or a politically incorrect reference using unspeakable symbology (e.g., using the word "holocaust" to amplify a concept which is removed from the extermination of Jews and others during World War II), the critic is asked to vacate the advocate's substantive claims regardless of merit. Presumably, the blameworthy advocate's claims become so tainted, they become warrantless.

An ideational kritik blames the advocate for wrongheadedness. The substantive claims are premised on concepts which are valueless and fundamentally flawed (e.g., using the hierarchy of capitalism or patriarchy to manage plan solvency).

A thinking kritik blames the advocate for methodologically incommensurableness. The substantive claims are built with a proverbial house of cards (e.g., legalism or scientific objectivism are self-referential systems of reasoning, hence silencing all voice but their own). Using this thinking crowds out truth seeking.

As such, this essay is a metakritik for it argues the kritik is mostly worthless and has little, if any, truthvalue in academic debate. Of course, This problem is hardly unique to debating. Indeed, it is the basis of one of the most serious criticisms of postmodern deconstruction.

> Conflicts in interpretation typically seek to resolve themselves by appealing to texts. But, we are told, the best one can get from a text is a reading, one among others. This relativism with regard to interpretation follows with logical rigor from the premises of semiological reductionism: if signifiers refer always and only to other signifiers, then there is no ground against which the truth of the interpretations can be measured. Defending a position becomes more a matter of stamina than truth or relevance (Dillon, 1995, 167).

The kritik, as an argument form, will need to meet the fundamental standards of good argument. The following are minimal to all argument. In sum, the criteria would include four factors:

1. explicableness
2. corroborability
3. falsifiability, and
4. ability to enhance truthvalue.

All good arguments should be explainable, especially good oral argument. Deference to tomes of literatures is a scoundrelous retreat for an advocate unwilling or unable to articulate warrants for an argument. All good arguments should be corroborated by proof. Whether deduced, induced, or even abduced, the reasoning should be discernible such that even the most profoundly new concepts can be evaluable. As suggested by Popper (1972), arguments must be falsifiable. Without the opportunity to challenge claims, the relative validity of the claims becomes asserted. The first three standards generally avoid the appeal to authority.

The fourth standard is different. We must ask ourselves: does the argument improve the truthvalue of the plan without the resolution (parametrics) or the resolution itself? Too often arguments are shrouded in complex language and generally obfuscate the truthvalue function of the debating process. White we cannot discover truth in an academic debate, we can approaching truthfinding, and that search is fundamentally valuable. With this latter point in mind, let us consider this question: Are we better able to make truth claims with the kritik? I argue below we are not.

II. INTERPRETATION - THE PROCESS

Denzin outlines steps in the interpretive process. These four steps are foundational to any interpretation. Denzin distinguishes between thick and thin description. While thick description builds on multiple, triangulated methods, is contextual, historical, and interactional, captures the actual flow of an experience of individuals or collectivities in a situation, captures meanings that are present in a sequence of experiences, and allows readers to experience vicariously the essential features of the experiences that have been described and are being interpreted (Denzin, 1989, 102), a thinner interpretative methodology might prove most useful to decide appropriate questions. The steps:

1. **CAPTURING** (locating and situating what is to be studied in the natural world).

2. **BRACKETING** (removing what is studied out of the world in which it occurs whereat it is dissected, its elements and essential structures uncovered, defined, and analyzed).

3. **CONSTRUCTION** (classifying, ordering, and reassembling

the phenomenon into a coherent whole).

4. **CONTEXTUALIZATION** (interpreting structures and giving them meaning by locating them back in the natural social world) (Denzin, 1989, 54-60).

For our purposes, the natural world is the debating environment, its setting. It begins as the first phrase is uttered ending when the participants cease to speak. In some situations, the defining limits have more to so with some point when the critic begins listening and ending when she stops, and this may have little, if anything, to do with the sweep of the minute hand or the cascade of digits on a chronometer, or even the speaking of the advocate.

The unnatural world occurs within the critic. Whether individually or collectively, it is a spoken or unspoken dialogue. Working within the general parameters of resolving claims made to postulate a resolution, the critic attempts to dispose of claims and counter-claims until an overall disposition of the debate itself becomes warrantable.

For purposes of illustration, consider the ideational kritik of militarism. In this kritik, an advocate maintains the "military" paradigm must be unmasked for what it is: violence. Hence, if an affirmative cleans up military waste, they sanitize the "military." Furthermore, by engaging the civilian world in the process, they convert civil society into complicitous agents, if not co-conspirators.

CAPTURING. The context is forsaken and the kernel of the idea is scrutinized. It is examined, statically, hence it is shielded from counterfactualized events: past, present and future. "Meaning deactivates the object, renders it intransitive, assigns it a *frozen* place in what we might call a *tableau vivant* of the human image repertoire" (1988, 1964, 189). Hence, textual analysis must remove a sign from time and space, arresting its potential mutability. However, freezing the text does not divest it of its time and space variables. These variables establish a first level context. Moreover, when the text is frozen again, maybe by a different reader, it is a different and sometimes a very different text. Trying to validate a mutable text by referring to other mutable texts demonstrates a foundational problem in textual analysis. In our example, this happens when military commentators addressing one phenomenon about the military are transposed as warrants for a similar, yet unintended, claim.

Furthermore, the advocates of the military kritik may employ a force or power unintended by the original commentator. Indeed, a military commentator might find the application of some of her conclusions used to delegitimize a paltry plan act as nearly inconsequential or trivial.

Maybe better than other concepts, **BRACKETING,** as a concept explains why advocates of the kritik claim the kritik is impervious to post-fiat, case derived, substantive rebuttal. Moreover, it explains the basis for the pre-fiat versus the post-fiat disposition of kritiks.

Isolated from its grander context (the case), the kritik sheds its catalyst until the ultimate subtext of the idea associated with the kritik is revealed. By bracketing the subject of the kritik, the deconstruction becomes manageable.

For example, the advocate of the military kritik extricates the realm of the affirmative remediation from its socio-politico-cultural setting or context and demands the merits of the kritik be evaluated exclusive of any issues which may occur post-fiat. Hence, long-term impacts which might expose military conspiracy are moot. Problematically, the bracketing might further distance the kritik from intrinsicness assaults in the form of hypothetical counter-counterplans or permutations.

CONSTRUCTION. Once interpretation has stopped and the critic lists, orders, and relates interpretations, she attempts to bind together her observations. Attempts to resolve a kritik involve collecting the warrants supporting the kritik and packaging them into a conclusion. Responses are packaged as well.

In the military kritik, the critic would ask any or all of the following questions.

- Is the critic situated to resolve the kritik? Since the disposition of kritiks is generally premised on the existence of fiat, a paradigm without fiat would complicate the disposition (see Berube, 1994, 222-241).
- Is the evidence bolstering the kritik contextually valid? For example, if the sources to support the kritik would never advocate rejecting the plan, using their texts to win the debate may be unacceptable.
- Is the kritik more important than the plan? While evidence

supporting a decision rule may have been introduced by the advocate of the kritik, the evidence may not justify rejection of the plan. For example, but for the plan, the kritik might not have even surfaced. The plan by provoking the kritik might be equally powerful in engendering similar ideas beyond the debate itself.

- Which sources are better? The authoritative warrants for the kritik may be less valid than those of the rebuttalists. For example, Heidegger, Hume, Kant and their ideas have rebuttalists.

- Can the plan be adopted outside or beyond the kritik? I guess this a what colleagues mean when they permute the kritik. In other words, if the affirmative plan is justifiable beyond the realm of the kritik, it denies the essential or necessary character of the kritik. For example, when the affirmative backs away from banning land mines to improve warfighting, instead arguing the ban is humanitarian by protecting innocent civilians, they attempt to avoid linkage. Since I believe all permutations, except replanning, are intrinsicness arguments by their very nature, the semblance between the permutation against kritiks and the intrinsicness arguments does not seem to bother me.

- Can the kritik be offset? Much like the exclusion permutation against counterplans, the affirmative can choose to argue we should embrace the post-fiat implications of the plan while unmasking military ideas elsewhere. Wholly dependents on the quality of the decision rule evidence embodied in the kritik and the apparent seemingly intrinsicness nature of this approach, the tactic is highly problematical, but it still remains a potential step in the construction process.

- Is the kritik kritiked? Beyond the incommensurableness of some kritiks, advocates often choose to argue the kritik is meaningless in the context of a debate. This is examined elsewhere, above and below.

In practice, most of the post-fiat substantive claims tend to be discounted. For a justification of this procedure, see Berube (1976, 16-17). Once the critic decides a conclusion is achievable, she moves into the final step.

CONTEXTUALIZATION. This step involves setting the kritik text within the text of the debate. At this point, the question of blame becomes pertinent and problematical. The critic must conclude that advocate against whom the kritik has been argued is blameworthy or sufficiently responsible for the alleged abuse. For example, the critic examines the text of the affirmative debate and asks whether the affirmative is sufficiently guilty of military ideation to trigger the decision rule embodied in the kritik. The critic is asking herself: does the affirmative text sufficiently link to the kritik text such that the substantive issues should become moot.

This process is further complicated once we examine the theory behind deep textual analysis and the kritik.

III. INTERPRETANT ANALYSIS - THEORY

What is a text?

A text is a device conceived in order to produce its model reader. I repeat that this reader is not the one who makes the 'only right' conjecture. A text can foresee the model reader entitled to try infinite conjectures. The empirical reader is only an actor who makes conjectures about the kind of model reader postulated by the text. Since the intention of the text is basically to produce a model reader to make conjectures about it, the initiative of the model reader consists in figuring out a model author that is not the empirical one and that, in the end, coincides with the intention of the text. Thus, more than a parameter to use in order to validate the interpretation, the text is an object that the interpretation builds up in the course of the circular effort of validating itself on the basis of what it makes up as a result. I am not ashamed to admit that I am so defining the old and still valid "hermeneutic circle" (Eco, 1992, 64).

All texts are made for a model reader. That is true of the secondary sources advocates use for evidence as well as the text the advocates make in a given debate. When texts are deconstructed and rearranged with bits from other deconstructed tests, the result is constructed for a different model reader. Experts whose writings are strung together to form a narrative might be appalled to learn their bits of information have been used as blocks of information drawing claims very unlike those they attempted to communicate to their model readers.

C. S. Peirce found even more difficulties with textual analysis and turned to semiotics to explain them. He struggled with the concept of *interpretant*. An interpretant is the idea given rise by the meaning of a sign. He claimed it is "essential to the function of a sign that it should determine an *interpretant*, or a second correlate related to the object of the sign as a sign is itself related to the object; and this interpretant may be regarded as the sign represents it to be, as it is in its pure secondness to the object and as it is in its firstness" (Ms 914, 1904, 3).

He attempted to distinguish between logical interpretants. Peirce defined the *logical interpretant* as the "intellectual apprehension of the meaning of a sign" (Ms 318, 1907, 176). A *first* logical interpretant consists of conjecture called up by the sign suggesting them. The *second* logical interpretant may be *higher* or *lower*. A slight modification of the conjectures makes them more carefully defined; this is the process by which we reach *lower* second logical interpretants. *Higher* second logical interpretants occur as forms of conjectures are abstracted with ensuing generalizations. When external experimentation or quasi-experimentation on conjecturing about the sign occurs, we reach *third* logical interpretants. Peirce admits a resulting logical interpretant will itself call forth a logical interpretant, and so forth ad infinitum.

If the meaning of a sign is calculated to produce the intended meaning, we must ask ourselves not only when an interpretant analysis moots the powers of the signer, but also at what level of analysis a further deepening of meaning is relatively unproductive. On one level, the answers lie within the dynamic of the communication event. For example, in a debate, arguments are judged as signs made by the arguers. Overstanding the signs may simply distance the arguments from the signers such that the interpretant being evaluated might be quite unlike that intended to be made by the arguers. Additionally, the time constraints on the arguers compels her to make choices, sacrificing the potential of an interpretant simply because thickening the analysis become problematical. For example, signing any meaning about the complexities of governmental regulatory policies in five minutes or within five pages produces a dynamic which trades potential off against actuality.

A. OVERINTERPRETATION AND OVERSTANDING

Peirce found an inherent fallibilism in every interpretative conclusion. Though he tried to construct a minimal paradigm of acceptability of an interpretation, he was less than successful. Not unlike Gadamer's idea of an interpretative tradition, Peirce suggested community consensus. While community consensus has proven useful as a guide to living, it is much less useful when it becomes nearly impossible to identify the intended community. Unless the model reader(s) can be identified and are willing and able to communicate her consensus, Peirce's paradigm is hopelessly mired in supposition and regressive reinterpretation.

> One might imagine *overinterpretation* to be like *overeating*: there is proper eating or interpreting, but some people don't stop when they should. They go on eating or interpreting in excess, with bad results (Culler, 1992, 111).

Overinterpretation can be undesirable. Culler hypothesizes such, though he defends the obverse.

> Moreover, if our interest is not so much in the receiving of intended messages but in understanding, say, the mechanisms of linguistic and social interaction, then it is useful from time to time to stand back and ask why someone said some perfectly straightforward thing such as, "Lovely day, isn't it?" What does it mean that *this* should be a casual form of greeting? What does that tell us about this culture as opposed to others that might have different phatic forms or habits? What Eco calls *overinterpretation* may in fact be a practice of asking precisely those questions which are *not* necessary for normal communication but which enable us to reflect on its functioning... Understanding is asking the questions and finding the answers that the text insists on. "Once upon a time there were three little pigs" demands that we ask "So what happened?" and not "Why three?" or "What is the concrete historical context?", for instance (Culler, 1992, 113-114).

Culler has a second reservation: too little understanding from over-interpretation.

> *Overstanding*, by contrast, consists of pursuing questions that the text does not pose to its model reader (Culler, 1992, 114).

Eco's overinterpretation may be compared to Booth's concept of *overstanding*.

> What do you have to say, you seemingly innocent child's tale of three little pigs and a wicked wolf, about the culture that preserves and responds to you? About the unconscious dreams of the author or folk that created you? About the history of narrative suspense? About the relations of the lighter and the darker races? About big people and little people, hairy and bald, lean and fat? About triadic patterns in human history? About the Trinity? About laziness and industry, family structure, domestic architecture, dietary practice, standards of justice and revenge? About the history of manipulations of narrative point of view for the creation of sympathy? Is it good for a child to read you or hear you recited, night after night? Will stories like you – *should* stories like you – be allowed when we have produced our ideal socialist state? What are the sexual implications of that chimney – or of this strictly male world in which sex is never mentioned? What about all that huffing and puffing (Booth, 1979, 243)?

B. TALKING TEXTS

Booth insists we must first determine what texts want of us. The questions a text may ask can be exceedingly narrow and simple or expansive and complex. What kinds of questions are essential or proper or even appropriate shift from text to text. *Boundaries of appropriateness* are set by the text as it moves in us. As examples, Booth considers two of the most open or ambiguous texts ever written: Beckett's The Unnamable (1958) and Derrida's Glas (1974).

> However indeterminate the work, it will still ask us to rule out cer-

tain inappropriate questions. *Glas,* for example, which is difficult to classify according to any traditional literary or philosophical category, insists that we *not* ask it to answer the Three Little Pigs kind of question ("Who will do what to whom?"). It also insists that we finally reject such questions as "In what traditional literary genre shall I place you?" It is important to underline the universality of this kind of demand. It is true that different readers will infer different boundaries (or 'horizons') of appropriate questions, depending on their previous experiences and their critical presuppositions. But about what we might call the text's central preoccupations there is an astonishing agreement among us all; that is what makes it possible for us to use generic terms without total confusion (Booth, 1979, 241).

Do different texts appropriate different questions? Of course, they do.

Some texts will try to set a single direction of questioning, and some will not. But *all* texts try to present boundary conditions which all experienced readers will recognize (Booth, 1979, 242).

Is criticism outside some hermeneutic circle of appropriate questions justified? Of, course, it is.

I will no more accede to all the demands of <u>Mein Kampf</u> or <u>Justine</u> than to the demands of the con man's text when it insistently rules out the question "Are you lying?" That question is totally 'inappropriate' to overt forgery; yet, if I do not insist of asking it, I shall be gulled (Booth, 1979, 242).

Misreading a text in order to overstand it is not valueless. However, Booth drew this conclusion.

Yet obviously no one will, except perhaps in theory, embrace *all* such improper questions as valid or even interesting. It is thus useful to distinguish improprieties according to what is violated and according to the source of validation that the critic offers for the violation (Booth, 1979, 244).

C. WEAK VERSUS STRONG READERS

"The best one can get from a text is a reading, one among others" (Dillon, 1995, 167). (Repetition intended.) The reading is both a function of the text and its reader. While some texts are undoubtedly better than others, so are some readers. If some readers are strong and others are weak, the meaning derived from reading an identical text may differ appreciably. While any judgement detailing interpretative merit may be inappropriate to conclude, it is enough to say variable, if not outrightly incompatible, interpretations can be fabricated from different readings of the same text.

A second level of elusiveness rests with the ephemeral quality of texts. The same readers, strong or weak, never read the same text the same way. The virginal interpretation is immediately lost. Subsequent readings do not only differ appreciably, the texts themselves change as well. Consider the literary text, Mary Shelley's Frankenstein. On first glance, it can be interpreted as a classic horror novel, and that label adroitly characterizes most readers' first experience at interpreting that text. A second reading of the same text may lead to interpreting the story as a critique of hubris. A third time, it might be a study on humanity or an evaluation of scientific ethics. The novel reads different at each subsequent reading.

The apparently thick character of textual analysis challenges readers. Different readers read differently. Seemingly, identical texts are never actually identical. The elusiveness of fixed textual validation demonstrates the futility of returning to earlier texts to validate, especially affirm, later interpretations.

Furthermore, overstanding via deepening interpretant analysis outside the parameters regulating advocates' choices divests the signers of their power to make actual arguments. By investigating the potentiality of interpretants through retextualizing the debate engages second level logical interpretant analysis. Though a defensibly productive exercise, this overstanding textual construction places the critic in a thicker dialogical reality than actually occurred in the debate. What is being evaluated is not the actual debate but rather the potential debate.

Peirce called this communicational event, a search for final interpretant. However, it is clear what occurs in a debate is not that search, rather it is a search (if that) for an immediate interpretant which Peirce articulated as a much lower grade of meaning.

> [A definition:] the interpretant in the intention of the utterer, ie., the state of information the utterer intends to result from the semiosis, including the purpose of the communicative act as it is conceived by him and the information for which he will assume responsibility (Johansen, 1993, 172).

It is intentional, intended, objective, naive, and rogate.

Finally, there is the *contract of dialogue*. Peirce argues the parties participating in symbolic action are not exterior to the analysis of meaning per se.

> As a logician Peirce is mainly interested in the act of affirmation (or assertion), and his favorite way of analysis is by comparing it to the legal act of going before a notary public and making an affidavit to the content of a proposition. This action has penalties attached to its; swearing to the truth of something may move an interpreter to act accordingly and at his expense because he believes in it. The only difference between swearing to a proposition and merely affirming it is that the commitment and the penalties in the latter case are less (Johansen, 1993, 198-199).

D. RHETORICAL TRUTHVALUE AND SPACE

A reconstruction is nearly never the same as its source texts, hence the grounds for comparison and validation are seldom useful per se.

At its best, this process might be utilized to discredit a claim but not for affirming one.

> [W]e can accept a sort of Popperian principle according to which if there are no rules that help to ascertain which interpretations are the "best" ones, there is at least a rule for ascertaining which ones are "bad." We cannot say if the Keplerian hypotheses are definitely the best ones but we can say that the Ptolemaic explanation of the solar system was wrong because

the notion of epicycle as defended violated certain criteria of economy and simplicity, and could not coexist with other hypotheses that proved to be reliable in order to explain phenomena that Ptolemy did not explore (Eco, 1992, 52).

The major problem surfaces when a reader asks whether an interpretation is affirmed. This process is moderated by a series of rules. For example, "the relationship between utterer and interpreter ... depends on the right understanding of the utterer's intentions by the interpreter. Without this understanding it would be impossible for the interpreter to analyze the utterance as a deed or action even if he understands the text's propositional content" (Johansen, 1995, 201).

Intentions are especially problematical to decode in a debating situation. We read differently. We interpret texts differently. We construct texts differently. And, maybe most important, we advocate texts for many different reasons. Unfortunately, these variables are very important factors in calculating the relationship between utterer and interpreter. Unable to fathom the basis of this relationship mitigates textual analysis as an affirming construct.

IV. THE CONTRACT

The role of penalty needs to be detailed at this point. Though the penalty may be less in a debate situation, it still exists.

[An] affirmation is an act of an utterer of a proposition to an interpreter, and consists, in the first place, in the deliberate exercise, in uttering the proposition, of a force tending to determine a belief in it in the mind of the interpreter. Perhaps that is a sufficient definition of it; but it involves also a voluntary self-subjection to penalties in the event of the interpreter's mind (and still more the general mind of society) subsequently becoming decidedly determined to the belief at once in the falsity of the proposition and in the additional proposition that the utterer believed it to be false at the time he uttered it. (Peirce, NEM 1976, IV: 249-250).

The penalty is not a negative phenomenon but rather an essential part of the contract between utterer and interpreter, a ground for a formative relationship. The basis of the relationship is the deictic structure of the utterance.

> ...[T]he utterer, besides being responsible for the conse-quences bound up with the mode of utterance that he selects, is also determining the *deixis,* or deictic system, of the utter-ance. Consequently the interpreter has to follow the directions of the utterer to be able to identify the topic of the discourse (Johansen, 1993, 199).

The utterer designed the parameters of the dialogue between the utterer and the interpreter.

> ...[B]y using the universal selective (e.g., *all* men [sic] sin) the utterer transfers the right of selecting an instance to falsify the proposition to the interpreter. Using the particular selective (e.g. *some* men [sic] sin), the utterer reserves the right of choosing an instance, which proves his argument, for himself [sic]. In the use of a proposition with a singular selective *(this* man [sic] sins), neither the utterer nor the interpreter has free-dom of choice. Since the utterer chooses the mode of the utter-ance, gives the directions for identifying the topic of discourse, and decides the range of the utterance's applicability, what is then left to the interpreter? First, the interpreter plays an important role in the capacity of being the addressee in the intention of the utterer (Johansen, 1993, 199).

Hence the formative role of the interpreter as addressee has a strong parallel in debate. The constructive role of the critic/audience as addressee involves simply constructing the meaning of the utter-ance. This constructing is not fortified by exiting the dynamic rela-tionship even to consider the kritik.

V. CONCLUSION

Kritiks are not good arguments because they fail the fourth criteri-on of good argument: they do not enhance truthvalue in the debate.

While there are ideal settings for discussing kritiks, interscholastic and intercollegiate debate does not qualify. Kritiks are best disposed in seminars and the banter of advocates and respondents in scholarly journals. Deep textual analysis, especially the sort associated with kritiks in debate, produce overstanding and overinterpretation, marginalize textual voices, fails to discriminate between different readers, devalues rhetorical truthvalue and space, and invalidates the dialogic contract in an academic debate.

Too much debate theory is based on power rather than reason. Kritiks are used as big sticks to avoid one of the duties closely associated with debating – research. Advocates argue their kritiks almost irrespective of their opponents' positions. By using highly overtotalizing rhetoric, they engage mini-max extended arguments and overclaim the power of their criticism. In other instances, they use kritiks to batter less experienced readers.

It is true theory tends to follow practice in debate. It is my hope this essay will raise some serious questions about kritiks and their application in competitive debating. None of the above statements directly attributable to me should be used as evidence in a debate round.

WORKS CITED

Barthes, Roland, "The kitchen of meaning," (Le Nouvel Observateur), *The Semiotic Challenge*, tr. Richard Howard, NY: Hill and Wang, 1988, 1964, 157-159.

_____ "Semantics of the object." (Colloquium at the Cini Foundation in Venice), *The Semiotic Challenge*, tr. Richard Howard, NY: Hill and Wang, 1988, 1964, 179-190.

Beckett, Samuel, *The Unnamable*, NY: Grove Press, 1958.

Berube, David, "Kritiks: The attitude of the Diet explained," *Southern Journal of Forensics, 1*, Spring 1996, 13-30.

_____ *Non-Policy Debating*, Lanham, MD: University Press of America, 1994.

Booth, Wayne C., *Critical Understanding: The Powers and Limits of Pluralism*, Chicago: University of Chicago Press, 1979.

Culler, Jonathan, "In defence of overinterpretation," *Interpretation and Overinterpretation: Umberto Eco with Richard Rorty, Jonathan Culler,*

Christine Brooke-Rosa, NY: Cambridge University Press, 1992, 109-124.

Denzin, Norman K., *Interpretive Interactionism*, Newbury Park, CA: Sage Publications, 1989.

Derrida, Jacques, *Glas*, Paris: Editions Galilee, 1974.

Dillon, M. C., *Semiological Reductionism: A Critique of the Deconstructivist Movement in Postmodern Thought*, Albany: SUNY Press, 1995.

Eco, Umberto, "Overinterpreting texts," *Interpretation and Overinterpretation: Umberto Eco with Richard Rorty, Jonathan Culler, Christine Brooke-Rosa*, NY: Cambridge University Press, 1992, 45-66.

Husserl, Edmund, *Ideas: General Introduction to Pure Phenomenology*, London: George Allen & Unwin LTD, 1931.

Johansen, Jorgen Dines, *Dialogic Semiosis: An Essay on Sign and Meaning*, Bloomington, IN: Indiana University Press, 1995.

Peirce, Charles Sanders, *Collected Papers: I-VIII*, C. Hartshorne, P. Weiss, and A. Burks, eds., Cambridge, MA: Harvard University Press, 1931-1958.

Popper, Karl, *Objective Knowledge: An Evolutionary Approach*, Oxford: Clarendon Press, 1972.

Silverman, Hugh J., *Textualities: Between Hermeneutics and Deconstruction*, NY: Routledge, 1994.

David Berube (Ph.D., New York University) is an Associate Professor of Speech Communication and Director of Carolina Debate at the University of South Carolina in Columbia, South Carolina. This essay was originally published as "Criticizing Kritiks: Textual Analysis Re-examined" in volume 18 (1997) of *Contemporary Argumentation and Debate*, pp. 68-81.

CRITIQUE ARGUMENTS AS POLICY ANALYSIS: POLICY DEBATE BEYOND THE RATIONALIST PERSPECTIVE
Pat J.Gehrke

Policy is not choking debate. An inflexible, narrowly defined vision of policy threatens debate (Shanahan A8).

While critique arguments were once rare in academic debates, today they are part of nearly every debater's experience. Contemporary debates frequently grapple with arguments that indict or advance values, systems of knowledge, and language choices. It is difficult to know whether this growing popularity is due to advances in critique theory, a growing dissatisfaction with traditional models of policy debate, or the competitive success of critiques in debate. What is apparent in debate literature and discussion is that a substantial amount of controversy still exists about the saliency of critiques to academic policy debate. Some policy debate advocates claim there is no place for critiques in the comparison of policy options, while advocates of critiques often consider such arguments broader than a policy perspective, arguing that critics should consider critiques before resolving policy questions. Whether one subscribes to Roger Solt's view that "the *kritik* is on balance bad for debate" (*Anti-Kritik* ii) or William Shanahan's view that "*kritiks* allow debate access to another of its fundamental assumptions" (A5), it is clear that at least for the near future critiques will play a major role in the practice of academic policy debate.

At this point, the controversy over critique argumentation is at an impasse. Both sides of this controversy marginalize critique arguments by positioning them outside of policy deliberation. The predominate notion among both supporters and opponents of critiques is that they are argued as a sidebar to the policy debate. While I am sympathetic to, and often agree with, the philosophical potential envisioned by those who endorse critique arguments, their reasoning often fails to address the questions raised by those who doubt the role of critiques in policy debate. We cannot transcend these differences without repositioning the relationship between critique arguments and policy deliberation. This essay contends that meaningful policy evaluation often includes arguments similar to those labeled "critiques" in academic debate. Specifically, it argues that critique arguments, rather than serving as *a priori* or tangential issues, are relevant dimensions of policy analysis and should be treated as substantive issues in policy debate.

The idea that the issues raised by critique arguments are relevant to the substance of policy disputes is consistent with arguments made by innovative policy analysts and policy scholars. Many policy theorists argue for including in the policy discussion process arguments that mirror certain forms of critique argumentation. This position may seem unusual, given that some debate theorists tend to believe that policy analysis excludes critique arguments (Jinks A14; Shors and Mancuso A15; Solt, *Anti-Kritik* xxiii; Solt, "Demystifying" A9). However, a considerable body of policy studies literature clearly supports the inclusion of critiques based upon competing value orientations and critiques based upon the communicative aspects of the policy process.

THE STATUS OF CRITIQUE ARGUMENTS IN ACADEMIC DEBATE

In contemporary academic debate, critique arguments encompass a wide range of philosophical issues. Shanahan originally focused on the German existential philosopher Martin Heidegger's call to explore how we think about being in the world. This continental pedigree gave rise to the commonly used German spelling, *kritik*. Shanahan contends that traditional policy debate "functions on a foundation of unquestioned assumptions" (A4). He calls for debaters to advance arguments that can uncover and investigate these assumptions. Shanahan holds that the focus ought not be on the results of such a questioning, but rather that the process of thinking and questioning itself is to be valued (A4). Since Shanahan, debaters have expanded critiques from their existential origins to include a broad diversity of philosophical and political perspectives. Recent critiques have been based on Riane Eisler's feminist anthropology, Herbert Marcuse's theory of repressive desublimation, Immanuel Kant's categorical imperative, and Ayn Rand's objectivism.

A second origin of critique argumentation is Kenneth Broda-Bahm's theory of the language-linked value objection, or "language critique." Broda-Bahm indicts academic debate for operating under the assumption that language is transparent and purely referential. He uses Ludwig Wittgenstein's theory of language games to argue that words and their use have effects, and that critics should consider objections to certain language choices when adjudicating debates. As originally conceived, the language-linked value objection focused "more directly on the actual language practices of an opponent" (Bahm 69). Broda-Bahm gives language critiques primacy as voting issues because they make claims to immediate and tangible impacts that "uniquely happen as a direct result of our advocacy" (Bahm 76). More recently, theorists and debaters have fashioned critiques involving such diverse arguments as evidence challenges, morality arguments, and objections to particular styles of delivery (Berube, "Kritiks").

For the purposes of this essay, critiques conveniently may be divided into three argument forms: value critiques, epistemology critiques, and language critiques. This classification system is relatively common in critique literature. David Berube refers to ideational (value), thinking (epistemology), and language critiques ("Criticizing" 68). Solt separates critiques into practical philosophical critiques (value), pure philosophical critiques (epistemology), and language critiques (*Anti-Kritik* ii-vii). While these classification schemes are neither universal nor comprehensive, they are functional for discussing the relationship between critique argumentation and policy deliberation.

Value critiques establish or indict value systems or advance ethical or moral claims. These take the shape of deontological critiques, decision rules, value hierarchies, ethics violations, and moral obligations. When an affirmative claims a moral obligation to implement their policy, they are advancing value arguments in an attempt to justify their policy position. Likewise, these arguments are frequently advanced by negatives contending that an affirmative's proposed policy is discriminatory (i.e., racist, patriarchal, heterosexist, etc.) or morally unacceptable as a course of action (such as the pacifist's opposition to committing violent acts). Value critiques were the stock and trade of "value" debate, usually referred to as criteria and value objections arguments (Zarefsky 15).

Epistemology critiques establish or indict means of creating or finding truths. These include arguments such as Paul Feyerabend's critique of scientific method and Murray Edelman's theory of enemy construction. Epistemology critiques predominantly question the reliability of particular methods of making predictive and descriptive claims inherent in a particular policy advocacy. Every policy case advances causal and predictive claims. These claims are each the result of a particular way of coming to or creating knowledge, such as laboratory study, romantic introspection, field research, or humanist investigation. Epistemology critiques indict a method of coming to or creating knowledge, thus undercutting the claims derived through that method. The best of these critiques will also advance an alternative knowledge system that produces results contrary to the claims advanced in the opponent's positions.

Language critiques can be differentiated from value and epistemology critiques in two respects. First, they focus upon communicative or interpretive aspects of either particular word choices or the broader advocacy of debaters. Language critiques indict what an advocate communicates, intentionally or otherwise, and what others who endorse that advocacy might communicate. Debaters have called these arguments language-linked value objections, language objections, language critiques, advocacy critiques, advocacy-linked disadvantages, and a host of other names. Second, the most controversial element that differentiates these arguments from other objections to policy advocacy is the claim that their implications supersede the impacts of particular policy actions. Advocates of language critiques often claim fiat to be illusory, that language creates reality, or that advocacy has "real-world" or "in-round" effects upon critics, debaters, and others. For example, a language critique might argue that an opponent has employed sexist language, such as using "mankind" as an androgynous term. The team advancing the critique may argue that a critic who fails to reject the sexist language likewise advocates using sexist language, and consequently perpetuates and reinforces sexism in the culture. Conversely, the policy issues debated are only fictions or imaginations used to simulate a policy decision in the debate. In actuality, when the critic votes, no policy is enacted. Yet, the critique proponents argue, the effects of the language are real and immediate. Thus, the debaters ask the critic to ignore the illusory or imagined impacts of the proposed policies and decide the debate based upon the real and immediate impacts of language.

Some critiques, such as Critical Race Theory, cross these categories. Since Critical Race Theory indicts the American legal system for being racist, which makes its predictive and descriptive claims inaccurate, it combines a value critique and an epistemological critique. Similarly, debaters sometimes combine value arguments with language critiques to create a dual set of impacts for their positions. With the sexism example previously discussed, the critiquing team may add an argument that says that individuals have a moral obligation to reject sexism when they encounter it. Thus, in addition to the language critique of the use of the term "mankind," the critiquing team would also advance a value critique, holding that there is an obligation to reject sexism. The distinctions between value, epistemology, and language critiques are not always clean, and may leave out some critique arguments. Critique argumentation is in a constant state of mutation as debaters find new ways to think about particular issues. The classification scheme used here should be considered functional only for the purposes of this discussion.

One of the primary criticisms leveled against all such critiques is that they fail to address policy questions (Jinks A14; Shors and Mancuso A15; Solt, *Anti-Kritik* xiii; Solt, "Demystifying" A9). Most debate theorists who oppose critique arguments advance a rational-

ist paradigm of policy evaluation. In their minds, a strict cost-benefit analysis, particularly a quantitative analysis based on the preser-
vation of human life, is the only means by which an advocate can justify or dejustify a policy. In his criticism of scientific models of public policy, Robert Formaini, the former vice president for public policy at the Cato Institute, explains the rationalist policy paradigm:

> According to the policy rationalist, if the risks are "accept-
> able" and the "benefits" are greater than "costs," what per-
> son can argue that the proposed policy ought not be done,
> and on what inductive basis? It will not work to say that the
> proposed policy is "wrong," "immoral," "unjust," and a
> "waste of time and effort." These arguments are "unscien-
> tific" and "value-laden" with the citizen's personal, irrational
> prejudices. (69)

In policy debate, the rationalist perspective marginalizes critiques by
mistakenly representing a particular approach to policy evaluation
as the essential means of policy deliberation, implying that one theoretical perspective is both appropriate for all policy questions and
preferable to all other means of policy comparison.

Marouf Hasian and Edward Panetta argue that "both the promise
and the peril of the critique come from its use as a method of questioning some of the assumptions behind 'policy' debate itself" (47).
They continue, "the use of 'the critique' in policy debate means a virtual abandonment of many of the cherished assumptions of policy decision making" (53). If by policy debate and policy decision making,
Hasian and Panetta are referring only to the conventional practices of
academic debate, they would be correct. However, their criticism is
not that critiques simply challenge academic policy debate as we commonly practice it, but rather that critiques are "politically irrelevant and
counterproductive" (54). This conclusion is arrived at by giving primacy to rationalist policy models, including claims such as that "debating is an inherently rationalistic activity" (54).

Faith in rationalism as the core element of policy debate leads
Derek Jinks to posit that if critiques have any theoretical legitimacy, "they should take the form of disadvantages, counterplans, solvency arguments, etc." (A14). Jinks argues that resolutions imply

the context for academic debates, and since contemporary resolutions are interpreted as policy questions, they should be addressed from a policy perspective (A12). While this line of reasoning may bear some merit, Jinks begs the question of whether the rationalist model is the only possible policy perspective. Jinks relies on a rationalist cost-benefit analysis model for decision making. He argues that policy decisions cannot be made without comparing unique costs and benefits of proposed courses of action (A14). Jinks likewise contends that policy debate should begin from a set of shared assumptions about the values at stake, which should simply be taken as true (A13).

Matthew Shors and Steve Mancuso propose an extreme division between critiques and policy discourse. Shors and Mancuso make the same error as Jinks by generalizing from rationalist policy models to all policy deliberation. They claim that critiques are "utterly irrelevant" and that critiques ask us to believe that "it is pointless to discuss policies" (A16). Shors and Mancuso would have us believe that critiques "ignore policy issues altogether" (A16). It is because critiques do not argue unique commensurable costs or benefits that they contend that critiques carry "little, if any, weight in policy comparison" (A16). Only by failing to recognize the broad diversity of policy perspectives can Shors and Mancuso come to conclude that "the Critique is wholly incompatible with, and non-germane to, policy debate" (A17).

Perhaps the most vehement opponent of critiques has been Solt. Solt makes many of the same assumptions about policy analysis as do Jinks, Shors, and Mancuso. Solt so strongly believes that critiques challenge the assumption that "what we are essentially engaged in is a policy debate" that he recommends the first response to critiques be to reestablish the policy framework ("Demystifying" A9). For Solt, "the *kritik* is a non-policy argument" (*Anti-Kritik* ii). He sees debate as a policy forum, and critiques are considered not to be "germane to the subject at hand" (*Anti-Kritik* xxii). Solt argues that "at root, the kritik misunderstands the nature of the policy calculus" (*Anti-Kritik* xxiii). Solt's rationalist assumptions are apparent in arguments encouraging us to "take an *a priori* ethical and political framework for granted" ("Demystifying" A11). Similarly, he ignores a whole body of interpretive and communicative policy analysis literature when he claims that "ideas are more important than the rhetoric with which they are expressed" ("Demystifying" A11). Here, Solt is attempting to refute language critiques by retreating to a separation of policies and the words that express, present, and form those policies. For Solt, the policy has a pure form outside of language, and it is that form that is to be evaluated, rather than any of the words that might malign it. Such a position is distant from much of both contemporary communication studies and policy studies literature.

The arguments against critiques advanced by the policy debate rationalists are suspect because they are grounded in the traditions of academic debate rather than contemporary theories of policy studies. Consequently, they dismiss questions they can not force-fit into policy rationalism as neither worthwhile nor relevant to policy discussions. As two policy analysts wrote of the hegemony of the rationalist paradigm, "When all you have is a hammer the whole world looks like a nail" (House and Shull 163-164).

Berube attacks critiques from a perspective not overtly founded on policy rationalism, holding that critiques are fundamentally pre-fiat arguments and that they disregard post-fiat substantive claims ("Criticizing" 68-72). Nonetheless, he bases his arguments upon similar assumptions about the relationship between critiques and policy debate. Here, "fiat" is a stand-in for "policy focus," in that fiat represents an enacted policy. To claim that critiques disregard issues that arise after fiat is to claim that they disregard questions raised by enacting policies.

Berube's argument is also predicated upon the assumption that academic debate should extend no further than "intentional, intended, naïve, objective, and rogate" meanings ("Criticizing" 77). This means that debaters and critics should not question any of the assumptions or presuppositions of texts or advocacies, uncritically accepting the premises inherent in propositions. In the context of policy analysis, Berube's standards require that policy advocates and analysts not ask of each other: "But what are your assumptions? Are they valid, or consistent, or morally acceptable?" This position is extraordinarily dangerous. Wayne Booth argues that we must consider precisely those questions texts attempt to foreclose:

Each literary work implicates within itself a set of norms about what questions are appropriate. Hemingway, to choose a favorite example of the new feminist critics, does not demand of us that we ask of his works, "Is it good for men or women to accept uncritically my machismo bravado?" Indeed, he seems to work quite hard to prevent our asking such a question. But surely, the feminist critics say, and I think they are right, surely *any* teacher who teaches *A Farewell to Arms* without inviting, somewhere along the line, a critical consideration of Hemingway's heroes as human ideals, and of his portraits of women as reflecting a peculiarly maimed creative vision, and of his vision of the good life as a singularly immature one—surely any such teacher is doing only half the job. (301)

Similarly, we might say that any policy debater who does not seek a critical consideration of the questions that a policy proposal tries to foreclose is only doing half the job of a policy analyst.

Additionally, Berube assumes that we have pure and direct knowledge of the meanings of a text. However, in order to understand the meanings of a text we must interpret that text. When advocates speak, we inevitably interpret what they say. Meanings are found in the act of interpretation, and those meanings differ, at least slightly, between interpretations. There is virtually no text in a debate that can inspire one universally agreed upon interpretation. As listeners and readers, we can never find ourselves at a point where the intentional, naïve, and rogate meanings of a text are objectively transparent to us. Determining what questions a text invites requires interpreting the text, and these interpretations will vary, producing contrary readings of what questions may be asked of that text. There is no way to reconcile interpretations objectively. In order to evaluate competing interpretations, one would have to engage in precisely the critical textual analysis Berube attempts to foreclose. Since every interaction with a text is interpretive, Berube's objective standard for encountering a text never can be met.

While opponents of critiques might be expected to position critiques outside of policy discussion, some advocates of critique arguments in debate have done the same. Many critique proponents advance either the position that we should not consider ourselves policy analysts (Berube, "Kritiks" 21), or that critiques supersede policy questions (Bahm 76; Broda-Bahm and Murphy 21). These arguments unwittingly lend assistance to opponents of critiques by disconnecting critique arguments from policy discourse. Stepping outside the policy focus is not inviting to those who hold resolutely to a policy perspective, rationalist or otherwise. Rather, it makes it all the more difficult to recognize the unique role critique arguments can play in the enhancement of policy analysis and policy debate.

Broda-Bahm probably has done more to popularize language critiques than any other theorist, but he clearly positions these arguments outside of policy deliberation. Broda-Bahm and Thomas Murphy define a critique as "any argument which does not provide an answer to the resolutional question" (21). In this context, they refer to "the resolutional question" not merely as the resolution itself, but as the affirmative case which advocates it (31 n3). They make the same assumption often used as a premise against critiques, that we can and should separate policies from the language that advances them. Broda-Bahm separates policy and language by arguing that critiques do not answer substantive advocacy, but rather focus "more directly on the actual language practices of an opponent" (Bahm 69). This is reinforced with attempts to give primacy to the "more immediate and more tangible" effects of language by claiming policy proposals to be fictions of debate rounds (Bahm 76).

While positioning critiques outside of policy discourse is a common error amongst critique advocates, Shanahan is an exception. Much of Shanahan's essay is esoteric and philosophical, but he does recognize at least a potential for critiques to be a part of policy analysis. Making use of literature about development assistance, Shanahan considers "the possibility that the *kritik* is policy debate" (A8). Shanahan was nearest the mark when he claimed that "the *kritik* supplements, not supplants current debate practice" (A4). However, critique proponents have either ignored or simply reiterated these claims, and opponents of critique argumentation scoff at Shanahan's conception of policy analysis. Most likely, this is because Shanahan's theory is so deeply embedded in Heidegger's philosophy that it is difficult to read a policy focus beneath the existential vocabulary. This may also be because neither proponents nor opponents of critique argumentation have considered the policy studies literature that reinforces the need for critiques in policy discussions. If one truly takes a policy perspective toward debate, one inevitably finds that critique argumentation is a necessary element of policy evaluation.

The impasse hence arises because opponents of critiques hold that the purpose of debate is to discuss policies exclusively, and assume that policy rationalism is the only mechanism debaters can use to do so. Many proponents of critiques maintain the impasse by arguing that critiques somehow supersede or exist outside of policy argumentation. The marginalization performed by both sides of this controversy disconnects critique argumentation from politics, policy deliberation, and real world debates. To move past the impasse and integrate critique argumentation and policy deliberation, we must reposition critiques within the spectrum of policy analysis.

TRANSCENDING RATIONALISM

Policy studies literature is a useful aide to those seeking to understand the relationship between policy, values, and communication. The applicability of policy literature to academic debate depends, to some extent, upon the purposes and goals of debate. One of the primary goals of debate is to foster better thinkers, better decision-makers, and responsible citizens. That contemporary debate focuses upon questions of public policy reinforces the position that debate politicizes participants by informing and shaping political consciousness. As citizens and consumers, we are all, at least indirectly, policy makers. Oddly enough, in an attack upon the theoretical legitimacy of critiques Solt argues exactly this point:

> It is through the process of making the judgments that our moral and political worldviews are developed. The judgments we come to at the end of debate rounds may only be provisional, based on the evidence and arguments in that round, but over time the sum of our provisional judgments is what ultimately constitutes our moral and political belief system. Policy debates are important. As citizens in a democracy, we have individually small but collectively large inputs into the policies our government chooses. And even if our own input into the policy process is small, we live (as Bob Dylan says) "in a polit-

ical world," and to keep our bearings in that world, we need to make some informed judgments about what we believe. ("Demystifying" A9-10)

While contemporary academic debate is largely engaged in training students to think about and advocate policy options, this is also the domain of policy studies. Debaters do the work of policy analysts in their day-to-day debating. They research issues, construct and analyze problems, and propose and oppose courses of action. Policy studies theorists use political philosophy and other disciplines to generate constructive and critical thought about policy choices and advocacy, and policy analysts often perform in adversarial or debate formats where they advocate for particular interests or issues.

In a widely used policy analysis text, David Weimer and Aidan Vining isolate three roles that policy analysts play when they approach a policy question: the objective technician, the client's advocate, and the issue advocate (17-18). Objective technicians position themselves as unbiased arbiters of the public good, advocating policy options based purely on objective analysis. However, since personal histories and cultural locations influence them, it is impossible to consider any analyst truly objective. Client's advocates construct policy analyses and advocate policy options that benefit their clients. Issue advocates construct policy analyses and advocate policy options to advance their particular issues or causes. Most policy analysts reject the role of the objective technician, claiming to be client or issue advocates who, much like lawyers, construct arguments for particular points of view (Durning and Osuna 649; Majone 21). Academic debaters can be likened to issue advocates, making arguments for their side of a policy issue.

Policy studies literature is not alien to academic debate. Don Brownlee and Mark Crossman used policy studies literature as the grounding for their discussion of the use of cost-benefit analysis in academic debate. Some policy theorists have even initiated an argumentative turn in policy studies, citing argumentation and debate literature in their attempts to apply argumentation theory to policy studies (Dunn; MacRae). While classical academic debate has limited policy argumentation to a rationalist perspective, a broader perspective on policy deliberation invites the incorporation of critiques.

CRITIQUES AND POLICY CRITERIA

One form of critique is the advocacy of value positions. These arguments may critique the results produced by a policy option or they may focus upon an evaluation of a policy option as an act, independent of the results. Either way, these arguments introduce into the deliberations another way to compare claims to value advanced by competing policy advocates. In many ways, these arguments attempt to establish value hierarchies similar to the criteria arguments that were common in the Cross Examination Debate Association during the 1980s. Often referred to as "value" or "non-policy" debate, many of these debates fundamentally dealt with policy issues. The primary difference was that debaters advanced explicit value models to justify their policy positions. While still about public policy, these debates embraced a multiple theory perspective on the possible benefits that could justify or indict a policy. These debates not only engaged in descriptive and predictive arguments about policies, they investigated what values policies should seek to realize and the means acceptable to accomplish those ends. Today, policy debate has jettisoned the explicit discussion of values and morality in favor of a rationalist policy perspective.

Policy narratives both rely upon and reinforce basic value assumptions about human beings and the world that we construct. If we fail to take value assumptions and implications into account, we cannot consider that we have a meaningful analysis of a policy question. Connie Bullis and James Kennedy note that policy analysts too often ignore values because of rational models of policy evaluation (543). The primacy of the rational model of policy evaluation similarly undercuts academic debate's ability to consider policy options. Garry Brewer, a policy scholar at Yale, and Peter deLeon, a policy analyst for the RAND Corporation, note that theories and models for social description and policy choice involve making value judgments (135-137).

The long term implications of any policy option are perhaps best reflected by the value systems that support them and the options they reflect and reinforce (Bullis and Kennedy 543). When one implements a policy, one also implements a value system. While the implementation and technical aspects of the policy may shift through agency and interpretation, the fundamental core value assumptions of the policy may be more enduring and have broader implications. The intrinsic connection between values and policies were not ignored by early non-policy debate theorists. For instance, David Zarefsky's notes the importance of criteria for the evaluation of quasi-policy propositions (9-10) and Jan Vasilius comments that "values precede policy formation, influence policy implementation and assess policy results" (35).

Policy debate that fails to incorporate value discussions may be deceptive and misleading. A belief in the ability of humans to produce an analysis of human interaction not laden with values can only be a grave self-deception. Value-free policy analysis is neither possible nor useful. This is in part because both policy analysts and policy makers inextricably inhabit "a world structured by values" (Vickers 95). Thus, as one sets forth to clarify and evaluate options, one inevitably ends up clarifying and ordering values. This is especially true in policy debate, where the entire argument rests fundamentally on some conception of what is the public good.

Thus, it is inevitable in debates over policy options that we engage in the construction of value systems and moral premises. The real question is whether we should do such *a priori*, behind a veil of objectivity, or as a part of the subject of the debate itself. The latter alternative is far preferable. No strict ethical rule or community standard can replace debate about value choices. Nor can the policy rationalist perspective account for value choices. The policy rationalist relies upon methods such as cost-benefit analysis to strive for scientific objectivity and authority in policy evaluation. Brownlee and Crossman note that cost-benefit analysis is unable to incorporate value conflicts into policy deliberations because cost-benefit analysis relies upon objective commensurable measurements that are often not possible with values (4-6). Rationalist policy analysts "either omit certain values or force them into inappropriate comparisons" (Brownlee and Crossman 6).

It would be a grave mistake to push normative value considerations out of the debate round and behind some mystical curtain. As one senior policy analyst put it, "Simply, values are too central to the various stages of the policy process to permit them to be covertly inserted, neglected, or left to some hidden marginalist hand 'muddling through'" (deLeon 39). We can reasonably expect to find our way through such issues only if we continually open them to discussion and include them in policy deliberations. We should consider that public policies and policy debates are about things that are happening. Debate is not fiction. The evidence and advocacies of our authors do not mystically originate in a vacuum, nor do they come from some entity creating game pieces for our amusement. It is essential that as policy advocates and analysts we not lose sight of these normative roots.

CRITIQUES AND INTERPRETIVE ANALYSIS

Not all critique arguments focus on value hierarchies. There is a general trend toward critiques focused on values implicit in the arguments advocates construct or the ways they are expressed. Similar movements in policy studies to incorporate interpretive theories and theories of communicative action have begun to overturn the presumption that a policy communicates only its own implementation. Interpretive perspectives on policy offer unique advantages in repairing our policy deliberation model, as well as the pedagogical benefits of deeper understanding of both specific policies and the policy process. It is important that we not think of policies in purely rational modes, but realize what we say through them to others and ourselves. Policy discourse and policies themselves can have profound communicative implications from the beginning to the end of the policy cycle. Since public policy is by definition interactive (that is, it must occur between people), policies have no option but to exist predominantly as communicative events. As a society "we live in and are confined to a communicated and communicable world" (Vickers 25), and we can not separate our policy options from the communicative acts they represent and the communications by which we represent them. The existence of the resolution itself and an affirmative team's operationalization of that resolution are profoundly communicative.

Policy scholar James Rogers argues that policy advocacy can alter belief systems, provide new paradigms, have an agenda setting effect, affect how policy issues are problematized, and change the way solutions are viewed and evaluated (22-27). Policy discourse begins, as do most affirmative cases, with an explication of the problems with existing policies. However, practical problems must be constructed, interpreted, and made sense of in the complex contexts at hand (Forester, "No Planning" 60). Hence, debaters as policy evaluators and advocates begin by problematizing the status quo. This act simultaneously creates some identities and roles while negating others. It communicates not only a what, but also a who, a why, and much more. The first impact of any affirmative case is to mark and modify the social and political world. Policy discourse communicates values and interpretations about a policy, its subjects, the objects it acts upon, and the world in which advocates seek to implement it. These communications shape the way that agents implement or carry out those policies (Bullis and Kennedy 543). Cornell professor of city and regional planning John Forester argues that public policies "alter the 'communicative infrastructure' of institutions that mediate between structural processes of social learning and the practical, situated claims-making process of social interaction" (*Critical Theory* 146).

Thus, as policy analysts and policy makers, debaters and critics must explore methodologies that can account for the communicative impact of policy discourse. Initially we may find such an approach in an interpretive perspective on policy. An interpretive approach to policy analysis focuses on the meanings of policies, on the values, feelings, and/or beliefs that they express, and on the processes by which those meanings are communicated to and interpreted by various audiences (Yanow 8-9). From this view, debaters may look to policy discourse as a rhetorical artifact subject to critical rhetorical analysis or similar analyses.

We can not neatly separate policies from the language and advocacy that brings about their implementation. Policies communicate both through action and through the arguments which advocate action. In light of the nationalist and racist rhetoric of extreme anti-immigration politicians, we should not be surprised to hear of border patrol officers abusing non-white people at the U. S. borders. Or, consider what the United States communicated through the Tuskegee experiments. Over 20 years after the conclusion of the Tuskegee study, what it communicated and continues to communicate about the attitudes of governments and medical institutions toward blacks is still having profound impacts. AIDS education program developers have found that the Tuskegee experiment left a legacy which leads many blacks, especially in the rural south, to believe, "that HIV . . . was deliberately created to kill black people, that AZT . . . was a plot to poison them, that condom distribution was part of a government plan to reduce the number of black births and that needle exchange programs were designed to foment drug use in minority communities" (Stryker E4).

Arguably, some policies may intend no more than their implementation. However, that does not free such policies from responsibility for far more than they intend. While methods for considering these interpretive and communicative aspects of a policy are beyond the rationalist perspective, any evaluation of policy options must consider these communicative perspectives. To limit these interpretations to the intentional and the naïve is to limit policy discourse and policy analysis, destroying our ability to consider the communicative effects and influences of policy advocacy. In her analysis of the published reports of the Tuskegee study, Martha Solomon notes that one reason the Tuskegee experiment continued for as long as it did was that the rhetorical conventions of the scientific community obscured and encouraged neglect of crucial human concerns (243-244). Her focus necessarily extends far beyond the intentional, naïve, rogate meanings of the Tuskegee texts. While recognizing these language choices were not intentional attempts to deceive or manipulate, Solomon accounts for their occurrence and impact upon the policy process. Attempts at similar analysis of proposed policies might act as a check against policy actions such as the Tuskegee study.

Ignorance of these aspects of policy analysis may persuade debaters that policies that meet rational cost-benefit criteria are always the most effective and preferential policy options, regardless of how they characterize individuals or communicate roles and obligations. Similarly, it will leave debaters unable to account for the often enduring and dramatic effects of the communicative aspects of policies and policy advocacy.

IMPLICATIONS OF CRITIQUES AS POLICY ANALYSIS

These two views of critique arguments — critiques as policy criteria and critiques as interpretive policy analysis — expand our conceptions of policy debate by demonstrating the roles of critiques in policy discourse. Some may find the implications of these views uncomfortable. Policy analysis critiques should not replace all other theories of critique argumentation or methods of policy analysis. Rather, this theory expands the ways that we can think about and discuss policies. Any debater, theorist, coach, or critic who advocates a policy focus has little theoretical basis from which to exclude critique argumentation from their decision making process. The further one entrenches oneself in the policy literature the more necessary critiques become.

Time is always at a premium in debate rounds, and debaters may already feel they are dealing with too many issues. However, we should remember that there was a time when debates moved, in general, much slower and included a justification of decision criteria in the affirmative case in addition to the requisite policy evaluation. Constrained by time, some debates will focus more on policy instrumentalities, some more on competing values, and some more on communicative implications. This is simply a reflection of the fact that the art of policy analysis "lies in realizing when inadequate data or social values other than efficiency make the narrow benefit-cost approach inappropriate" (Weimer and Vining 311). Critiques enhance our current model of policy discourse and can improve our ability to perform policy evaluation and advocacy.

A caveat here must be that viewing critiques as a dimension of policy analysis does not seem to provide a model from which we may comfortably evaluate arguments that critique the policy focus. Arguments that question the project of policy making may be ill-suited to the perspective of critiques as policy analysis. We should not indict or reject critiques that we can not frame as policy analysis. Rather, these positions simply must ground their relationship to policy advocacy in something other than the models outlined here. However, the vast majority of critiques do not break with the assumption that we are debating about what we should do. Whether one critiques patriarchy, statism, legal objectivism, modernism, essentialist ontology, democracy, capitalism, or a host of other subjects, these arguments most often attempt to shape our actions — our personal, social, and political policies.

Repositioning critiques within the realm of policy analysis provides an opportunity to overturn some common assumptions about critiques found in claims made by both proponents and opponents of critique argumentation. Perhaps most disturbing to some is that incorporating critiques into policy analysis revokes their status as *a priori* issues. However, we should resist so privileging any argument form. Placing critiques before all other arguments generates a structure that stultifies and stagnates the critical investigation of issues. Instead, we should place specific arguments in contingent hierarchies for the purpose of evaluation in a particular debate. Critiques are additional methodologies for discussing our shared world and shared action — the realm of policy debate. Hence, the implications of a particular critique for a particular decision should be grounded in the particular arguments advanced in that particular debate.

Accepting critiques as a part of policy analysis may help us to redefine the relationship between debate and politics. Even the most radically esoteric critique arguments may be deeply political, and positioning critiques as policy analysis asks us to think of ourselves as policy analysts and policy makers. This very proposition politicizes debate and revives the reality of the debate forum. Thinking of debate and critiques as policy advocacy, policy analysis, and policy making explodes the distinction between debate and the "real world" by erasing the fictionality of debate rounds.

Once debaters and critics recognize themselves as real citizen/policy makers rather than imagined governmental bodies, they will find it more difficult to exclude values, ethics, and morals from their decisions. Critique opponents may argue this personalizes the politics of debate, making decisions more arbitrary or dependent upon a critic's subjective value system. We might more accurately say that it *uncovers* politics. If the policy theorists and analysts discussed here are correct, then the rationalist model is no less political or personal; rationalism merely denies and masks its political and personal biases. In attempting to maintain the rationalist position, a body of value hierarchies and epistemological assumptions are enforced as given truths. Toppling the hegemony of the rationalist paradigm has the pleasant side effect of unmasking the non-rational and emotional bases for decisions made under the guise of the rationalist model.

Debaters and critics will need to struggle with how these issues can be adjudicated in a debate round. Considering critiques as substantive issues removes the easy hierarchy of issues that gave critique arguments their trump status, and will require that critics and debaters develop more sophisticated practices of comparison and evaluation. Non-policy theorists such as Zarefsky may provide some guidance, but much work will have to be done in the debate rounds. For value critiques, debaters might advance both a criteria for the adjudication of the issues at hand, and a value hierarchy that helps to place the competing values in the debate in relation to one another.

Language and advocacy arguments might be advanced as substantive issues in a debate when a team argues that the critic, as a citizen/policy maker, should not specifically endorse the other team's advocacy. This could be as philosophical as a moral obligation to not engage in or endorse particular communicative behaviors, or as instrumental as a discussion of the implications of advocacy for policy implementation and interpretation. Executive and judicial bodies often interpret policies based upon the advocacy that advanced them. This is especially apparent in judicial attempts to interpret international treaties (Bederman 972-976; Koh 343).

Solt may have provided grounds for language and advocacy arguments as substantive issues within the policy frame: "If language is so abused that the integrity of the debate process has been undermined, then it probably should be a voting issue" ("Demystifying" A10). If a citizen/policy maker feels that the language choices have impeded effective consideration of the issues, they may opt simply to reject the proposal of the offending party. Solt's argument against critiques is that such abuses are uncommon in debate. This is not a criticism of the theoretical legitimacy of language critiques, but rather questions the common practice of relying upon tenuous links between arguments.

Ethics violations or critiques that are equivalent to "calling fouls" in the debate "game" could also be reconsidered as substantive reasons why a citizen should not endorse a particular advocacy. Ethics violations question the reliability and character of the debaters, as well as all of their argumentation. Politically these are powerful arguments. In debate, we often remove them from the realm of debatable propositions in favor of having critics or tournament administrators adjudicate them independently. In politics they are openly discussed and debated and result in political ramifications for propositions, policies, and advocates long before any judicial body mandates criminal or civil penalty. If one can adequately convince a citizen/policy maker that an advocate of a proposition is lying, it is unlikely that the citizen/policy maker will entertain many of the arguments of that advocate.

Of course, reconsidering critiques as policy analysis is not an unassailable proposition, and it may be subject to criticism for its focus on academic policy literature. The theorists discussed here include policy analysts and advocates from the RAND Corporation and the Cato Institute, and a variety of policy analysis educators and scholars. Their work does not comprise the entirety of perspectives on policy analysis, and there are many in the policy field who take issue with their positions. However, Dan Durning and Will Osuna do provide a quantitative analysis of the perspectives of working policy analysts. They conclude not only that most policy analysts are not objective technicians, but also that the majority of policy analysts recognize that no policy problem has a single right solution. Additionally, the majority of analysts do not believe that a single unified theory of policy analysis can explain or solve all policy situations (649).

It could also be claimed that the model of critiques as policy analysis is unrealistic in terms of what a policy analyst must do, which is to convince a client to follow their advice. While the rational policy model may manifest hegemony in academic debate, such is not always the case in policy analysis. Consider some advice from Weimer and Vining: "Sometimes doing good simply requires analysts to advise their clients to forgo some current popularity or success to achieve some important value. You are doing exceptionally well when you can convince your client to accept such advice" (408).

Just as Weimer and Vining seek to ensure that the training of policy analysts considers perspectives other than policy rationalism, so must we as debate educators and critics ask ourselves if limiting academic debate to a rationalist perspective pays too high a price in the values it sacrifices and messages it sends. If policy debate is to train better citizens and political activists, then we must consider the inclusion of value arguments critical to this education. Political deliberation rarely relies solely upon instrumental rationality. Even given the tendency of some policy analysts to take a predominantly instrumental perspective, the inclusion of normative value claims is prerequisite to a meaningful and compelling justification or dejustification of a policy. Policy rationalism fails for the same reason Brownlee and Crossman specifically indicted cost-benefit analysis: "In the attempt to replace consent with reason, [it] typically omits vital steps in the debate over values" (1). Arguments focused upon value systems are a much-needed corrective to the weaknesses of the rationalist policy paradigm (Anderson 31).

In academic debate, it is critical that the training and experience of the students, coaches, and critics include the consideration and evaluation of competing value claims. Value conflicts are increasingly central to politics in the United States. Brownlee and Crossman note that conflicts between constituencies over regulatory or redistributive policies are usually centered around "the absence of a common set of value priorities" (1). If debaters, after spending hundreds of hours in the activity, are left with the impression that decision making only entails considerations of instrumentalities within the bounds of formal rules or ethical guides, academic debate will be responsible for proliferating amoral and value ignorant policy advocates, and citizens who are ill-equipped to cope with the value-laden issues of contemporary politics.

WORKS CITED

Anderson, Charles W. "Political Philosophy, Practical Reason, and Policy Analysis." *Confronting Values in Policy Analysis: The Politics of Criteria.* Eds. Frank Fischer and John Forester. Newbury Park: Sage, 1987. 22-44

Bahm, Ken. "Meaning as Language Use: The Case of the Language Linked Value Objection." *CEDA Yearbook* 12 (1990): 67-78.

Bederman, David J. "Revivalist Canons and Treaty Interpretation." *UCLA Law Review* 41 (1994): 953-1034.

Berube, David M. "Criticizing Kritiks: Textual Analysis Re-examined." *Contemporary Argumentation and Debate* 18 (1997): 68-81.

—. "Kritiks: The Attitude of the Diet Explained." *The Southern Journal of Forensics* 1 (1996): 13-30.

Booth, Wayne C. *The Vocation of a Teacher: Rhetorical Occasions*

1967-1988. Chicago: University of Chicago Press, 1988.

Brewer, Garry D., and Peter deLeon. *The Foundations of Policy Analysis*. Chicago: Dorsey, 1983.

Broda-Bahm, Kenneth and Thomas L. Murphy. "A Defense of Critique Arguments: Beyond the Resolutional Question." *CEDA Yearbook* 15 (1994): 20-32.

Brownlee, Don and Mark Crossman. "Advocacy, Values and Cost/Benefit Analysis." *CEDA Yearbook* 10 (1989): 1-11.

Bullis, Connie A., and James J. Kennedy. "Value Conflicts and Policy Interpretation: Changes in the Case of Fisheries and Wildlife Managers in Multiple Use Agencies." *Policy Studies Journal* 19 (1991): 542-552.

deLeon, Peter. *Advice and Consent: The Development of the Policy Sciences*. New York: Russel Sage Foundation, 1988.

Dunn, William N. "Policy Reforms as Arguments." *The Argumentative Turn in Policy Analysis and Planning*. Eds. Frank Fischer and John Forester. Durham: Duke University Press, 1993. 254-290.

Durning, Dan, and Will Osuna. "Policy Analysts' Roles and Value Orientations: An Empirical Investigation Using Q Methodology." *Journal of Policy Analysis and Management* 13 (1994): 629-657.

Edelman, Murray J. *Constructing the Political Spectacle*. Chicago: University of Chicago Press, 1988.

Eisler, Riane. *The Chalice and the Blade: Our History, Our Future*. San Francisco: HarperCollins, 1987.

Feyerabend, Paul K. *Against Method*. New York: Verso, 1988.

Forester, John. *Critical Theory, Public Policy, and Planning Practice: Toward a Critical Pragmatism*. Albany: State University of New York Press, 1993.

—. "No Planning or Administration without Phenomenology?" *Public Administration Quarterly* 14 (1990): 55-65.

Formaini, Robert. *The Myth of Scientific Public Policy*. New Brunswick: Transaction, 1990.

Hasian, Marouf, Jr., and Edward M. Panetta. "The Promise and the Peril of the 'Critique' in Academic and Competitive Debate." *Speaker and Gavel* 30 (1993): 46-56.

House, Peter W., and Roger D. Shull. *Rush to Policy*. New

Brunswick: Transaction, 1988.

Jinks, Derek. "Rethinking Critique Arguments." *Health Care Policy: Debating Coverage Cures.* Eds. Roger E. Solt and Ross K. Smith. Winston-Salem: Wake Forest University Debate, 1993. A12-A14.

Kant, Immanuel. *Grounding for the Metaphysics of Morals.* Trans. James W. Ellington. Indianapolis: Hackett Publishing, 1981.

Koh, Harold Hongju. "The President versus the Senate in Treaty Interpretation: What's all the Fuss About?" *Yale Journal of International Law* 15 (1990): 331-344.

Lain, Brian. "Verb, That's What's Happening: Kritiking Theory and Practice" *Juvenile Crime.* Eds. Roger E. Solt and Ross K. Smith. Winston-Salem: Wake Forest University Debate, 1996. A12-A16.

MacRae, Duncan, Jr. "Guidelines for Policy Discourse: Consensual versus Adversarial." *The Argumentative Turn in Policy Analysis and Planning.* Eds. Frank Fischer and John Forester. Durham: Duke University Press, 1993. 291-318.

Majone, Giandomenico. *Evidence, Argument, and Persuasion in the Policy Process.* New Haven: Yale UP, 1989.

Marcuse, Herbert. *One-Dimensional Man: Studies in the Ideology of Advanced Industrial Society.* Boston: Beacon Press, 1964.

Rand, Ayn. *Introduction to Objectivist Epistemology.* New York: New American Library, 1979.

Rogers, James M. *The Impact of Policy Analysis.* Pittsburgh: University of Pittsburgh Press, 1988.

Shanahan, William. "Kritik of Thinking." *Health Care Policy: Debating Coverage Cures.* Eds. Roger E. Solt and Ross K. Smith. Winston-Salem: Wake Forest University Debate, 1993. A3-A8.

Shors, Matthew, and Steve Mancuso. "The Critique: Screaming Without Raising Its Voice." *Health Care Policy: Debating Coverage Cures.* Eds. Roger E. Solt and Ross K. Smith. Winston-Salem: Wake Forest University Debate, 1993. A14-A18.

Solomon, Martha. "The Rhetoric of Dehumanization: An Analysis of Medical Reports of the Tuskegee Syphilis Project." *Western Journal of Speech Communication* 49 (1985): 233-247.

Solt, Roger. *The Anti-Kritik Handbook.* Denton: Paradigm Research, 1995.

—. "Demystifying the Critique." *Health Care Policy: Debating Coverage Cures.* Eds. Roger E. Solt and Ross K. Smith. Winston-

Salem: Wake Forest University Debate, 1993. A8-A11.

Stryker, Jeff. "Tuskegee's Long Arm Still Touches a Nerve." *New York Times* 13 April 1997, natl. ed.: E4+.

Vasilius, Jan. "Presumption, Presumption, Wherefore Art Thou Presumption?" *Perspectives on Non-Policy Argument* 1 (1980): 33-41.

Vickers, Geoffrey. *Policymaking, Communication, and Social Learning.* New Brunswick: Transaction, 1987.

Weimer, David L., and Aidan R. Vining. *Policy Analysis: Concepts and Practice* 2nd Edition. Englewood Cliffs: Prentice-Hall, 1992.

Yanow, Dvora. *How Does a Policy Mean? Interpreting Policy and Organizational Actions.* Washington, DC: Georgetown University Press, 1996.

Zarefsky, David. "Criteria for Evaluating Non-Policy Argument." *Perspectives on Non-Policy Argument* 1 (1980): 9-16.

Pat J. Gehrke (Ph.D., Pennsylvania State University) is the Director of the Center for Public Speaking and Civic Engagement at The Pennsylvania State University in University Park, Pennsylvania. This essay was originally published in volume 19 (1998) of *Contemporary Argumentation and Debate*, pp. 18-39.